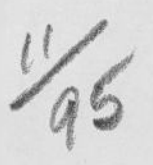

D1013033

TIES THAT STRESS

The New Family Imbalance

TIES THAT STRESS

The New Family Imbalance

DAVID ELKIND

Harvard University Press
Cambridge, Massachusetts
London, England
1994

Printed in the United States of America

This book is printed on acid-free paper, and its binding materials
have been chosen for strength and durability.

Library of Congress Cataloging-in-Publication Data

Elkind, David, 1931–
Ties that stress : the new family imbalance / David Elkind.
p. cm.
Includes bibliographical references and index.
ISBN 0-674-89149-X
1. Family—United States. 2. United States—Social conditions—1970– I. Title.
HQ536.E44 1994
306.85'0973—dc20

94-11126
CIP

To Debbie, with love

Acknowledgments

At a working breakfast recently, a young colleague asked me, "How do you write a book?" A medley of different explanations came to mind, but I finally answered with what I believe is true for the writing of most books, namely, "You don't do it alone." First there are your family and friends, who must listen patiently while you talk on and on about your current preoccupation. I know my wife and sons were getting pretty tired of hearing about the postmodern family. They were nonetheless patient and genuinely supportive over the years while this book was germinating and being written. I appreciate them and love them for that, among other things. I also want to thank my friends Emory Cowen, Bernie Eisman, and Joe Stewart, who answered my sometimes despairing, sometimes euphoric, correspondence with good humor and calming reassurance.

In addition to family and friends, there are all the people who were more directly involved in the enterprise. I owe a big debt of gratitude to Jason Sachs, my graduate research assistant, who conducted much of the library research for this project in addition to his many other duties. I also want to thank Kathy Hourigan for reading early drafts of the book and offering many helpful suggestions. My deepest thanks go to the editors at Harvard University Press. I am most indebted to Angela von der Lippe, Senior Editor for the Behavioral

Sciences. She saw past the crudeness of the early version and guided me through the several revisions that have resulted in a more balanced and more solidly documented book than I might otherwise have written. I also want to thank Susan Wallace Boehmer, Senior Editor for Manuscript Development, who helped tighten the book's organization and provided many vivid examples to further substantiate the arguments.

Last, but certainly not least, I want to express my gratitude to the hundreds of children, parents, and educators I have worked with, or met with, over the last quarter century. Talking and writing about the plight of children and youth in our society is often disheartening and depressing. But even when I am feeling most discouraged, I listen to a children's choir, see a chalk game on the cement of a school yard, or watch a child consoling a friend, and I feel renewed. Or I meet men and women who, despite all the pressures and demands, are doing a really decent job of parenting, and my spirits rise. Sometimes I visit a classroom and hear the quiet hum of activity that, to me, is always the music of healthy schooling, and I feel rejuvenated. Talking with a principal who has introduced multiage grouping, has cut back on testing, and is encouraging remedial teaching within the classroom has the same uplifting effect.

These encounters help me to remember that, despite all that is wrong with our families, classrooms, and school administration, there is also a great deal of healthy parenting, creative teaching, and imaginative governance going on. If I am guardedly optimistic about the future of children and youth in our society, it is because I meet so many people who are genuinely committed and dedicated to the well-being of our young people.

Contents

TIES THAT STRESS

The New Family Imbalance

Family Imbalance

1

From Nuclear to Permeable

Over the past half century, profound shifts in our ways of perceiving, valuing, and feeling about ourselves and our world have radically altered American society and reconfigured the American family. We find these changes—which have been described as the movement from modernity to postmodernity—both liberating and stressful. The modern nuclear family, often idyllically portrayed as a refuge and a retreat from a demanding world, is fast disappearing. In its stead we now have a new structure—the postmodern permeable family—that mirrors the openness, complexity, and diversity of our contemporary lifestyles.

The nuclear family provided clear-cut, often rigid, boundaries between our public and our private lives, between the homeplace and the workplace, between children and adults. In the permeable family, these dividing lines have become blurred and difficult to discern. The postmodern family is more fluid, more flexible, and more obviously vulnerable to pressures from outside itself.

The solid boundaries of the idealized nuclear family were particularly beneficial for children and adolescents. Firm divisions between public and private, homeplace and workplace, parents and children offered the young a social envelope of well-defined limits and standards. That envelope of security and protection made it possible for children and youth to devote all of their energies to the demands and conflicts of growing up.

These firm boundaries also provided a haven for some parents. But for many others they were unbearably confining and demeaning. Mothers often felt discouraged from pursuing fulltime careers, on the assumption that a nurturing mother should devote her time to driving children to afternoon ballet classes or baseball practice. Many fathers felt overburdened by the demands of the breadwinning role and of adaptation to corporate or industrial life. Parents whose marriage was unhappy often felt compelled to stay together "for the sake of the children" and to avoid the stigma of divorce, even if it meant resigning themselves to an unsatisfying lifelong relationship. The nuclear family's strong boundaries served the needs of children to a greater extent than they met the needs of parents. This was the old, modern family imbalance.

The old imbalance was, to be sure, relative. The ideal nuclear family was largely a white middle-class fantasy, rarely fully realized even in that socioeconomic milieu. In many lower income homes the family had always been permeable in the sense that children often worked alongside parents in family businesses near or in the home, blurring the distinctions both between homeplace and workplace and between the responsibilities of children and of adults. The immigrant family also was permeable to outside influences as children were exposed to American values and suffered the loss of old traditions. At the same time, however, these parents believed in working hard and sacrificing so that their children could have a better life. In this limited sense, many lower income and immigrant families reflected the old nuclear family imbalance, which met the needs of children better than it met the needs of adults.

But even among middle income families, the old imbalance was a relative one. Some parents thrived within the protected confines and clear role definitions of the nuclear family. In contrast, many children and adolescents suffered from overprotection and frequently blundered as innocents into the adult world of work, sexual relations, and ruthless competition. Perhaps that helps explain why the postmodern parents of today—many of them the overprotected children of yesterday's modern parents—are more willing to prepare their own children for the real world, rather than to protect them from it. Nonetheless, the old imbalance between the needs of children and the needs of adults was prevalent in the typical family of the 1950s.

With the emergence of the postmodern permeable family, the need imbalance has tilted in the opposite direction. In many respects, the cave-in of the nuclear family's divisions and boundaries has been beneficial to parents. As a result of this collapse, parents living in permeable families have many more lifestyle options than did parents living in nuclear families. Childcare by paid professionals is rapidly becoming the national norm, as large numbers of women with children under schoolage enter the fulltime workforce. Single-parent families have become the fastest growing family structure in America in the 1990s, as more and more parents choose divorce over marital dissatisfaction and as greater numbers of women make the decision to bear children out of wedlock. Blended families, consisting of stepsiblings and half-siblings from two and sometimes three marriages, are not unusual.

These many ways of loosening the old constraints of the nuclear family have come about because parents have demanded relief from the stresses of family life that accumulated in the modern period. Yet the crumbling of these divisions has been detrimental to most children and youth. Growing up is difficult when family rules, boundaries, and values are ambiguous and in flux. In the permeable family, therefore, the needs of parents and adults are better served than the needs of children and youth. This is the new, postmodern family imbalance.

Like the old imbalance, the new imbalance is relative. Postmodern parents are not necessarily more self-indulgent or less self-sacrificing than modern parents. It is simply that the demands of postmodern life are different from those that obtained in the modern world. Like passengers on a jetliner whose cabin has suddenly depressurized in midair, postmodern parents know they have to put their own oxygen mask on first, before they can attend to the safekeeping of their children. The postmodern global economy makes unceasing demands on adults to constantly update job skills or to change occupations, and has robbed postmodern parents of their sense of vocational security. For parents at all income levels, the demands of family and work, in a time of declining income and job scarcity, are a source of unceasing stress. With the telecommunications revolution, postmodern parents can no longer control the information flow to their children and have to be content to help them, as best they can, to cope. These crumbling boundaries and mounting pressures, combined with an appalling lack of institutional support for families, certainly does not make life in a permeable family easy for many postmodern parents.[1]

Moreover, just as the nuclear family had some benefits for parents despite its costs, the permeable family has some benefits for children. It enables them to realize abilities and to demonstrate competencies that went unrecognized in the modern era. Perhaps the most striking example of this positive side of the new imbalance is the widespread postmodern acceptance of the value of early childhood education. Although the ability of young children to profit from age-appropriate instruction was argued by Friedrich Froebel and Maria Montessori, the education of young children did not become accepted in the United States until the reform movements of the 1960s altered our perceptions of children and of the family.[2]

This said, and recognizing the many hardships confronted by contemporary parents and the new opportunities available to their children, I still believe that, overall, the imbalance in the family's ability to meet the needs of its members has shifted during the postmodern period in favor of adult needs over those of children and youth. Moreover, this shift is not limited to families but is aided and abetted by all of those social institutions that serve the family.

Origins of Family Need Imbalances

The nuclear family's heyday, as the media remind us, was the decade of the 1950s. But as early as the first decades of this century the basic substrate of the modern family imbalance was already in place—the result of two related historical changes. One change was the acceptance, during the nineteenth century, of childhood and adolescence as distinct stages of life, with their own developmental tasks. The other change was the gradual restriction, during that same period, of the family's function to the sole task of meeting the emotional needs of family members. The first change brought about a separation between the needs of children and adolescents and the needs of adults, while the second transformation raised the issue of which family members' needs should predominate.

The unique developmental characteristics of childhood and adolescence had been recognized since the beginnings of recorded history. Aristotle gave a description of adolescent behavior that might well have been written today:

> Young men have strong passions and tend to gratify them indiscriminately. Of the bodily desires, it is the sexual by which they are most swayed and in which they show absence of control . . . They are changeable and fickle in their desires which are violent while they last, but quickly over: their impulses are keen but not deep rooted.[3]

Yet only in the modern period did we begin to conceive of childhood and adolescence as entirely devoted to education and to preparation for adult life rather than to the performance of the tasks of adulthood.

In the premodern world no such role differentiation obtained. Children and adolescents were on a functional par with adults and contributed in meaningful ways to maintaining the family. On the farm, even young children collected eggs, fed the animals, and picked fruit and vegetables. There was no reason to make any clear role distinctions between grownups and children. In the premodern family, the needs of children and adolescents and their contributions to the fulfillment of those needs were largely coextensive with those of their parents—a difference in degree only, not in kind.

Philippe Ariès contends that the invention of modern perceptions of children and adolescents was brought about by the introduction of universal public schooling in the mid-1800s. Prior to that time, childhood was brief, and it continued to be brief for a long time in the working classes. But with the ascendancy of the middle class, when schooling became the principle activity of the young, the meaning of childhood changed.[4]

The perception of childhood and adolescence as periods devoted to schooling paralleled the family's progressively narrow focus on meeting the emotional needs of its members. Glenna Matthews, in *Just a Housewife,* describes the family's divestiture of other functions in this way:

> Let us look at the four significant functions that the home had gained by 1830 and assess their status one hundred years later . . . As we have seen, the political function of the home had been eroded by changes in the late nineteenth century, chiefly the emergence of an evolutionary perspective that saw the home as irrelevant to human progress. The capacity of the home to serve as an arena for the display of female prowess had been greatly undermined by a combination of technological innovation and the arrogation to themselves of domestic expertise by the home economics profession. The religious function was unlikely to be salient in an increasingly secular age.
>
> What was left, then, of the original foundation of the ideology of domesticity was the heightened emotional role home had gained by 1830. If anything, that role had become even more important by the early twentieth century. Yet the importance was tied to a new self-consciousness—not to say anxiety—about how well the women in charge of the home could meet their families' needs.[5]

As Matthews points out, the family's narrowed mission to fulfill the emotional needs of its members was not an equally distributed responsibility; it fell almost exclusively on the shoulders of mothers. The differentiation of child and adolescent needs from those of adults, together with the family's concentration on meeting its members' emotional needs, raised the question of whose needs should be given priority. It was the eventual acceptance of Charles Darwin's theory of evolution that tipped the balance in favor of children and adolescents.

Darwin published *On the Origin of Species* in 1859 with some trepidation and only after he learned that A. R. Wallace was about to put forth a similar theory. In Victorian England, in an era that celebrated creationism and natural theology, Darwin was justifiably concerned about a negative reception of his heretical ideas. Particularly controversial was his suggestion that humans were simply another animal species and therefore subject to the same forces of variation and natural selection that drove the evolution of all species, from flatworms to redwoods to squirrel monkeys.[6]

From a Darwinian perspective, human children, like the young of many other animal species, require security and protection while they acquire the skills (through adult tutelage) that make it possible for them to survive on their own. Looked at in this way, parents have an inherent biological drive to nurture their offspring and to provide them with a time period, free from work and responsibility, to complete their education. And, by implication, children who are not afforded these opportunities for growth would suffer irreparable damage.

By the early decades of the twentieth century, the nuclear family's focus on the successful rearing of children at the expense of parental (particularly maternal) opportunities for personal and vocational growth gave rise to the old imbalance. The unhappiness created by this imbalance, in turn, undoubtedly contributed to the social revolutions of the 1960s and eventually to the emergence of the postmodern permeable family. The walls of the modern family, undermined by unhappiness within and besieged from without by social forces beyond its control, eventually gave way. The prevalence and influence of television, the clashes of the civil rights movement, the revolution in sexual mores, the rise of a drug culture among middle-class youth, the disillusionment of Vietnam and Watergate, the growth of telecommunications and computers, and many other social developments all helped to overturn established relationships between the generations and to introduce new discourses that have come to be known as postmodernism.

Many of today's parents—offspring of the modern nuclear family but also products of the social upheavals of the 1960s and 70s and the economic pressures of the 1980s and 90s—no longer regard themselves as solely responsible for meeting the emotional needs of their offspring. Many of them do not think of children and youth as requiring a full helping of security, protection, firm limits, and clear values, and many of those who still believe in the goodness of those things no longer have faith in their ability as parents to provide them in today's complex world.

As a consequence, postmodern young people are often left without the social envelope of security and protection that shielded earlier generations. Because today's children and teenagers are resourceful, they can cope, to some extent, with these new demands for independence and maturity. But ironically, this demonstration of adaptability often encourages parents, and the larger society, to provide even less security and direction than they might otherwise have done.

The debilitating effects of both the old and the new imbalance can be documented statistically. With respect to the old imbalance, as recently as 1975, in a large survey of a "normal" population of married couples, married women consistently reported more depression than married men of comparable age, education, income, and number of children.[7] Today, by contrast, it is the legitimate needs of the young that often go chronically unmet. A recent survey found that 20 to 25 percent of all schoolage children experience physical symptoms that are largely caused by psychosocial factors.[8] While we cannot, nor should we wish to, turn the calendar back, we do need to figure out new ways to take some of these damaging pressures off of contemporary children and youth.

Psychodynamics of Family Need Imbalances

Whenever one group meets its own needs at the expense of another, the stage is set for stress and conflict. Modernity itself grew out of an imbalance between the needs of the common people and those of the aristocracy and the clergy. The American Revolution was fought in part because the needs of the colonists were continually subordinated to those of the English monarchs. The French and Russian revolutions were fought for similar reasons. Obviously this is a vast oversimplification of the forces operative in these events, but need imbalances did play their part.

An ongoing imbalance within families can do serious psychological damage because it requires individuals to subordinate their personal needs and ambitions to the needs and ambitions ascribed to them by their social roles. Family members in this position feel put upon and uncared for.

• *THE NUCLEAR FAMILY IMBALANCE*

In the old imbalance, mothers were the ones who most often felt exploited. In a society that emphasized self-reliance, self-realization, and self-determination, women were asked to subordinate their needs for self-expression to the nurturance needs of their husbands and children. The pathological effects are poignantly described by Anne Sexton, who listed herself as a "poet" on her income tax only after she had won a Pulitzer Prize:

> Until I was twenty-eight I had a kind of buried self who didn't know she could do anything but make white sauce and diaper babies. I

> didn't know I had creative depths. I was a victim of the American Dream, the bourgeois, middle-class dream. All I wanted was a little piece of life, to be married, to have children. I thought the nightmares, the visions, the demons would go away if there was enough love to put them down. I was trying my damnedest to lead a conventional life for that was how I was brought up, and it was what my husband wanted of me. But one can't build little white picket fences to keep nightmares out. The surface cracked when I was about twenty-eight. I had a psychotic break and tried to kill myself.[9]

Sexton was not alone. Stephanie Coontz, in *The Way We Never Were: American Families and the Nostalgia Trap*, informs us that "tranquilizers were developed in the 1950s in response to a need that physicians explicitly saw as female. Virtually nonexistent in 1955, tranquilizer consumption reached 462,000 pounds in 1958 and soared to 1.15 million pounds merely a year later. Commentators noted a sharp increase in women's drinking during the decade."[10]

In the modern era, the emotional needs of women were not being met by the family, and the consequences can be seen in drug and alcohol abuse. It was only in 1963, however, that Betty Friedan, in *The Feminine Mystique*, gave public voice to "the problem that has no name" afflicting middle-class housewives.[11] The volcanic nationwide response to her book was clear evidence of the extent to which women living in modern families were suffering. It could no longer be doubted that the out-of-balance social expectations for nurturance placed on women in a marriage can be as emotionally destructive as, say, the out-of-balance social expectations for violence placed on soldiers conscripted to fight in a war.

But the women's movement was far from being the whole story in the transformation to the postmodern family. While some writers, even today, would like to lay responsibility for the dissolution of the nuclear family at the feet of what was once called "women's lib," that movement was an effect, more than a cause, of postmodernism, as we will see in Chapter 2. A return to nuclear family roles, as some writers advocate, will not redress the new imbalance. The new imbalance has evolved from a complex set of social changes, not just one.

• THE PERMEABLE FAMILY IMBALANCE

The effects of the new imbalance are comparable to those of the old one. Like all those whose needs are not being met over the long term, postmodern children and adolescents are feeling victimized. They believe that they must suppress their own needs for security and protection to accommodate their parents' and the society's expectations that they be independent and autonomous. Like modern mothers, postmodern young people either turn their anger on themselves (for letting themselves be used) or at the world around them.

The new imbalance and its stressful consequences are receiving increasing professional and public attention. In the early 1980s several books appeared that described the erosion of the markers that set childhood and adolescence apart from adulthood. These books—Neil Postman's *The Disappearance of Childhood,* Marie Winn's *Children without Childhood,* and my own book *The Hurried Child*—all made many of the same points.[12] Contemporary children were no longer protected and shielded from some of life's harsher realities, exempted from adult decisionmaking and responsibilities, or given opportunities to engage in the play and pastimes unique to childhood.

The resulting harm has been documented in the reports of a number of national commissions and study groups. In their report on the state of the nation's education, the National Commission on Excellence in Education entitled its publication *A Nation at Risk.* Among their conclusions:

> Average achievement of high school students on most standardized tests is now lower than 26 years ago when Sputnik was launched.
>
> The College Board's Scholastic Aptitude Tests (SAT) demonstrate a virtually unbroken decline from 1963 to 1980.
>
> There was a steady decline in science achievement scores of US

> 17-year-olds as measured by national assessments of science in 1969, 1973 and 1977.[13]

The Children's Defense Fund, reporting on the state of the nation's children in 1990, concluded: "As the wealthiest nation on earth and the standard bearer for democracy we have an 'A' *capacity* to care for our children but an 'F' *performance* on many key indicators of child well-being. By every measure the U.S. performance is unsatisfactory." Among the many negative comparisons of the treatment of children in the United States with that afforded the young in other countries was the following: "America invests a smaller portion of its GNP [gross national product] in child health than 18 other industrialized countries. It invests a smaller proportion of its GNP in education than six other countries."[14]

Studies of contemporary adolescents also reflect the negative effects of the new imbalance. In 1991 the Carnegie Corporation commissioned a task force on Youth Development and Community Programs. The Yale psychiatrist James Comer, in the Commission's report, describes the plight of postmodern adolescents in the following terms:

> In my view, two massive sets of social and economic changes have occurred along parallel tracks, and they intersect most acutely at the point when young people attempt to make the transition from adolescence to adulthood . . . I see these two tracks as the following: a significant increase in the level and number of skills needed for successful adulthood, and a significant decrease in the ongoing support and guidance offered young people during their growing years. These two trends have created a serious problem in our country, indeed a crisis.[15]

Clearly, the new imbalance takes many forms and has many different and varied effects. At the very personal, individual level, however, children and youth often experience it as overwhelming stress. "When Linda Mohr joked recently that her son Shane's hair was too long, he pulled her up short. 'I really don't care about my hair,' the eight-year-old said, 'I just care about getting through. School's a war. The playground's a war. The cafeteria's a war. Life is a war.'"[16]

Although the stress experienced by postmodern children and youth and its damaging effects are being given increasing media attention, we still lack a systematic approach to correcting this problem. Stress reduction and management programs for adults exist in abundance, ranging from brown-bag luncheon courses at the workplace to aerobics classes to individual psychotherapy and couples therapy. No such comprehensive network of services exists for children until antisocial behavior brings them to the attention of law enforcement officials or school authorities. The new imbalance is thus echoed in the bias of the helping professions toward the prevention and reduction of adult, but not childhood, stress.

Toward Rebalancing the Scale

While it would be an oversimplification to attribute all of the problems of today's young people to an unequal distribution of resources within the family, this imbalance certainly makes a significant contribution. In part at least, the postmodern correction of the old imbalance has itself gone too far and fails to adequately meet the needs of children and youth. Further adjustment is in order to redress the balance in such a way that the needs of children and youth are more equally weighted against those of parents and adults.

In Chapter 2 we will explore the meaning of "modern" and "postmodern," in order to understand two sets of cultural ideas that have had enormous influence on our changing views of family life.

In Chapters 3 and 4 we will turn to the sentiments and values of the modern nuclear family—expressed as romantic love, maternal love, domesticity, unilateral authority, and togetherness—and we will examine how they have fared in the postmodern permeable family.

In Chapters 5, 6, and 7 we will look at the different family members in turn—parents, children, and adolescents—and assess the impact of postmodern ideas on their role in the permeable family.

Chapter 8 will present the views of health professionals on child and adult development, and will assess the contribution of these "helping professions" to the modern and postmodern family need imbalance. Three postmodern societal stressors, and the damage they are doing to contemporary children and youth, are the subjects of Chapter 9.

Then in the final chapter, I will introduce a new family pattern which seems to be emerging: the vital family. This vital family incorporates the best of nuclear and permeable family life, by putting the needs of children and youth on an equal footing with those of their parents and other adults. I hope this book will help us move more quickly to the establishment of the vital family and the amelioration of the symptoms of overwhelming stress that every day become more evident among our nation's youth.

Family Ties

2

From Modern to Postmodern

I arrived at this formulation of a new postmodern family imbalance after an extended intellectual journey. For the past two decades, as a child psychologist and child advocate, I have been trying to understand and explain the decline in the health and emotional well-being of our children and youth. In my earlier books—*The Hurried Child, All Grown Up and No Place to Go,* and *Miseducation*—I described a number of the immediate stresses and pressures on contemporary young people, and some of their negative consequences.[1] As I continued to think, write, and lecture about these matters, it became clearer to me that what was happening to children and youth was part of a larger set of tectonic upheavals that have transformed our society since midcentury.

When I reviewed the literature, however, I could not find an overriding perspective that placed the alterations in the condition of children, youth, and families within the context of the larger society.[2] Nor could I find a terminology to describe the disruptions, confusion, and distress experienced by contemporary parents and their offspring. At about the time I began to feel discouraged about my chances of ever finding the approach I was looking for, I became acquainted with postmodernism. Although I had come across the term in a number of discussions, it often seemed rather esoteric or elitist (for example, deconstructionism in literary criticism and minimalism in art). But when I read Michel Foucault, I began to appreciate the broader significance of postmodernism as a critique of our established ways of talking and thinking about social institutions, including the family.[3]

What is unique about Foucault, as is true for all original thinkers, is the type of questions he asked. The difference between the questions Foucault poses and those asked by modern writers is perhaps best illustrated in a 1973 debate between him and the linguist Noam Chomsky on Dutch television on the topic "Human Nature: Justice vs. Power."

For Chomsky the most important question to ask about human nature is: How do individuals, out of their isolated, fragmented, and often contradictory experiences, manage to learn a common language and use language in a generative, creative way? Chomsky's answer is that there must be "something biologically given, unchangeable, a foundation for whatever it is we do with our mental capacities."[4] Chomsky has devoted his scientific career to describing the language devices which he sees as inherent in human nature—devices that are, according to Chomsky, both rational and universal.

Foucault takes a different tack. He is not concerned with determining the universals of human nature; indeed, he questions whether such universals exist. Rather, for Foucault the most important question to ask about human nature is this: What functions has the concept of "human nature" served at different times and in different places within human society? In Foucault's view, human nature is not a preexisting reality that awaits discovery by psychologists, anthropologists, linguists, or others. Rather, the concept of human nature is part of a social discourse that arises at particular times and places to serve particular purposes.[5]

Postmodernism is, therefore, first and foremost a critical attitude toward the values and beliefs of modernity, including such cherished notions as rationality and individual freedom. Foucault and his followers claim that both truth and the human subject that knows truth are cultural productions, not universal constants. Their emphasis is on the embeddedness of all human knowledge in a social, historical, and linguistic context.

The postmodern perspective has been extended to many different domains and issues, ranging from literary criticism to legal studies, and from economics to education.[6] But it has not been systematically applied to the remarkable changes that have taken place in the last half of the twentieth century in the lives of children and youth, parents and families. As I set about analyzing and conceptualizing the family from first a modern and then a postmodern perspective, I began to understand the problems of today's children and youth in a way that I had not appreciated before. It is that description and perspective that are presented in the chapters of this book.

Before we turn to this discussion of the postmodern family, it will be useful to contrast some of the major themes of modernity with those of postmodernity, so that later we can see how modern themes are played out in the institution that most of us know as the nuclear family. Postmodern themes, by contrast, come on stage in the permeable family, which is in many ways a correction of the outmoded underlying assumptions and the functional failures of the nuclear family. But the postmodern permeable family, like its predecessor, is a system out of balance.

Modern Themes

In the broadest sense, modernity arose in the seventeenth century as a revolt against the autocracy of the premodern world. It eventually overturned medieval forms of government, religion, science, art, and education. Modernity was a continuing revolution in the sense that it did not occur all at once or in one particular country or one specific domain of society. Rationalism, humanism, democracy, individualism, romanticism were all modern ideas that took root and flourished at different times and in different places. Moreover, modernism was largely a Western phenomenon; even today, in some parts of the world, societies that are more feudal than modern can be found.

Although modernity did not emerge all at once, it did have a central, unifying theme: celebration of the individual over established authority. René Descartes is often credited with being among the first to express this individualistic theme with his assertion, "I think, therefore I exist." Descartes rooted authority not in learned theologians but in the thought and reasoning of individual human beings. The supremacy of reason, of the individual, and of individual freedom has been the abiding theme of modernity—in the Protestant religions, in movements celebrating self-expression in the arts and letters, in experimentation in science, and in democracy in government.

At liberty to observe, experiment, reason, and write, modern thinkers eventually put in place three conceptual foundationstones upon which many nineteenth- and twentieth-century developments rested; and each of these, as we will see, had implications for the modern family. First was the belief in *progress*—the idea that society and the lot of individuals within it are gradually improving. The idea of social progress was closely tied up with faith in the continuing growth of scientific knowledge and its benefits for mankind. In the modern world, knowledge is cumulative, a product of scientific endeavor. Through the growth of knowledge and its application, humankind could move toward a world in which all individuals enjoy the unalienable rights to "life, liberty, and the pursuit of happiness" that eighteenth-century political theorists had found self-evident.

A second self-evident truth of modernism was *universality*. The belief was that nature operated everywhere according to universal principles—natural laws—which human beings, through the exercise of rational and creative thought, could discover and understand. It was this belief that encouraged the grand unifying theories of Newton, Darwin, Marx, Freud, and Einstein, among others. The belief in universality led to a third foundationstone of modernity, the notion of *regularity*. The belief in the regularity, and therefore predictability, of natural phenomena was a reaction against the often arbitrary and willful dictates of premodern religious and civic authorities. Modern science was established as the search for the universal natural laws that governed the physical and social worlds in some regular and predictable way.

For example, Newtonian physics—perhaps the first great scientific accomplishment of modernity—established the regularity and predictability of celestial phenomena based on the laws of motion. In a like manner, Gregor Mendel's careful experiments with peas established the regularity and predictability of certain types of genetic inheritance. In chemistry the regularity of Dmitri Mendeleev's periodic table of the elements allowed the existence and structure of several rare elements, such as gallium and scandium, to be accurately predicted before they were discovered. Similarly, Albert Einstein, in his general theory of relativity, predicted in 1916 that the path of a ray of starlight passing near the sun would be deflected by the sun's mass. Three years later, observations made by A. S. Eddington during a solar eclipse confirmed Einstein's prediction and hence the regularity of gravitational effects.

As our scientific understanding of the world became more complex, the belief in regularity was translated, in later phases of the modern movement, into a conception of causality that recognized different "levels" of phenomena. Though surface events might appear irregular and chaotic, they could always be explained by underlying principles and structures. Freud attributed irregular surface events, such as slips of the tongue or bizarre dreams, to underlying regularities in our unconscious impulses and desires. Irregular surface features such as eye color were explained by underlying molecular structures within the nucleus of cells—the genes. Similarly, the atomic and subatomic theories of matter, as well as the germ theory of disease, scientifically explained events at one level of observation by reference to events at another level.

Postmodern Themes

The themes of progress, universality, and regularity were incorporated into all modern social institutions, including the nuclear family. But alongside the flowering of modernism, the seeds of postmodernism were germinating. Postmodernism arose not so much as a revolt against the beliefs of modernity as a set of attitudes designed to correct and modify modern ideas that had been perverted or had proved to be overly broad or overly narrow. For example, while modernism regarded reason as the engine of human progress, rational arguments were also used to justify such barriers to human progress and human rights as slavery, colonialism, imperialism, and fascism. Likewise, modernity stressed the freedom of the individual, but the individual in question was usually an Anglo-Saxon, Christian male. The modern belief in the unmitigated benefits of science and technology did not anticipate their use to create ever more powerful weapons of human destruction nor their contribution to the degradation of the environment. Modern beliefs were not entirely wrong; but they were often overly idealized and blind to the dark side of human behavior and of technological development.

At the apex of human knowledge for the modernist, as we have seen, is science—a way of knowing that is considered by its practitioners and promoters to be separate and apart from the natural phenomena it describes. Nature exists, according to this view, and it is the task of the modern scientist to observe, explain, and predict nature as accurately and objectively as possible. For Foucault and his followers, by contrast, it is this very assumption of the objectivity of science that is in error. They argue that we can never lift ourselves out of the framework within which we speak, live, and work, and that all of our forms of knowledge, including scientific knowledge, are subjective. From this way of looking at things, it is not religion, as Freud claimed, that is an illusion but rather it is scientific objectivity.[7]

The directive of this embeddedness motif is that we must now question many of the basic concepts that we heretofore took as self-evident in all academic disciplines, particularly those behavioral and social studies that attempted to model their methods on the physical sciences.[8] Because Foucault saw himself as rooted in a particular place at a particular time, and steeped in the prevailing discourse, he described himself as a "genealogist" rather than as a historian. Genealogies—lines of descent, whether of families or ideas—are highly particular. Grand histories, by contrast, such as Oswald Spengler's two-volume *Decline of the West* (published in 1945) and Arnold Toynbee's twelve-volume *A Study of History* (1946–1961), presuppose an ability to place oneself outside the sequence of human events and to observe them from a distance.[9] For Foucault, such a stance is impossible.

If our thought and action are socially and culturally embedded, any particular discourse, including scientific discourse, must always serve a social function. Divisions of knowledge are divisions of power.[10] To illustrate the difference between a modernist and a postmodernist perspective on the way we approach knowing, we might look at some of the so-called helping professions. A modernist would ask: How is psychology different from psychiatry? How is medicine different from nursing? How is administration different from teaching? The modern answer is based on the assumption that these divisions correspond to objective differences in knowledge, skill, and training. A postmodernist, by contrast, would ask a functional question: What purposes did these divisions serve when they were first introduced, and what purposes do they continue to serve today? The postmodern answer is that the divisions between psychiatry and psychology, between medicine and nursing, and between administration and teaching are clearly divisions of power as well as divisions of knowledge and skill.

Understanding this knowledge/power relationship has led to many recent revelations regarding the abuse of power derived from knowledge—the sexual harassment and abuse of patients by doctors, of children by priests, of students by teachers, of employees by employers. From a modern "objective" perspective, knowledge and power are always separate; from a postmodern "embedded" perspective, they never are.

The 1980s and 90s have witnessed an explosion of writing about the postmodern. While commentators share the same embeddedness perspective, they are not always in agreement as to whether the world they see from this new window is better or worse than the world once seen through the glass of modernity.[11] Indeed, there are probably as many different interpretations of postmodernity as there are postmodern writers. This diversity is in itself, of course, postmodern—evidence of each individual's embeddedness in his or her own experience and interpretation of phenomena.

Nonetheless, most postmodernists are in agreement that language is a better model for the way human transactions are accomplished than is logical discourse. The ascendance of language over reason began in the last century, with philosophers such as Nietzsche, Wittgenstein, and Kierkegaard, who played "language games" to demonstrate that there is no such thing as pure reason and that our thinking can never be abstracted from our modes of linguistic expression. Through their use of parody, irony, and satire, they demonstrated that language is inherently ambiguous, and that the truths of reason, which employs language, must therefore be ambiguous as well.[12]

When language rather than reason is ascendant, a different set of themes moves into prominence. Languages change, but they do not necessarily progress; in the postmodern worldview, things change quickly, but they do not necessarily get "better." Franglais and TexMex are language developments that many would not regard as linguistically progressive. However, they share an important characteristic of all living languages, which is the mixing of regional variations, dialects, and lexicons. Accordingly, rather than the celebration of progress and improvement, a major postmodern theme is sensitivity to *difference*. Postmodernists recognize difference, but not superiority.

Many postmodern writers are much more concerned with elucidating differences in outlook and agendas than they are with describing progress toward some universally accepted goal.

Moreover, although reason may be taken as universal to mankind, language surely is not. Language is always particular to a given culture at a given time. Every language contains much surplus cultural meaning that cannot be translated. Correspondingly, postmodern writers are much more concerned with the *particular*, with domain-specific issues and discourses rather than with grand unifying theories.

And finally, language—in contrast with logic—is often as irregular as it is regular. To be sure, there are regular grammatical and spelling rules, but there are also many exceptions. While "boy" and "girl" are regularly pluralized as "boys" and "girls," "man" and "woman" are irregularly pluralized as "men" and "women." Indeed, regularity in language, when it takes the form of hackneyed phrases and metaphors, is considered undesirable. For many postmodern writers, the *irregular* is as legitimate and as worthy of exploration as the regular.

These postmodern themes of difference, particularity, and irregularity come together in the postmodern celebration of diversity. The postmodern openness to diversity appears in many different domains. In the United States, for example, the image of the melting pot has been replaced by the image of the rainbow. The civil rights movement, the women's movement, the gay movement, and new provisions for the people with disabilities are all reflections of the postmodern tendency to honor human diversity.

Nor is this emphasis on diversity limited to civil rights. In the arts and architecture, many people welcomed "pomo" as a liberating movement, one that encouraged them to cut across historical, disciplinary, and artistic boundaries and methods. The playful mixing of styles from different periods within the same work, the notion of *pastiche* in the arts and architecture, has become a major postmodern theme. And in science, while the search for grand unifying theories continues, there is also a growing acceptance of microtheories and explanations—of miniature systems as well as great structures. In psychology also, concern with the basic principles of learning that held across all species has given way to emphasis on domain-specific principles of learning, as well as on individual differences in learning styles. Intelligence, rather than being considered one unified, quantifiable attribute, is now said to come in many diverse forms.[13]

Industry, too, has come a long way since the days when Henry Ford said that his cars could be any color so long as they were all black. Today, the automobile industry has a car for every age group, for every pocketbook, for every ego trip. The large motion picture theater has given way to the multiplex, where many different films, to suit different tastes, are shown at the same time. Video stores across America make thousands of movies available for less than the cost of a TV dinner. The fear frequently expressed in the first half of this century that mass-media technology would homogenize us has not been realized. In fact, the electronic revolution promises to do the opposite: to allow for a much fuller expression of human diversity. Since the 1970s, the explosion of new multimedia electronic products and networks, from laptop computers, interactive video games, and CD-ROMs to cable channels and electronic bulletin boards, has allowed consumers to tailor their electronic environment to meet their personal needs. The result has been a positive, if dizzying, sense of endless, individualized workspaces, entertainments, and education.

Postmodern diversity has its own dark side. In the political arena, particularly on university campuses, an obsessive concern with diversity has sometimes resulted, ironically, in a "political correctness" that can be as confining in its insistence on cultural relativism as it is liberating from the authority of "dead white men." In the industrial arena, the entertainment, information, and communications industries in particular have fueled a new and heightened consumerism by targeting and catering to the diverse interests of the buying public. Within this differentiated climate, children and adolescents have become markets toward whom a whole panoply of goods has been targeted.

Some voices have cautioned us that the long-term danger of the electronic revolution may not be an Orwellian loss of privacy and personal autonomy as once feared, but rather a sense of individual isolation and social fragmentation. Ithiel de Sola Pool, an authority on the social impact of telecommunications technologies, expressed the problem this way:

> What will it mean if audiences are increasingly fractionated into small groups with special interests? What will it mean if the agenda of national fads and concerns is no longer effectively set by a few mass media to which everyone is exposed? Such a trend raises for society the reverse problems from those posed by mass conformism. The cohesion and effective functioning of a democratic society depends upon some sort of public agora in which everyone participates and where all deal with a common agenda of problems, however much they may argue over the solutions.[14]

One of the many ironies of the postmodern world is that, with so many sources of information and avenues of communication available at our fingertips, we run the risk of a loss of community, of a shared view of the common good.

The postmodern emphasis on multicultural diversity has led some to charge that postmodernism is completely relativistic and denies any abiding human moral principles. That is not entirely the case. Modernism saw itself as superior to premodernism on the basis of its discovery of transcendental principles of ethical behavior. Indeed, modernity constantly defined itself in opposition to premodernity. Postmodernism does not define itself in that way, nor does it regard itself as superior to modernism. To do so would be to suggest that it has discovered even truer and more transcendental principles than modernity. Rather, the postmodern attitude is that universal principles must arise out of consensus, not out of some rational argument or sacred text. All religions, for example, share some values in common, and it is these commonly held values that can provide us with a general, nonrelativistic ethical code.

My own view is that there is much to be valued and much to be discarded in modernism, and much to be valued and much to be discarded in postmodernism. The aim in this book is not to argue that the modern family is superior to the postmodern, or vice versa. Both family configurations have their strengths and weaknesses. Rather, I hope to provide a discourse of the family that will reveal its intimate embeddedness in, and ongoing dynamic interaction with, the social institutions of media, school, law, and the helping professions. If we wish to counteract some of the negative effects of postmodern life, we can only do this by making changes in all of the institutions that affect the family, not just the family alone.

Writing about postmodernism exposes one to many pitfalls. I am, in many ways, rooted in the modern perspective, and it is not easy to free myself from established categories and ways of thinking. Indeed, in trying to describe the postmodern family in general terms, I am in some ways falling back on the modern search for broad generalities. Such contradictions are inevitable. It is really not possible to be outside a social system and within it at the same time. In the end, my aim is to provide a language with which to talk about what has happened to families and to children and youth in contemporary society. Having such a language enables us to frame problems in fresh ways, and this is often the first step toward their solution.

Modern Family Ties

To put the needs of children and adolescents in balance with the needs of their parents, I believe we will have to rethink the socially determined family ties that hold both nuclear and permeable families together. Up until about midcentury, kinship bonds within the nuclear family, and the institutions that nourished them, reflected the basic beliefs of modernity: a faith in progress, universality, and regularity. As we have moved into the postmodern era—with its emphasis on difference, particularity, and irregularity—our undergirding assumptions about kinship have undergone a paradigmatic change. In the rest of this chapter we will look at these changing concepts and how, under their influence, the seemingly invulnerable boundaries of the nuclear family have been shot full of holes by postmodernist attacks.

• *PROGRESS AND THE NUCLEAR FAMILY STRUCTURE*

During the modern period, social scientists did not hesitate to apply the notion of social progress to the evolution of the family. They argued that the family, like other social institutions, had evolved to its current ideal state—monogamy—after passing through the more primitive stages of sexual promiscuity, group marriage, and polygamy.[15]

In its ideal form, the nuclear family had the following characteristics: it consisted of two adults and at least one child who is the biological offspring of the two adults; the couple were married before they had children; all parental and marital tasks were performed exclusively by the married couple; and family members belonged to only one nuclear family and had boundaries that were legally, geographically, and biologically explicit.[16]

The idea that this evolved, monogamous nuclear family exemplified the highest form of kinship relations resulted in the widely held myth of the nuclear family as "the focus of everything good and warm in human relationships, a center of love, solidarity, harmony where each person fulfills personal needs contributing to the well being of other family members." The myth recognized dysfunctional families but assumed that these exceptions were attributable to the personal failings of family members, not to problems in the family structure itself.[17]

In other words, it was the structure of the nuclear family that was ideal, not necessarily the individual family members. Of course the many discrepancies between the nuclear family ideal and the reality of particular families were recognized by modern psychology and psychiatry. Sigmund Freud described some of the disturbances created by the powerful emotional ties of the nuclear family. The Oedipal conflict and sibling rivalry are only two of many examples. Yet, while Freud argued for more enlightened childrearing, he never suggested altering the kinship structure of the nuclear family.

The neo-Freudians Karen Horney, Harry Stack Sullivan, and Erich Fromm, while they rejected Freud's biological, sexual emphasis, retained his faith in the nuclear family structure. Though some specific families were pathological, the remainder fit the myth of the nuclear family as the most highly evolved, progressive structure for healthy kinship relations.[18]

• *UNIVERSALS AND FAMILY ROLES*

The modern belief in universals was mirrored in the rigid social roles members of nuclear families were required to play. Under the influence of Darwinism, the idea took hold that a society, like a species, evolves in the direction of increased specialization of function. The wings of birds, like the claws of squirrels, are highly specialized adaptations. As societies evolve toward greater complexity, their members, too, became increasingly specialized. Rather than one person performing many different functions, specialization resulted in each person performing only one function or a related set of functions. This specialization of functions within a society was called role differentiation. Although societies evolved at different rates, all were assumed to move toward increasing role differentiation of its members.

The sociologist Talcott Parsons was one of the many advocates of the role differentiation theory in the 1960s. Parsons contended that the premodern multiroled priest, magician, mathematician, medicine-man has evolved, in modern times, into a number of individuals, each of whom takes one and only one of these roles. Such role differentiation, Parsons argued, allows advanced societies to attain levels of cultural and economic productivity that were not possible in earlier societies with multiroled individuals.[19]

Within the nuclear family, this belief in role differentiation led to the definition of the universal father role as the "breadwinner" and the universal mother role as the "homemaker." In turn, children and adolescents were seen as "pupils" or "students." Social scientists regarded these clearly delimited and universal social roles as the "fittest" end product of the evolutionary progress of differentiation and specialization of function.

The relegation of modern parents to the roles of breadwinner and homemaker was stifling to many modern parents. On the other hand, the role designation of children as pupils ensured parental and societal efforts to meet young people's needs for protection and guidance. The belief in universal role differentiation, therefore, added its weight to the old imbalance.

• *REGULARITY AND PARENT-CHILD CONTRACTS*

In the nuclear family, parent-child interactions were dictated by a set of underlying contracts—unverbalized rules, understandings, and expectations that assured orderly and predictable attitudes and habits, that is to say, regularity. These contracts were based on the unquestioned unilateral authority of parents to set rules, limits, and standards for their offspring.[20]

Three basic parent-child contracts predominated in the modern family. In the first, parents provided freedom when young people demonstrated the requisite types of responsibility. For example, an infant is allowed to feed herself if she gets more food into her mouth than on the floor and walls, but not if the reverse is true.

A second contract involves parents providing support in return for the achievements of their offspring. To illustrate, as parents we show in many different ways our joy, happiness, and relief when our child says her first word or toilet trains herself.

The third contract requires parents to demonstrate commitment in return for a child's demonstration of loyalty. When our infant clearly prefers us to a stranger, we glow, and recommit ourselves to the child's well-being.

These contracts ensure that the child is properly socialized and able to function productively in the larger society, where similar reciprocal arrangements prevail.

In the normal course of development the contracts are implicitly rewritten to take account of the child's growing knowledge and skills.

Once a youngster is of school age we might allow her the freedom to ride her bike to a friend's house if we are convinced that she is responsible when crossing streets. Likewise, we support a schoolage child's achievements by complimenting her on the work she brings home and by attending piano recitals and soccer games. When a child demonstrates loyalty, as when she abides by family rules in our absence, we show our commitment by the time we devote to activities that she enjoys.

The socialization of children by means of implicit contracts takes a good deal of time and effort on the part of parents. It is not always easy to say no. But children understand that a parent who takes the time and makes the effort to set limits and standards cares enough about the child to do so—even if it means angry confrontations. As a young teenager once asked me, in relation to a friend who apparently had unlimited access to his parent's liquor cabinet, "I guess they don't love him or they would say no, wouldn't they?"

Contracts are thus often difficult for parents to teach but very beneficial for children to learn. The regularity in the lives of children provided by parent-child contracts, therefore, weighted the balance in favor of the needs of children over those of their parents.

Postmodern Family Ties

Since midcentury, several kinds of evidence have undermined the myth of the nuclear family as the ideal structure for nurturing healthy kinship relations. First, recent studies make clear that family violence was much more prevalent in the nuclear family than we previously assumed. It occurred in the absence of mental illness and in all social classes. The mistreatment and abuse of children in nuclear families, we now know, was widespread. Murders by people the victim knows well were—and still are—much more common than murders by total strangers, and many of the former occur within the confines of the family home.

Second, studies of family interaction patterns reveal that behaviors which seem most pathogenic—parents expressing affection in words but hostility in action; alliances between different family members; keeping secrets, scapegoating, expressing sarcasm, and belittling—are also observed quite regularly in "normal" families.[21]

By midcentury, then, scholars of the family were beginning to deconstruct the myth of the nuclear family as necessarily creating a warm, harmonious, comforting refuge and haven. Research findings about abuse, incest, and addiction in nuclear families, together with the sociopolitical revolutions of the 1960s and 70s and the astronomical rise in the divorce rate, have all contributed to the postmodern dethronement of the nuclear family. This deposition cleared the way for the emergence of a different notion of kinship structures.

• *DIFFERENCE AND THE PERMEABLE FAMILY STRUCTURE*

In the 1960s the many demands for the recognition and legitimization of human diversity—by minorities, women, and gays, among others—challenged the idea that only one kind of kinship structure was suited to the function of meeting the emotional needs of family members. The postmodern permeable family includes not one but many different relationship patterns. It is a true pastiche of kinship structures. Two-parent working families, single-mother families, single-father families, stepfamilies, multigenerational families, adoptive families, unmarried families, like-sex parent families, surrogate mother families—all are now recognized, if not fully accepted, as ways to put together a family.

Although some writers still contend that the classic nuclear family, consisting of two married parents and their biological offspring, is the best environment for rearing children, the evidence to support this contention has not been overwhelming.[22] To be sure, a strong, emotionally healthy, financially secure nuclear family may be the least stressful arrangement for childrearing. But not all nuclear families approach that ideal. We now recognize that abuse and neglect may be as frequent in nuclear families as love, protection, and commitment are in nonnuclear families.

What appears to be crucial to effective childrearing is not so much the particular kinship structure as the emotional climate of the family. Authoritative parents, who set firm limits with love and thoughtfulness, are more effective than either strict, authoritarian parents or permissive, laissez-faire parents. And this is true regardless of the particular kinship structure of the family.[23]

The postmodern acceptance of many different family structures has contributed to the erosion of the walls between our public and our private lives. Divorce is a publicly visible, yet private, hurt. Our children, cared for outside the home, are free to talk to strangers about what goes on within it. Moreover, the demolition of the myth of the happy nuclear family has led to the public airing of much of what is wrong with modern family life. What were once private family matters have now become scripts for amateur theatrics. Television talkshow hosts such as Oprah, Donahue, Geraldo, and Sally, among others, daily reveal the innermost secrets of private family life to the public television audience.

In general, the proliferation and acceptance of these new kinship patterns and living arrangements have benefited parents and adults more than it has children and youth. The many options now available to parents, for example, have not been accompanied by a comparable expansion of programs that provide quality, accessible, and affordable childcare. Despite the efforts of childcaregivers, many of whom display heroic altruism in their devotion to children's welfare, many children today are not being adequately cared for by the nonfamily members entrusted with their nurturance.

Likewise, the loss of privacy generally does more harm to children than to adults. Children need boundaries and protected spaces. The openness of the permeable family kinship forms can contribute to children's feelings of insecurity. While these facets of permeable family life are also uncomfortable for many parents, their overall impact is greater on the young than on the fully grown.

•*PARTICULARITY AND ROLE DE-DIFFERENTIATION*

Just as the modern belief in universals contributed to the belief in progressive role differentiation, the postmodern belief in human diversity and particularity is leading to the reverse, namely, role de-differentiation. Although we still have a way to go, there has been a significant de-differentiation of, for example, gender and occupational roles. Women in executive offices, in jetliner cockpits, or on construction sites are one side of role de-differentiation. Male stewards on airlines and househusbands are the other side of the pattern.

Unfortunately, this postmodern de-differentiation of gender and occupational roles has not always been accompanied by widespread institutional acceptance. The modern ideal of role differentiation dies hard. As Jeanne Bodin and Bonnie Mitelman write:

> We determined that women who are struggling to combine careers and families sense an undercurrent of nonacceptance, be it direct or indirect, on the part of the established order of America today. They seem to feel somehow that their priorities, lifestyles, and values are not being taken seriously. They feel that our schools, our government, our institutions, our organizations, and our industries do not substantively, seriously, and consistently reflect the realities of many American families, that is, that the mother works. Again and again working mothers give examples of the message they hear all too often: the "normal" American mother is at home all the time and is always available to her family.[24]

It is not just the larger social institutions that have failed to recognize role de-differentiation. Many contemporary fathers persist in their convenient commitment to modern role differentiation. As Arlie Hochschild reports in her book, *The Second Shift:*

> Although most working mothers I talked with did most of the work of the home, they felt more permission to complain about it than did working women fifty years ago. Many of them wanted to share or wanted to believe that they already did. A hundred years ago, American women lacked social permission to ask for a man's help in "women's work." As Gwendolyn Hughs pointed out in 1925, in her book *Mothers in Industry*, earlier in this century supermomming

> wasn't a strategy, it was a way of life. Today, women feel they are allowed to ask for help at home; but on the other hand, they still have to ask. A hundred years from now men may presume it's their role to share. We're in the middle of a social revolution.[25]

The postmodern recognition of the particularity and multifacetedness of individual interests, abilities, and talents should, in theory, lead to the de-differentiation of rigid gender, occupational, and parental roles. Unfortunately, in fact, postmodern ideas have not yet displaced the modern ideal of differentiated social roles. This levies a heavy labor tax on the many mothers who now work outside the home and who must also do most of the work within it. The United States does not have a family leave law on the books, and government provides precious little public support for daycare and preschooling. The resulting pressures on mothers increase absenteeism and labor turnover and eat into their productivity on the job.[26]

The permeable family, while freeing postmodern mothers to work and to pursue careers, has not liberated them from the modern role perception of childcaregiver and homemaker. It is only half of a revolution. For many contemporary mothers, at all income levels, elements of the old need imbalance persist. Many working mothers often have neither the time nor the peace of mind, given the poor quality of much childcare, to take a lot of pleasure in their new options.

Role de-differentiation has extended to children and adolescents as well as to their parents. In some homes children do much of the cooking and housecleaning. Many contemporary teenagers do much of the household shopping, and others have almost total responsibility for their younger siblings. Some young people in single-parent families actually assume the parental role. A single mother told me that her teenage son passes judgment on all of her dates and is not above telling her by what hour she should be home. To be sure, children and adolescents did similar things in the modern era, but these nontraditional child and adolescent roles are much more common in postmodern society.

The deconstruction of family roles, where it has occurred, has often contributed to the disintegration of the distinction between homeplace and workplace. With the advent of powerful personal computers, modems, fax machines, answering machines, electronic mail, and data-base access, together with the explosion of information-based occupations, approximately thirty million people now have space set aside at home where they do some or all of their work. The majority of businesses begun by women in recent years have been started in home offices. At the same time, more than 4,000 firms either support childcare services or have childcare facilities on their premises. In short, the workplace is now moving into the homeplace just as the homeplace is moving into the workplace.

With respect to role differentiation, therefore, the picture is mixed. While postmodern role de-differentiation has occurred in the breaking down of gender barriers to various occupations, we have remained modern in the expectation that working mothers should continue to do the king's share of the housework and childcare.

The solution, however, is not a surrender to confining and suffocating role differentiation. Rather, we need to provide what so many other Western countries already offer, namely, quality, affordable childcare for all those families that require it. Helping many contemporary fathers further de-differentiate their role perception of themselves and their wives would also not be amiss.

• *IRREGULARITY AND FAMILY SCHEDULES*

The postmodern emphasis on kinship diversity and role differentiation has also transformed the nature of parent-child relationships. Parent-child contracts were created on the assumption that regularity was desirable and healthy. The irregularity forced on many parents by the pressures of family and work has meant that contractual relationships have lost some of their allure. Although many postmodern parents still work very hard to maintain some semblance of contractual interactions, it is often exhausting for overworked postmodern parents to hold up their end of the bargain: to support their children's achievements by attending plays, ball games, and recitals, chaperoning fieldtrips, or helping out with the school newspaper. The economist Victor Fuchs contends that children have lost from ten to twelve hours of parental time per week since 1960.[27]

What often replaces contracts in permeable family life are schedules and lists. Unlike the contract—an underlying agreement which remains the same despite changes in content—schedules and lists are variable and irregular with no underlying agreement. The schedule tells children what they should be doing and when they should be doing it. Lists are of the same order. In busy families, with everyone going his or her own way, transitory scheduling and lists, rather than abiding contracts, have become the major currency of family interactions.

Schedules and lists teach children the skills of organization and discipline, both of which are basic to survival in the postmodern world. But they shift the balance of authority and respect within the family, and this can have unsettling consequences. When parents establish contracts, they operate under unilateral authority, in which they hold the power to give or withdraw support, freedom, and commitment. Unilateral authority is the kind of authority we all have to obey when we stop at traffic lights or pay our income tax. With schedules and lists, however, a different form of authority comes into play, namely mutual authority. In making out schedules and lists and doing what needs to be done, parents and children are on a par. Children, for example, may have to remind parents of what is on their schedule—soccer practice, guitar lessons—or what has to go on the list—goalie gloves, haircut, book report. Mutual authority is the type that exists between friends and between husbands and wives. Mutual authority exists when equals create, accept, and enforce the rules of the relationship.

Clearly, both unilateral and mutual authority are necessary to a democratic society. But in establishing contracts under the umbrella of unilateral authority, the parent clearly distinguishes between adult and child. In the exercise of mutual authority, in the making of lists and schedules, however, the differences between children and adults are minimized. For this reason postmodern parents often find it difficult to exercise unilateral authority when it seems necessary. This is frustrating for parents, and it can be harmful to young people, who often need adults to be in charge.

As we shall see in succeeding chapters, the shift in emphasis from unilateral to mutual authority within the family is coupled with a similar change in the surrounding society. This postmodern shift in the locus of authority is a major contributor to the new imbalance.

Family Feelings

3

From Child-Centered to Parent-Centered

Our most binding family ties are the emotional ones—the feelings that attach us one to the other. In the modern nuclear family these binding sentiments were largely child-centered in the sense that they gave preference to the well-being of children and required the self-sacrifice of parents. In the postmodern permeable family, however, the sentimental ties have been transformed and are now more likely to be adult-centered to the extent that they favor the well-being of parents and adults and require self-sacrifice from the young.

This is, of course, a generalization. Many contemporary families remain primarily child-centered in their sentiments. For example, many middle-class black families of today resemble white middle-class families of two decades ago. In these families, the well-being and education of the children are often placed above the needs of the parents. Likewise, many contemporary low-income and immigrant families remain child-centered in their sentiments. These parents may work at menial jobs so that their children can get an education and do better than the parents. So, while the trend toward adult-centered family feelings is a very real one, there are many exceptions to the pattern.

As Edward Shorter described in his book *The Making of the Modern Family,* the emotional ties that bind the family together are of three kinds. First there are those that bind the parents to one another. Second, there are those that bind parents to their offspring. And, third, there are those that dictate the relation of the family and family members to the larger community. For many families, the character of these three sets of emotions has changed quite remarkably from the modern to the postmodern era.[1]

Sentiments of the Nuclear Family

The nuclear family was but one of many social institutions resulting from the industrial revolution and the emergence of democratic governments. As a large proportion of the population in the United States and Great Britain moved from the farm to the city, the family lost much of its independence and its communal character. Parents worked in factories that were often at long distances from the home. As a result, they became dependent on store-bought food, clothing, furniture, and appliances. This dependence often made the larger society appear exploitative and uncaring, while the home provided a place of nurturance, security, and relaxation. These circumstances contributed to the formation of three sentiments that, together, gave the nuclear family its unique emotional tone: romantic love (the tie of parents to one another), maternal love (the tie of parents to offspring), and domesticity (the tie of family to community).

• ROMANTIC LOVE

In the premodern era, when families were integral parts of larger communities, the community rather than individuals directly or indirectly chose marital partners. In parts of Europe, for example, male offspring were given acreage of the family farm as their birthright. It was important to choose the right partner who would bring an equal or a more valuable dowry to the marriage. Property and social status were more important than personal preference in the selection of marital partners. To be sure, young people "fell in love" then as they do now, but love relationships were not socially recognized nor given importance in marital decisionmaking.

All of that changed with the industrial revolution, the breakdown of community control, and the prevalence of city living. While property and status were, and still are, important, personal preference came to play the most prominent role in marital choice. It was at this point that the discourse of romantic love emerged and became a dominant sentiment of the newly emergent nuclear family. Romantic love entailed the idea that there was one and only one person on earth whom a person was destined to meet, to love, and to cherish for a lifetime. Romantic love became the rationale for sexual abstinence, for "saving oneself" for one's predestined lover.

Romantic love has probably been present in some form since the advent of humankind. This is a real possibility inasmuch as romantic love reflects, in part at least, the new mental abilities that emerge during adolescence and permit young people to construct ideals and possible realities, as opposed to extant realities. Thanks to these new mental powers, adolescents are able to idealize another person. Such idealizations are at the heart of romance, the belief in the perfection of one's fated partner. Romantic attachments were clearly present in premodern times but simply could not be acted upon. The concept of chivalry—the qualities associated with knighthood during the Middle Ages, such as courtesy, bravery, honesty—included the dedication of oneself to an unattainable woman. In the premodern period, Don Quixote's idealization of the peasant girl Dulcinea exemplifies this unconsummated romantic love.

With the ascendance of the nuclear family, however, romantic feelings became the most important factor in the selection of a marital partner. To be sure, many people then and now marry for reasons other than romantic love. It is the *option* to marry on the basis of romance that was new to the modern era, not always its execution.

One result of the emergence of romantic love as the basis for marital choice is what Shorter has called the "first" sexual revolution. Once courting and marriage became based on romance rather than convenience, the sexual behavior of couples who fell in love changed. In premodern times, premarital sexual intercourse, even between engaged couples, was proscribed by the community. With the collapse of communal control and the introduction of romantic love as the basis of marriage, premarital sex between engaged couples, and even between couples who were not yet engaged but fancied themselves to have fallen eternally in love, became more common. An increase in out-of-wedlock pregnancies was one manifestation of this first sexual revolution.[2]

In nineteenth-century fiction as in real life, romantic choice was a popular theme. Jane Austen, in *Pride and Prejudice,* has the sister of her heroine run off and marry an army officer without her parents' knowledge or permission. Thomas Hardy in *The Return of the Native* suggests that an attractive, unmarried couple are having sexual relations, although he never makes this explicit. Likewise, in the *Mayor of Casterbridge,* the mayor has an affair with an unmarried woman. Later this woman falls in love with, and marries, the mayor's rival. In the twentieth century, in both romantic fiction and in real life, romantic love came into full flower, and couples made their marital choices independently of family and community—sometimes in opposition to family values and societal mores.

Yet the idealized image of romantic love, the image of a lifelong happy marriage to a special person "made in heaven for you," started to fracture in the early decades of this century. Romantic love also embodied the notion that a woman was relatively helpless and dependent, in need of a prince charming, and that once he arrived on the scene she would be happy to devote her life to him and to their children. During the nineteenth century, these perceptions were made a little more bearable by the opportunity afforded women to engage in creative crafts within the home, such as baking, cooking, canning, weaving, needlecraft, and gardening. But in the twentieth century the romantic image of the helpless woman began to take on some reality.

The century's new infatuation with modern store-bought, machine-made goods effectively destroyed the craft skills that gave early nineteenth-century housewives outlets for their creativity and ingenuity.[3] Women were told—and believed—that white bread, baked in a factory and purchased at a store, was more nutritious and sanitary than bread baked at home. Coffee, preground and vacuum-packed, was tastier, they were assured, than coffee freshly ground in one's own kitchen. Clothing made in sweatshops, and bought in stores, was more stylish than what women could create on their own sewing machines. First and foremost, however—and this was the major selling point for all machine-made goods—they were more efficient and thus more economical than anything that was made at home. In this "Betty Crocker" prepackaged world, housewives were transformed into unskilled consumers who could be manipulated, via advertising, into purchasing the latest "labor-saving" products and gadgets.

As a result, the ideal of romantic love often became an increasingly empty excuse for increasingly empty lives. Vivian Gornick describes her own mother's dependence on the sentiment of romantic love to justify her existence:

> Papa's love did indeed have wondrous properties; it not only compensated for her boredom and anxiety, it was the cause of her boredom and anxiety. Countless sentences having to do with all in her life that was less than satisfactory began, "Believe me, if it wasn't for Papa's love." She would speak openly of how she hated to give up working when she got married (she'd been a bookkeeper in a Lower East Side bakery), how good it was to have your own money in your pocket, not receive an allowance like a child, how stupid life was now, and how she'd love to go back to work. Believe her. If it wasn't for Papa's love.[4]

The other side of the fracture in romance appeared in novels such as *The Man in the Gray Flannel Suit*, wherein the "bitchy housewife" made her appearance:

> She had a high art of deflating him, of enfeebling him, with one quick, innocent sounding phrase. By the most careless comment on

> his bulky new overcoat she could make him feel like a lout in it; by crisply suggesting that he "try for once to talk about something besides motors and stocks" while they rode to a formidable dinner with an elocutionary senator, she could make him feel so unintelligent that he would be silent all evening. The easy self-confidence which weeks of industrial triumphs had built up in him she could flatten in five seconds. She was, in fact, a genius in planting in him an assurance of his inferiority.[5]

In this century, therefore, the ideal of modern romance was splintered as many wives felt useless and neglected by their husbands and as many husbands felt undermined and demeaned by their wives. Again, this is a general characterization and does not take account of all those couples who maintained a loving and mutually respectful and supportive relationship, quite in opposition to the societal stereotypes.

• *MATERNAL LOVE*

While parents, particularly mothers, have always been attached to their infants, societal conditions frequently made this attachment difficult to maintain. First of all, the high rate of infant mortality in the premodern era meant that such attachments often ended in despair. Perhaps to prevent the depression that infant death entailed, a number of societal practices evolved which worked against early attachment of mother and child.

One of these premodern attachment-discouraging practices was to leave infants unnamed until they had survived into the second year. Another practice that discouraged maternal attachment was tightly wrapping, or swaddling, infants. Swaddling effectively prevented the close physical interactions (cuddling, stroking, and kissing) that are so much a part of modern mothers' and fathers' affection for their infants.

A third practice which had the same distancing effect was wet-nursing. Breast-feeding was not fashionable among the well-to-do in the early modern era; infants were often nursed by lactating women hired for the purpose. In some places, such as nineteenth-century France, city infants were sent to the country to be nursed by lactating farm women. Often a wet nurse would neglect the city infant and feed her own child first, leaving little milk for the urban child—who, in many cases, died. In Rouen, the mortality rate for home-reared legitimate children was 19 percent, whereas the mortality rate for children sent to a wet nurse was 35 percent.[6]

During the nineteenth century a new humane concern for, and understanding of, the needs of infants came about through the dissemination of new medical knowledge about the importance of nutrition, cleanliness, fresh air, and exercise. This new health orientation toward infants was evidenced by the many parents who gave up the practices of wet-nursing and swaddling, and who began to follow sound nutritional and cleanliness routines. As a result, infant mortality rates dropped markedly.

These changes in parental orientation were reflected in a new discourse that described mothers as warm, nurturant caregivers, a characterization that was hardly possible in premodern times. This new nurturant view of the maternal role became a popular theme in nineteenth-century literature. In Harriet Beecher Stowe's bestseller, *Uncle Tom's Cabin,* the heroine is a model of maternal affection and care. Stowe also wrote many books and articles extolling the nurturing of children and of animals as well. When urged by a friend to put aside some of her domestic duties to finish a story, she is said to have replied: "But my dear, here is a baby in my arms and two little pussies by my side, and there is a great baking down in the kitchen and there is a 'new girl' for 'help,' besides preparations to be made for housecleaning next week. It is really out of the question, you see."[7]

The affectionate, nurturant mother became a fixture in much of literature, and later in films, and still later in television. But those idealized images masked significant changes in the maternal role that took place in the early decades of the twentieth century under the influence of the new fields of child psychology and of psychoanalysis. Modern mothers were expected to understand child growth and development if they were to be "good" mothers. And they had to be psychologically healthy themselves to avoid damaging the psyches of their children.

In 1942 Philip Wylie in his book *A Generation of Vipers* railed against "momism," arguing that the large numbers of men who had been turned down by the draft were in such poor emotional shape because of improper maternal care. As Nancy Rubin puts this transformation of the sentiment of maternal love: "Slowly, the madonna-like mother so pervasive for a century of American culture was transformed into a she-devil or at the very least a troublesome demon dancing neurotically on the backs of her children in payment for their birthright." The idea of maternal love was thus turned on its head as the emotional problems of children were increasingly attributed to maternal overprotection and coddling or to narcissistic manipulation.[8]

A brief respite from these attacks came during World War II, when women were welcomed into the factories to fill the places left by men who went off to war. In all parts of the country, daycare programs to meet the needs of these working mothers were established. Some of these facilities were excellent and have yet to be emulated today. For example, the Kaiser shipyards in Portland, Oregon, established what Caroline Zinser calls "the best daycare that ever was." These daycare centers had large, airy classrooms, around-the-clock childcare, special provisions for sick children, and the Home Service Food Program: "By selecting from a weekly menu, a mother could order her family's evening meal to be picked up—precooked and packaged—at the center's kitchen when she collected her child at the end of the day shift."[9]

The acceptance of working mothers and the provision of quality childcare was, however, short-lived. Once the war was over and women were no longer needed in the factories, mothers who worked were derided as neglecting their maternal duties. The British psychoanalyst John Bowlby, in his book *Child Care and the Growth of Love,* published in 1953, had this to say about the child's need for mothering:

> The absolute need of infants and toddlers for the continuous care of their mothers will be borne in on all who read this book, and some will exclaim, "Can I then never leave my child?" Though far more knowledge is required before a proper answer can be given, some advice is perhaps possible. In the first place we must recognize that leaving any child under three years of age is a major operation only to be undertaken for good and sufficient reasons and, when undertaken, to be planned with great care.[10]

While it is certainly true that young children should not be placed in out-of-home care without a great deal of thought and effort as to the placement, Bowlby strongly intimates that mothers should really not do so at all. He and many other health professionals reinforced the sentiment of maternal love as a mainstay of the nuclear family.[11] Yet the concept of maternal deprivation, though supposedly based on research, nonetheless managed to ignore the data showing that many "maternally deprived" children, such as those in the Kaiser Childcare Centers, actually thrived.

As a result of this postwar attention to maternal deprivation, modern women were damned if they demonstrated maternal love, because momism was destructive to their sons, but they were damned if they did not demonstrate it, because neglect was not normal and was harmful to their children! Clearly the sentiment of maternal love as it developed in the early decades of this century was not sensitive to the predicament that it presented to women.

Though modern mothers may have been unhappy at their low status and lack of opportunity, most of them did not take it out on the children. Rather, childrearing became one arena where mothers could be creative in the activities, toys, and reading material they chose for their offspring. Thus, the sentiment of maternal love weighted the family balance in favor of children over mothers.

It should be said that modern fathers often were also not highly regarded, at least by the media. Analyzing the role of fathers in modern films, Martha Wolfenstein concluded:

> In American life, children are expected to surpass their parents. The father is not the model the boy will follow when he grows up. But the boy longs for a man who can induct him into the mysteries and powers of masculinity, who has the strengths and skill to which the boy aspires and who can show him how. Thus we have seen how the boy heroes of these American films [*Shane, The Little Fugitive, When I Grow Up*] are drawn to men other than their fathers to whom they can look with admiration, men who are masters of wonderful skills—the gunfighter, the cowboy, the acrobatic clown—who might impart to the boy the masculine prowess he longs to attain. And we have also seen the dream of the father who could be both strong and tender projected onto the past—great grandfather—not the father of today.[12]

While the boy's need for a masculine archetype could be met outside the family, the need of the hardworking, benign modern father to be a role model for his own son was undermined. For every wise, competent "Father Knows Best," there was at least one bumbling "Dagwood Bumstead." It is true, of course, that in many professional and business families, the sons pursued the same professions as their fathers. And in many factory towns like Rochester, New York, sons followed their fathers in working for Kodak or Bausch and Lomb. Nonetheless, the media image, if not the reality, was often of a father who, as a man, was not worthy of emulation.

• *DOMESTICITY*

The third sentiment of the family deals with its relation to the larger community. In the nuclear family Shorter calls this sentiment "domesticity"—"the family's awareness of itself as a precious emotional unit that must be protected with privacy and isolation from outside intrusion":

> Romantic love detached the couple from communal sexual supervision and allowed choice on the basis of sexual and personal attraction. Maternal love created a nest within which the modern family would ensconce itself and it removed many women from involvement with community life. Domesticity, beyond that, sealed off the family as a whole from its pre-modern integration within a community. Accordingly, family members came to feel far more solidarity with one another than they did with their various age and sex groups.[13]

In the twentieth century, while the home continued to be thought of as a place where mothers provided children with the basic values and attitudes required for citizenship in the community, at the same time it also became a refuge from the demands of communal life. But by the later decades of the century, as Christopher Lasch describes, the sentiment of domesticity could no longer deliver:

> As business, policy and diplomacy grow more savage and warlike, men seek a haven in private life, in personal relations, above all in the family—the last refuge of love and decency. Domestic life, however, seems increasingly incapable of providing these comforts. Hence the undercurrent of anxiety that runs through the vast and growing body of commentary on the state of the family.

As Lasch points out, the idea of the home as haven from a demanding, cruel world suggests that it is always a warm, welcoming place. The truth is, however, that nuclear family life is not, and never was, serene and unruffled. Unhappiness and conflict, as well as warmth and nurturance, were all part of nuclear family life. In many ways, the sentiment of domesticity denied the reality that the home could be as savage and warlike as the outside world.[14]

Nonetheless, the idea of domesticity kept many parents in marriages that were often unhappy and degrading. Such parents tried to "put up a front" for their children, frequently at great emotional cost to themselves. Children, of course, were not fooled. But what did come across to the children in such families was their parents' willingness to sacrifice for them. This willingness of modern parents to forgo their personal happiness for the sake of maintaining a safe haven for their children became the true meaning of the sentiment of domesticity.

Sentiments of the Permeable Family

Changes in American society since the 1950s are helping to transform the sentiments of the modern nuclear family into those of the permeable postmodern family. In place of romantic love, we now have consensual love; where maternal love once reigned, we now have shared parenting; and in place of domesticity, we find urbanity. Parents have benefited from these adjustments in how we feel about our loved ones and what we expect of family members, but children have, by and large, been the losers.

• *CONSENSUAL LOVE*

In the postmodern era, the feelings of parents for one another have changed from romantic love to what might be called consensual love. Romantic love was ushered in by the first sexual revolution, which freed individuals to choose their own marital partners. As Shorter's work makes clear, consensual love was ushered in by a second sexual revolution that made premarital intercourse among nonengaged couples socially acceptable. In realms where romantic love was idyllic and mystical, consensual love has become practical and realistic.[15]

The second sexual revolution occurred in the 1960s and resulted in our postmodern orientation to sexual behavior. Until the 60s, sexual activity among unmarried men and women was generally limited to couples who were going together or who were engaged. During the 60s, sexual activity between unmarried, uncommitted partners became, for the first time, socially acceptable. Having sex with numerous different partners before marriage has become, in the postmodern world, a common practice. The romantic idea that there is one and only one person in the whole world whom we are fated to be with, and the only person with whom we will ever have sexual relations, lives on in fiction and fantasy, but not in postmodern reality. Even in the wake of the AIDS pandemic, the sexual activities of people today have much more in common with those of the 1970s than with those of the 1950s.

The second sexual revolution has transformed the sentimental bond underlying the marital relationship. Romantic love presupposed a double standard, that nice women would not have sex before marriage, whereas this was permissible for men. Presumably the male ego could not stand the thought of another man having had intercourse with his wife, while women's egos could accommodate to this reality. At least part of the idea behind a woman's "saving herself" for her husband was that this evidence of abstinence would be reciprocated by the husband's fidelity once the marriage was consummated. Abstinence was the price a woman paid for the promise of lifelong commitment on the part of the husband. That this commitment was often not honored does not change the fact that fidelity was part of the marital contract founded on the sentiment of romantic love.

The advent of uncommitted premarital sex has changed the contractual assumptions of the permeable marriage. Neither men nor women expect their partner to be a virgin when the wedding vows are spoken. While romantic love is not dead, it is no longer the essence of marriage. What is critical is that there be consensus between the partners not only about their sexual activities (even when the agreement simply makes explicit their mutual intention to practice monogamy) but also about all facets of the marital relationship. No longer is the woman to be regarded as helpless and dependent, but rather as an equal and voting partner in the relationship.

In addition, while both partners presumably want the relationship to last, they also appreciate the fact that it may not be, and perhaps should not be, lifelong. The prenuptial agreement came into being to take account of this contingency.

This consensual understanding is even evident in current dating patterns. To illustrate, some young women now invite my sons to dinner and pick up the tab. Having grown up in the era of romantic love, when men always paid the bill, I have difficulty understanding how my sons can be comfortable with this arrangement.

Although she does not use the term "consensual love," Ann Swidler nicely describes this postmodern sentiment: "The obligation to sacrifice oneself for another is replaced by the duty to respect the other person's separateness, to recognize the other person's need for growth and change, and to give to the other in return for what one receives . . . We no longer believe that an adult's life can be meaningfully defined by the sacrifice he or she makes for spouse or children."[16]

The notion of consensual love is thus freighted (some would say overfreighted) by a concern with maintaining individual autonomy. While the concept of consensual love provides more freedom and equality for marital partners, it can have some less salutary consequences. For example, some young mothers with whom I have talked tell me they continue to work even though they would like, and can afford, to stay home with their young children. They work out of concern that the lost seniority and salary would put them in dire financial straits should they have to return to work in the event of a divorce. Anticipating that a divorce might occur, even at a time when the relationship is a secure one, highlights the difference between romantic and consensual love.

This transformation in our sentiments regarding love is evidenced in the changes in song lyrics that were written as we moved from the modern to the postmodern era. A content analysis of the top forty songs for the odd-numbered years between 1953 and 1971 shows how changes in music lyrics mirrored the transition from romantic to consensual love:

> Love and romance were far and away the most popular subject matter, comprising 65 percent of all themes. While the proportion of love songs did not change significantly over time, their mode of expression did. When the data were analyzed by splitting the time period covered by the study in half (1953–1961) and (1963–1971) love lyrics stressing older values or older "sentimentality" significantly decreased. That is to say, themes which spoke of love as eternal, as having one fated partner or as resulting from outside forces (such as angels, or "Mr. Sandman") declined.
>
> Also declining were songs describing relationships where one partner pledged continued fidelity or would never love again, or where hearts were broken. At the same time, love lyrics indicating a "new sentimentality" significantly increased. Themes grouped under new values included songs in which love had one or more of the following characteristics: it was often transient; partners, of which there could be many, were realistically appraised; relationships had to be actively worked for, and love was fun.[17]

The idea of love as a lifelong commitment has, of course, not been given up by everyone. Many couples at all age levels would like to think that their love, if not its romantic stage, is an abiding one, and for many it will indeed be so. But it will not be true for all couples. And the postmodern acceptance of differences, and rejection of ideal types, helps us to be more accepting of divorce. We appreciate that couples who divorce do so not because they are bad people, or unlucky, but simply because they are human. As humans, we continue to grow. Sometimes mistakes or simply immaturity gets us into marriages that sooner or later stop working, and sometimes our growth gets us out of them. While consensual love offers mixed blessings for parents, it does provide men and women with many more options than were available when romantic love was the prevailing family sentiment.

For children and youth, however, the demise of romantic love and of parental commitment to marriage has been detrimental. And this, again, not because the parents' split-up per se is damaging but rather because the message of parental sacrifice that staying in an unhappy marriage conveyed has been lost. Genuine self-sacrifice, when it is done without attempts to exact a return from children, is the clearest and most powerful evidence of parents' unconditional love and care for their children. Please understand, I am *not* saying that parents should stay in bad marriages for the sake of their children. I am saying that decent children do appreciate parents who put them first, and they often work hard to warrant that show of parental commitment. Parents who divorce need to show this caring and concern in other ways, and many, many divorced parents find a means to do so.

•*SHARED PARENTING*

The family sentiment dealing with the relation of parents to their children has also been transformed from the modern to the postmodern era. The women's movement of the 1960s effectively broke down the idea that only a stay-at-home mother could love her children and rear them properly. We now recognize that both men and women can fill multiple roles and fill them well. A woman can pursue a career and still be a loving, nurturing, and effective mother.

The de-differentiation of the maternal role has made it possible for women to care for themselves as well as for others, and they are often better for their loved ones as a result. It is also true, however, that many more women today than in the past work because of economic necessity rather than choice. Many women who might choose to stay home with their young children often find it economically impossible to do so.

With the deconstruction of the modern sentiment of maternal love, a new, postmodern sentiment has emerged, one that might be called shared parenting. In some ways, the idea of shared parenting is, like many other features of postmodern life, a throwback to an earlier social era. Shared parenting was the rule in premodern times when childrearing was part of extended family life and communal living; every adult was in some respects a parent to every child. In the postmodern world, shared parenting reflects women's desire "to develop a strong bond with our child and at the same time maintain our partnership, our adult friendships, as well as our involvements with the outside world. What we discover, even before we have a baby, is that our lives are thrown off balance once we become parents and we need time to establish a new equilibrium."[18]

The postmodern sentiment of shared parenting has evolved in several directions. First, in the more egalitarian, permeable family, fathers and mothers are expected to share equally the responsibility for childrearing. More and more men are now asking for paternity leave to be at home when a new baby arrives. And it is not at all unusual today to find a househusband who stays home and looks after the children while the mother works. In airports and aboard planes I am often amused to observe quite rugged-looking men cuddling babies and chattering "motherese" to them. (A more modest evidence of this new egalitarianism in childrearing is the introduction of changing boards into men's restrooms at major airports around the country.)

Shared parenting between husband and wife is, however, more often accepted in principle than it is in practice. In reality, research suggests that women continue to be burdened with an unreasonably large share of childrearing activities.[19]

As more women have joined the workforce and as the number of single parents has increased, shared parenting has expanded to include some grandparents, as well as day-care-center and home-care-center providers. Grandparents and these nonfamilial providers now look after infants and toddlers as well as preschoolers. More affluent couples may share childrearing with an *au pair* or a nanny, or a fulltime domestic—usually from an ethnic minority, it might be added.

Joint custody arrangements for the care of children after divorce have become popular in some parts of the country as a way of explicitly recognizing the shared childrearing responsibilities of both parents before and after the breakup of a marriage. In contrast, the alimony and child-support arrangements of the modern divorce spoke only to the financial contribution of one partner, usually the father, but not to his actual role in childrearing. While joint custody can work well, it can also present many problems when the parents are hostile toward one another or when they do not agree about such matters as which schools the children should attend.[20]

The large number of mothers in the workforce whose young children are cared for by others has led to a reassessment of Bowlby's concept of maternal deprivation. A number of studies of the effects of daycare on children have now been conducted. One of the dimensions assessed is the issue raised by Bowlby, namely, the security of the attachment between infants and their mothers under different parenting arrangements. These studies are based on a well-established difference between two types of attachment.

At about one year of age, securely attached infants explore and manipulate a strange environment when their mother is present and are minimally disturbed by minor separations but are enthusiastic about their mother's return. Insecurely attached infants may show one of two patterns. The infants in one group show little distress when the mother leaves and do not seek contact when she returns. Those in a second group display distress and crying both when the mother is present and when she is absent. In some samples of subjects, securely attached infants make up about 65 percent of the children and insecurely attached children make up about 35 percent.[21]

In a review of studies of children in daycare, Clarke-Stewart found that 29 percent of infants whose mothers were not employed, or who were employed part-time, were insecurely attached. Among fulltime working mothers, 36 percent of the infants were insecurely attached.[22] The difference is not large, though it is statistically significant, and the reasons for it are not clear. Fulltime working mothers may simply be more tired than part-time or nonemployed mothers, and this may affect their interactions with their children. In their review of the daycare research, Mavis Hetherington and Ross

Park, authors of a leading child psychology textbook, conclude: "There is little clear evidence that day-care is likely to cause disruptions in the infant-parent attachment relationship. In fact, day-care may have positive effects for some infants, particularly if the day-care is of good quality."[23] While there are still a few writers who decry the notion of working mothers, taken as a whole, postmodern social science has been supportive of the sentiments behind shared parenting.

While shared parenting has helped some parents to lead fuller and more rewarding lives, and has helped others make ends meet, it may nonetheless work a hardship on their children. The problem is not that children are going to be harmed by out-of-home care from an early age. Rather, the problem is that as a society we have not provided sufficient affordable, accessible, high-quality childcare for all those families who require it. Our inadequate childcare facilities have shifted the need balance in favor of parents. Leaving children in out-of-home care is hard for parents and for children, but may be harder in the long run for children when such care is not of the highest quality.

• *URBANITY*

The third family sentiment, which relates the family to the larger community, has also undergone transformation from the modern to the postmodern era. In part this has come about as a result of the demolition of the modern sentiment of domesticity, of the home as a nurturing haven. This deconstruction has occurred on many fronts. On the one hand, the media attacks against maternal overprotection and momism made the point that nurturance can be harmful as well as helpful. Likewise, the growing literature on the sexual abuse of wives and children challenged the idealized image of the home as a place of care and protection. Finally, domesticity, inasmuch as it presupposed the same two adults always in attendance as nurturant, protective parents, has also been undermined by the doubling of the divorce rate from 1965 to 1985.[24]

Christopher Lasch laments the demise of idealized domesticity in this way:

> The fear and rejection of parenthood, the tendency to view the family as nothing more than marriage, and the perception of marriage as merely one in a series of non-binding commitments, reflect a growing distrust of the future and a reluctance to make provisions for it—to lay up goods and experience for the use of the next generation. The cult of interpersonal relations represents the final dissolution of bourgeois optimism and self-confidence.[25]

Out of the rubble of domesticity has emerged the postmodern sentiment of urbanity. In relation to the larger society, the postmodern home is no longer a haven, a place for nurturance and protection. Rather it is more like a railway station, with parents and children pulling in and out as they go about their busy lives. In many homes, family meals are a relic of the modern nuclear family ideal. In middle-class homes, one parent comes home late from the office while the other parent is driving one or more children to piano lessons or scouts. In other homes one or both parents may be working a shift at the usual meal times. The independent schedules of permeable family members are one evidence of its new urbanity.

The permeable family is urbane in many other ways. As the barriers to information flow have come down, television and videos, rather than direct experience, play an important part in shaping children's attitudes toward the world. Children who watch a great deal of television overestimate the degree of danger and crime in the world, while they underestimate the helpfulness and trustworthiness of other people.[26] Fear and distrust are sophisticated attitudes in many urban settings, but they are not appropriate for all situations. Television news and drama, by making children and their parents aware of heinous crimes, lead to self-protective behaviors, but these behaviors come with a cost in the quality of everyday life.

Television also makes children more knowledgeable about products. Children watch more than 20,000 TV commercials a year, and these do have an impact on their choices and the pressures they exert on parents to buy advertised products. In one study, 85 percent of the children interviewed reported that they had asked their parents to buy something they saw advertised on TV.[27]

Unhappily, television has not made children more urbane in the sense of being more accepting of those different from themselves. Although television exposes children to ethnic, racial, and cultural diversity, research suggests that such exposure is more likely to reinforce preexisting stereotypes than to change them.[28]

Postmodern technological innovations also contribute to the urbanity of the permeable family. The prevalence of low-cost fast-food restaurants means that families eat out a good deal more than they did in the modern era, when going to a restaurant was a special, and expensive, outing. Because fast-food chains engage in a great deal of promotion, even young children are vocal with regard to the latest give-aways at the neighborhood pizza parlor. The near universal possession of cars together with state and national superhighways, as well as the advent of low-cost jet fares, have also made travel about the country and the world much more affordable and convenient than ever before. Both parents and children in permeable families tend to be more widely traveled, and more frequent travelers, than was true for the members of the modern nuclear family.

For work-oriented parents, the home as a station, to come to and depart from, is need-fulfilling. A railway station is a noisy hub of activity that provides food, information, and transportation much more than it provides nurturance. But for children and teenagers, the home as a station is often less than satisfactory. As in a station, no matter how many people are about, the young person often feels lonely and alone. And although the urbane home provides food and shelter, it may provide too little in the way of nurturance and security.

Again, it is important to emphasize that these are only trends and that in many contemporary families domesticity may be more prevalent than urbanity. For a good number of families, the home and loved ones represent the center of social life and the source of self-esteem. Yet, given the pressures of postmodern life and the lack of societal support for a nurturing family lifestyle, it is more difficult to maintain the sentiment of domesticity today than it was several decades ago.

From Unilateral to Mutual Authority

In many ways, the transition from the family feelings of the modern period to those of the postmodern era marks a transition from unilateral to mutual authority, both within the home and in the larger world outside. In modern America, unilateral authority tended to outweigh mutual authority. White, Christian males tended to be the unilateral authority in most institutions, from the presidency on down. Men in the professions were highly esteemed and seldom challenged either by clients or by the media. Religious leaders also enjoyed the respect that goes along with unilateral authority. In business and in factories there was a sharp separation between labor and management, echoed in the separation between administration and teaching in the schools. In all of these institutions, authority was from the top down and was unequally distributed.

The sentiments of the modern nuclear family were also largely unilateral at least until about the 1950s. Romantic love, to the extent that it viewed women as helpless and dependent on the wisdom and financial support of men, represented a notion of unilateral authority between men and women. But maternal love was also unilateral relative to children in that it placed the day-to-day responsibility for the care of young children almost exclusively in the hands of the mother. Finally, the sentiment of domesticity reflected unilateral authority to the extent that all family members had to subordinate their personal desires to the larger interests of the family unit.

All of this changed about midcentury, heralded by both the civil rights movement (against the unilateral authority of the white majority) and the women's movement (against the unilateral authority of the male gender). This reaction has been repeated in many facets of our society. The office of the presidency of the United States, for example, is unlikely to ever exert the unilateral authority it did before the Vietnam War and the Watergate scandal. Likewise, the professions of law and medicine are no longer regarded as highly as they once were. Both lawyers and doctors are constantly in the news, as much for their improprieties as for their achievements. Mainstream religion is also losing membership, and many Catholics defy the Pope's doctrines regarding contraception and abortion.

Within industry, a number of chief executive officers are now being called to task by their once rubber-stamp executive boards, and some are even being asked to resign. In both factories and schools, top-down management is being replaced by bottom-up or on-site decisionmaking. Finally, the concepts of no-fault divorce and no-fault insurance that came to prominence in the 1960s reflect the shift from unilateral to mutual responsibility and authority.

The movement toward mutual authority has been seen as a positive development by some writers and as a regression by others. As Lasch comments: "Conservatives lament the collapse of authoritative leadership, whereas progressives claim, once again, that the democratization of politics makes up for the raucous quality of modern political culture, the lack of deference shown to opponents and to authorities and the unthinking contempt for tradition."[29]

For some writers, the decline of unilateral authority coincides with an acceptance of a soft relativism and the disavowal of absolute standards. For others, it implies a new openness and acceptance of difference. Regardless of whether one views the glass as half empty or half full, the fact remains that we have moved away from unilateral authority.

Authority within the family has also became more mutual, in keeping with the shift in other social institutions. The sentiment of consensual love clearly reflects the idea of mutual authority in which both partners help make the rules that govern the relationship. Likewise, the sentiment of shared parenting is a sentiment of mutuality in which both parents cooperate in childrearing, or share those responsibilities with providers outside the family. Finally, the sentiment of urbanity, to the extent that it places the two-parent family on a par with other kinds of families and with other institutions rather than elevating it above them, also reflects mutual rather than unilateral authority.

Of course this shift is relative rather than absolute. There is still a great deal of unilateral authority in government, religion, industry, and education. And there was a good deal of mutual authority in the modern era. But the balance has shifted, and mutual authority is much more prevalent today than it was before midcentury, in the family as well as outside it.

The erosion of unilateral authority in the family, though it has been in many ways an adaptive response to changing economic conditions, has contributed to the new family need imbalance. While modern parents often set limits (say, the age for dating) and made decisions (regarding clothing) for their adolescents that would be regarded as tyrannical today, postmodern parents are much more likely to be overly mutual in their authority. They may fail to set clear rules and consequences (say, regarding drug use and sexual activity) and let their children make decisions regarding their own personal lives that might better be made by parents in consultation with their offspring.

One telling bit of evidence of this shift from unilateral to mutual authority is the number of postmodern children who call their parents by their first names. Calling a parent "Mom" or "Dad," though familiar, still bespeaks a degree of respect for the parent's authority. Calling a parent by his or her given name does not.

In many avant-garde schools, teachers are also called by their first names rather than by Miss or Mrs. or Mr., as in the modern era. I regard this tendency as unfortunate. Teachers must, of necessity, exercise some unilateral authority with regard to their students. The use of first names, however, suggests a false equality. When it comes time for teachers to exert their authority—for example, when they have to assess a student's work or issue grades—the student could rightly feel betrayed by an assumed equal who is suddenly "pulling rank."

At some point in development parents also feel the need to exercise unilateral authority, particularly when their offspring become teenagers. If parents start out emphasizing mutual authority, it is difficult, if not impossible, to assert unilateral authority when the children become adolescents. Children will accept a parent who moves from a pattern of unilateral authority to one of mutual authority, but not the reverse.

Imagine a boot camp where a tough, uncompromising sergeant is in charge. At the end of their training the recruits find that the sergeant, unbeknownst to them, has performed a number of kindly and thoughtful actions on their behalf. The recruits can believe this, and it only enhances their respect and affection for this officer. In contrast, imagine a drill sergeant who is easy on his recruits and who goes out of his way to be pals with them. If the commanding officer finds out, and pushes this sergeant to be tough and unrelenting, the soldiers cannot accept this change of heart. They feel betrayed. Psychologically, we are prepared to believe that a tough person can become soft, but we cannot believe that a soft person can become tough.

Modern parents who were unilateral could shift to mutual authority as their children grew older, and their children could accept this without losing respect or admiration for their parents. But postmodern parents, who use mutual authority with their children from an early age, find that their teenagers will not accept a conversion to unilateral authority. "You didn't tell me who I could be friends with when I was a kid, you can't start now." It is postmodern parents' inability to successfully employ unilateral authority that contributes to the new imbalance. Young people benefit most from considerable unilateral authority when young and considerable mutual authority as they grow older. In the permeable family, parents often do the reverse, and it does not work.

Family Values

4

From Togetherness to Autonomy

What we often take to be family values—the work ethic, honesty, clean living, marital fidelity, and individual responsibility—are, in fact, social, religious, or cultural values. To be sure, these values are transmitted by parents to their children and are familial in that sense. They do not, however, *originate* within the family. There is one value, however, that does originate in the family. It is the value of close relationships with other family members, and the importance of these bonds relative to other needs.

In the modern period, romantic love, maternal love, and domesticity gave rise to the value of togetherness, the commitment to place family before self. In the postmodern period, consensual love, shared parenting, and urbanity fuse to produce a new family value, autonomy. Autonomy means in effect that each family member is empowered to place his or her need for self-realization and self-fulfillment before the needs of the family as a unit.

We will see in this chapter that as the themes of first togetherness and then autonomy have taken center stage, the need imbalance within families has shifted in favor of adults over children. Both the change in family values and the change in the family need imbalance are reflected in the media, the schools, the legal system, and the helping professions. But these social institutions are not mere mirrors of the family: they also influence how the family views itself and how its members relate to one another and to the world outside the home.

Modern families demonstrated their commitment to the value of togetherness in many different ways. Going to church or synagogue together, going on outings, being together on birthdays and holidays were all regarded as essential to normal and healthy family life.[1] Togetherness worked to the advantage of modern children and youth. It ensured that they would be involved with their parents in meaningful ways on a regular basis. Such involvement satisfies young people's need for security and protection and allows them to devote their energies to the tasks of schooling and socialization.

Family togetherness was easier to achieve during an economic era when a single blue-collar worker could earn enough to comfortably support his family. But even under the most advantageous conditions, nuclear family togetherness was not always what it was imagined to be. Family meals could be the setting for emotional flare-ups, just as mandatory church attendance and participation in family outings could be the cause of intense conflicts. Nonetheless, even these battles over rebellion and autonomy gave young people a feeling of belonging, of being cared for enough to warrant a confrontation.

For parents the value of togetherness was somewhat less benign. Many parental options were proscribed as being a threat to family togetherness. Togetherness often denied mothers the possibility of realizing any of their personal ambitions. Divorce, another possible option for parents, was a social anathema because it posed the ultimate threat to family togetherness. Debt, which might permit parents to purchase a few luxuries, was equally regarded as an evil because it might place the locus of the family's togetherness, the home, in jeopardy. Strong attachments to nonfamily members and nonfamily avocations were also looked down upon. Togetherness, therefore, often limited parental freedom and worked against the satisfaction of at least some parental needs.

Individuals do, of course, differ widely when it comes to which values are personally comfortable and which are not. For some parents, togetherness is a very good fit for their personalities, and the absence of other options for fulfilling individual needs makes little or no difference and may even be a plus. Such parents are committed to the family and are fulfilled, rather than deprived, by having to forgo some facets of self-realization. So, while togetherness may have worked a hardship on many parents, it was far from being a burden on *all* parents.

The Social Mirror of Family Togetherness

During the modern era, the reigning family sentiments of romantic love, maternal love, and domesticity as they melded into a value of togetherness were mirrored and magnified by those social institutions most closely affiliated with the family: the media, the schools, the legal system, and the helping professions. Each of these social institutions made a contribution to the imbalance in the nuclear family between the needs of children and the needs of parents.

•*MASS MEDIA FOR THE MIDDLE CLASS*

Portrayals of family life in the media, particularly during the decades of the 1940s, 50s, and early 60s, often reflected the sentiments of romantic love, maternal love, and domesticity. As Peggy Charren describes in her book *Changing Channels:*

> In the 1950's and 60's the typical TV family lived in a home that was always spotless, with a mom and dad who were always caring and always available, and children (always cute) whose most traumatic crises were missed homework assignments and broken prom dates. In those antiseptic TV families, mother was always around to serve cookies and milk, and father really did know best. Even on shows featuring single parents (*The Partridge Family* and *The Courtship of Eddie's Father*) the families argued over issues no more meaningful than those that had troubled Andy Hardy or Henry Aldrich

[fictional adolescents from the 1930s and 40s]. Even though these typical TV audiences did not reflect the actual lives of most Americans, they attracted and entertained enormous audiences.[2]

By not acknowledging families of color, or families living in poverty, these programs provided a fantasy of white middle-class security and protection that children from all backgrounds, and all socioeconomic levels, watched and enjoyed. Of course, some children may have been made unhappy with their own parents and home by the images presented on TV, and they may have developed false hopes of a lifestyle they could never attain. But in general, as Bruno Bettelheim has argued, fantasy often works at many different levels and can meet unconscious needs and resolve unconscious conflicts.[3] For example, with respect to the Santa Claus fantasy Bettelheim writes:

> Children are only too keenly aware of parental and reality limitations every day of the year. Thus they have every reason to wish to believe that at least once a year, fairyland—or that paradise of infantile existence—can be regained, at least in make-believe for a few hours. These experiences are most reassuring to children, because they mean the golden age is not lost forever. This gives them the strength to go on with the difficulties of the present and holds out hope for the future.[4]

Television fantasies of ideal families can have many of the same beneficial effects and for similar reasons.

Television programs of the modern era helped meet children's needs in other ways as well. Family programs for children, and TV shows in general, accepted and respected the needs of children and adolescents to be shielded from some of the crueler aspects of real life. In situation comedies such as *The Donna Reed Show, Leave It to Beaver,* and *Father Knows Best,* overt sexuality, foul language, and physical and verbal abuse were not shown. The implicit message of this protective programming was very clear to young people—that adult society cares enough about us not to show material that would upset and disturb us. This unspoken communication of adult caring and concern, much more than the absence of troubling content itself, met young people's need for a sense of being looked after and protected.

If the content and concerns of modern television spoke to the needs of children and youth, they were largely silent with regard to the needs of parents. Parents on TV always seemed calm and knowledgeable, with plenty of time for, and ready solutions to, every problem presented to them by their wholesome offspring. For real-life parents, these sitcoms did not present relaxing, stress-reducing fantasies but rather portrayals of family life which spotlighted their own inadequacies. Committed to togetherness yet guilt-ridden over charges of momism and overprotection, mothers in particular often compared themselves with these mavens of balanced childrearing and came off second best or lower.

In addition, the portrayal of intact, happy, well-functioning families as the norm made parents who were experiencing difficulties in their own marriage feel that there was something wrong with them. Modern TV shows that modeled togetherness thus often provided a healthy fantasy for children, while it often made many of their parents feel inadequate and deviant.

Musical lyrics of the modern era, which idealized romantic love and lifelong relationships, also reinforced the value of togetherness. These songs, however, were not music to the ears of couples in joyless relationships. For these men and women, the songs of romantic love made their own unhappiness feel like an aberration. It made them feel that they were lacking that "special something" that was essential to the attainment of a loving relationship. For children, in contrast, the songs of romantic love reinforced their belief that their parents would stay together forever. Song lyrics played their part in perpetuating the old imbalance.

One of the most complete media portrayals of the family value of togetherness was given in Frank Capra's film classic *It's a Wonderful Life*, starring Jimmy Stewart and Donna Reed. In this film, which is now rerun every year at Christmastime, romantic love is realized when Stewart marries his childhood sweetheart, Donna Reed. Maternal love is glorified in Reed's apparent lack of any personal ambition beyond her total devotion to her children and husband. Domesticity is celebrated in Stewart's involvement with his family and his commitment to his friends and his savings and loan customers. The togetherness of family and community provide the happy ending to the story.

During the modern period, magazines and books for children and teenagers also reflected the media's respect for the sentiments of the nuclear family. Those who wrote for children had to avoid a number of taboo topics and off-color language. For example, in the 1960s I wrote children's stories for magazines such as *Jack and Jill*. At that time, children's magazines would not publish stories about families of divorce, alcoholic parents, or children with disabilities. If we writers of children's fiction wanted to see our work in print, we had to write about intact, happy families.

While these strict taboos may have been helpful in buttressing children's needs for protection and security, they did not necessarily shore up parental needs. Like the television programs and movies that reinforced togetherness, the modern literature for children was not supportive of those parents whose lives did not follow the nuclear family ideal. Parents who were divorced could find little in the literature that might help them, or their children, deal with marital separation as a normal life problem, not as a symptom of pathology. The same was true for families with two working parents, blended families, and families with a parent who was an alcoholic or had some physical disability. There were few stories dealing with ethnic minorities, and there were absolutely no stories about gay parents.

The modern literature for children and teenagers thus catered to the needs for security and protection among children and youth in the majority, while providing little in the way of help or support for those parents and children whose lives deviated from the white, middle-class ideal. Again, this imbalance was relative inasmuch as those modern children who might have benefited from stories dealing with illness, death, and divorce were not well served.

In its responsible monitoring of what was presented to children and youth, the modern media also reflected the unilateral authority so characteristic of the modern era. The Hayes Office, for example, exerted strict control over what could be shown in films. Unmarried couples could not sleep in the same room, nor could they appear unclothed. In the classic movie *It Happened One Night*, the characters are forced to share the one available hotel room after their car breaks down. Thanks to the Hayes Office, they had to hang a sheet between the two beds. Similar controls were exercised with respect to radio programs, and even the comedian Bob Hope was sometimes silenced when his jokes were a little off-color. Of course what was off-color then would be considered pure white in comparison with what we see and hear today.

• *THE SCHOOLS AND THE SINS OF OMISSION*

Schools have always shared childcare functions with the families of the children they serve. The extent of this sharing, however, always reflects and supports the sentiments and values of the predominant family structure. During the late modern era, when the nuclear family was in ascendance, schools mirrored the values of the nuclear family indirectly, by the childcare functions they did *not* perform. In postmodern times, however, the childcare functions carried on by the schools are a direct reflection of permeable family values. To fully appreciate this changed relationship between the home and school, a little history is in order.

In this country, universal free public schooling was fairly well established by the middle of the nineteenth century. The first public school curricula, however, were modeled after the classical curricula of the private schools that served the leisure class. These schools were based on the *faculty* view of mind—the idea that the mind is mapped out like a country that is made up of many independent municipalities, each of which functions autonomously from all of the others.

This faculty view of mind assumed a fixed and unchanging body of knowledge that was divided logically into subjects. These subjects, in turn, were woven into courses that could be completed in a specified period of time.

Subjects such as Latin and Greek, however, were of little value to working-class children growing up in industrial America. And the physics and biology of Aristotle looked increasingly primitive compared with the achievements of modern science. As a result, there was growing unhappiness with the classical approach to education. Voices such as those of Jean Jacques Rousseau, Johann Heinrich Pestalozzi, Johann Friedrich Herbart, and Friedrich Froebel had all challenged the faculty theory of mind and the education upon which it was based. But it was John Dewey who, at the turn of the century, translated the ideas of these innovative thinkers into a philosophy of education for American schools.[5]

For Dewey, the mind was a social product, dependent for its growth on the social environment. We learn not through direct experience with the environment but through the interpretation and *re*-presentation of that environment by the accumulated experience of the human race. The facts that are labeled geography, arithmetic, biology, and so on are not entirely external but are also rooted in social experience and needs. Education is part of life, not separate from it.

Although many of his ideas were quite postmodern (for example, his concept of the project method anticipated the integrated curriculum), Dewey nonetheless remained modern in offering a grand theory of progressive education. The educational historian Lawrence Cremin describes this sweeping, idealistic view of the aims of the modern educational agenda this way:

> First, it meant the broadening of the function of the school to include direct concern for health, vocation, and the quality of family and community life. Second, it meant applying in the classroom the pedagogical principles derived from new scientific research in psychology and in the social sciences. Third, it meant tailoring

> instruction more and more to the different kinds of classes of children who were being brought within the purview of the school . . . Finally, progressivism implied the radical faith that culture could be democratized without being vulgarized, the faith that everyone could share not only in the benefits of the new sciences but in the pursuit of the arts as well.[6]

Progressive education to varying degrees became the template for late modern education in the United States. It was theory-driven, with little input from parents. In the early decades of this century a large proportion of adults were immigrants who were themselves often illiterate, at least in English. Many nativeborn adults were also unschooled. As parents, they were easily intimidated by professionals and accepted without question the educational program offered by the schools. (Contemporary immigrant families are often in the same position.) And the schools, in the absence of parental participation, assumed that all children came from nuclear families.

Because public schools took the nuclear family as a given, they reflected its values through acts of omission rather than commission. The kindergarten during the first half of this century is a case in point. In many states and communities there were no publicly supported kindergartens. In school districts that did provide kindergartens, attendance was not compulsory. Kindergarten itself was a half-day program. Children who did attend dressed up for dramatic play, listened to stories, engaged in arts and crafts, and went on fieldtrips to farms and firehouses. The noncompulsory, play-oriented, half-day modern kindergarten thus supported the sentiment of maternal love by reinforcing the idea that young children should not be separated from their mothers, or their homes, for long periods of time. Full-day kindergartens, so common today, would have been (and in some circles still are) regarded as a threat to family togetherness.

Other modern educational practices also reinforced family togetherness by omission rather than commission. The personal information forms children and adolescents were required to fill out made no provisions for young people whose parents had divorced or remarried. Likewise, many elementary schools were built without lunchrooms because it was taken for granted that children would go home for lunch or bring their lunch to school. This presumed a mother at home with plenty of time to prepare lunch for her young offspring.

Family togetherness as a value was embedded in the public schools' focus on personal adjustment. Progressive education was meant to facilitate children's adaptation to the larger society. In the process, however, children met with frustration and—in the language of modern educational psychologists—were required to "adjust."[7] The focus on adjustment, as in the popular phrases "well-adjusted" and "maladjusted," emphasized the importance modern education placed on children's adapting themselves to the social world. Educators assumed that children would come to school already grounded in the basics of "social adjustment" thanks to the value of togetherness. Children's successful adjustment to the order of the school and the larger society was, therefore, premised on his or her prior adjustment within the family. If children did not adjust well to school, it was clearly the parents' fault.

Modern schools, therefore, paid little or no attention to the needs or concerns of parents, but then were ready to blame these same parents if their children were not well-adjusted. To be sure, there were parent-teacher organizations then as now, but these groups were focused on the well-being of children and seldom gave voice to the concerns and needs of parents. In their relationships with parents, schools exercised considerable unilateral authority.

Perhaps because it was so theory-driven, and not in touch with parental concerns, progressive education was often distorted, misinterpreted, and sabotaged. By midcentury it had been pretty much discredited. Its earlier political-reform agenda had been all but abandoned, and its practices had come to be associated with a suspicion of "book-learning" and with overly permissive classrooms.[8]

The demise of progressive education coincided with the emergence of the postmodern family. Postmodern parents were a new breed—they would not be taken for granted by the schools. In the postmodern world, as we shall see, educational practices would reflect the sentiments and values of the permeable family directly, by commission rather than by omission.

•*LEGISLATING CHILDHOOD*

During the modern era, the value of family togetherness was accepted and reinforced by the laws of the land. In the early decades of the nineteenth century, the obligation of parents to nourish, protect, and educate young people was so well accepted by the society at large that it was seldom thought to require enforcement by "human laws."[9] In the same way, it was generally thought that "the promptings of parental affection and wholesome public opinion" would be more than sufficient to prevent the abuse of parental authority.[10]

Yet these assumptions about the acceptance of parental responsibility on the part of all mothers and fathers proved to be ill-founded. The horrors of child labor in the latter part of the nineteenth century led the states to pass and to enforce laws to ensure that parents did indeed safeguard, nurture, and educate their children. Parents who neglected their responsibilities were very much on the minds of reformers, who stressed the duty of the state to protect children from the authority of parents who neglected their children's well-being. The efforts of these reformers led to more effective regulation of child labor by the states, creation of juvenile courts, establishment of the Federal Children's Bureau, and improvement in child welfare services at all levels.[11]

The overall thrust, then, of the "rights of childhood movement" during the modern era was to protect children from others and to recognize the special developmental needs of children and adolescents. Childhood, and to a lesser extent adolescence, was regarded as a special period of life that was unique and valuable. Fictional young people, such as Tom Sawyer, the sisters in *Little Women,* and

Penrod Schofield, concretized the image of childhood that the laws sought to preserve and protect.[12]

Laws geared to the protection of children and youth, however, did not always work to the benefit of parents. With respect to marriage and divorce, the legal system spoke with unilateral authority. Stringent divorce laws, for example, kept many adults in unhappy relationships simply because of the high social, legal, and financial hurdles that had to be surmounted to attain a divorce. Parents who stayed together because they had to were not the happiest husbands and wives. Nonetheless, the majority resolved to make the best of a bad bargain and to enjoy and fulfill their role as parents, if not as marital partners. That is to say, most parents who felt constrained to stay in bad marriages did not take it out on the children. Children, not parents, were thus the indirect beneficiaries of stringent divorce laws.

• *THE "HELPING" PROFESSIONS*

In the modern era, psychologists, psychotherapists, psychiatric social workers, educational psychologists, and others in the helping professions—all steeped in the discourse of Freud and of psychoanalysis—took the sentiments and values of the nuclear family as given and reflected them in their diagnoses and treatment.

With respect to romantic love, for example, modern mental health professionals paid little attention to the emotional problems created by divorce. When divorced patients came for treatment, their problems were often interpreted as arising from their childhood experiences, not from their present life circumstances. In the same manner, the assumption of maternal love—the idea that women instinctively wanted, and needed, to devote their lives to their children—often blinded mental health professionals to the plight of those women who were unhappy and depressed because they had no outlet for their abilities and talents. The sentiment of domesticity made it hard for therapists to accept as real a patient's accounts of abuse and violence in the home.

Modern helping professionals also took as an unchallengeable given the value of togetherness and the importance of adjustment to the status quo. In Freud's later theory, the ego was the adjusting instrument of the personality. The ego had to reconcile the demands of the id (unconscious impulses and desires) with those of the superego (the internal residue of society's morals and prohibitions). Freud saw the goal of treatment as a readjustment of personality such that "where Id was, there shall Ego be."[13] In its focus on the ego, and on adjustment to the status quo, modern mental-health theory and practice reinforced the nuclear family value of togetherness.

It is also true that modern health professionals generally had unilateral rather than mutual relationships with their patients. Psychoanalysis, in particular, by having the patient lie on the couch with the therapist seated behind him or her, built the unilateral authority into the physical arrangement of the consulting room.

The Social Mirror of Individual Autonomy

What is important to the permeable family is that each family member be independent, competent, achievement-oriented, and able to go it alone. The sociologist Robert Weiss describes the transition from the family value of togetherness to that of autonomy as "the development of a new relationship in which the children are defined as having responsibilities and rights in the household not very different from the parent's own."[14]

This autonomous new relationship is related to a broader, exaggerated individualism that has been described negatively as the excesses of "affluence," the selfishness of a "Me decade," or the prevalence of a self-centered "narcissism," to take just three of the more well-known formulations.[15] Recent survey studies show that a commitment to personal autonomy is widespread among adults in America. A survey by Daniel Yankelovich reports that by the late 1970s, 63 percent of Americans were spending a great deal of time thinking about themselves and their inner lives. In another survey Robert

Bellah and his colleagues found that the language of personal autonomy was extremely prevalent in white middle-class America.[16]

The shift from modern togetherness to postmodern autonomy as a basic family value is perhaps most easily observed at mealtime. Whereas in the modern family, eating together was the first priority, it is no longer so in the permeable family. For permeable family members, a couple of free theatre tickets, or a deadline at work, or a late soccer practice, a scouts meeting, a friends' birthday party—each is considered a legitimate reason to miss the evening meal and the attendant conversation about the day's events.

Like the family dinner, church and synagogue attendance by families has also declined in the postmodern era. In part this might have come about because today's parents just cannot face another morning of getting everybody dressed up and rushing out the door. The tight schedules of the work week and the back-to-back extracurricular events of Saturdays (when many parents try to make up for some of the lost parenting time of the week before), not to mention the grocery shopping, or a trip to the department store, or visits from family friends—all of this leaves most postmodern parents, even religious ones, exhausted on the weekend.

In many families the pressure for autonomy may come from economic necessity rather than from choice. Contemporary economics often requires that one or both parents work longer hours in order to manage family finances. This translates into less time for children, as working parents readjust family schedules to accommodate the demands of fulltime work.

But as tired and harried as postmodern working parents may appear, they do have more autonomy and more options than did modern parents. Children and youth, however, do not fare as well. Latchkey children, who spend their afternoons at home alone, learn that they must rely on their own resources and that they cannot count on having their parents around a great deal of the time. Children are simply on their own more often in permeable families than they were in nuclear families. And too few provisions have been made by the larger society to fill this vacuum of adult support, guidance, and direction.

Divorce, reviled when togetherness was the core family value, has today, thanks to autonomy, become commonplace and acceptable. Children in single-parent families often see one parent only episodically, and this usually translates into less overall parental time for children. It is estimated that by the time they reach the age of eighteen, at least 50 percent of American children and youth will have spent some time in a single-parent home.[17]

Debt is another fact of postmodern life that in some ways expresses the autonomy of parents and works against the ideal of togetherness. Contemporary parents are encouraged to go into debt to buy luxuries ranging from sports cars and boats to elaborate stereo equipment and Camcorders. Postmodern parents feel freer to spend on themselves and less compelled to save for their children's future than did their modern counterparts. While economic constraints in the 1990s are quite real, social constraints against "spending on oneself" are largely gone.

Single-parenting, two working parents, divorce, and debt frequently have repercussions that reduce the family's ability to spend time together and to meet the emotional needs of children. This shift from togetherness to autonomy does not hold for all contemporary families, however. Many parents and their children maintain a sense of togetherness despite the many demands and time constraints of postmodern life. Middle-class black families, for example, may remain quite nuclear in their orientation and their emphasis on togetherness. And many other kinds of families may invent ingenious techniques for communicating and sharing even in the absence of physical togetherness.

I have heard of one hard-working professional woman—a single mother—who bought a beeper expressly for the purpose of communicating with her nine-year-old son, who was feeling insecure after his parents' divorce. A California mother confided to me that her family opted to purchase a hot tub instead of a new car, so that they could all spend some time together relaxing and talking. Autonomy is not a universal pattern, but it does appear to be the dominant trend.

The new imbalance that favors the needs of parents over those of children is, again, relative. Postmodern parents would like to spend more time with their children and frequently feel deprived and guilt-ridden because they need to work long hours to keep the family afloat. Nonetheless, postmodern options for divorce and self-realization put childrearing in competition with autonomy, a phenomenon that was relatively unknown in the modern era. The value of autonomy was, and is, present in nuclear families, just as the value of togetherness is present in permeable families; what has changed is the emphasis and importance attributed to these values. The result is a shift in the family's allocation of resources to adults rather than children.

• *THE ELECTRONIC HOMESTEAD*

Contemporary TV programs and films convey the sentiments and values of the permeable family in much the same way that the programs of the 50s and 60s brought forth the sentiments and values of the nuclear family. The long-running *Love Boat* and *Hotel* were paeans to consensual love and recreational sex. Consensual love is also taken for granted in the more recent TV hit *Seinfeld*. Shared parenting is a common theme in contemporary TV sitcoms such as the popular *Murphy Brown,* in which a single-mother newsanchor shares parenting of her infant son with a male artist. The urbanity of the permeable family is echoed in the frequency with which these shows deal with topics such as AIDS, drugs, family violence, infidelity, unemployment, and deviant behavior.

Norman Lear revolutionized the genre of situation comedies with programs that tore apart old TV clichés. *Maude* was to sentimental family fare what *M*A*S*H* was to *Dr. Kildare*. As Charren points out, "Maude had an abortion, a nervous breakdown, and when she went through menopause on a show she helped more people understand this crisis than most documentaries ever could."[18]

In the 1990s some family TV shows have gone beyond portraying family life as it really is and are devoted, instead, to ridiculing the values of the nuclear family. Families such as the cartoon Simpsons, the Connors of *Roseanne*, and the Bundys of *Married with Children* are as unreal in their portrayals of family life as were the Cleavers in *Leave It to Beaver.* As Harry Waters expressed it in *Newsweek:*

> If you buy the argument that television mirrors us more than it molds us, then suddenly it's sending out an intriguing message about ourselves. We're beginning to revolt against the tube's idealized images of domestic life—and at the same time, lovingly embracing messed up families with collars of blue.
>
> *The Simpsons* is a joke on traditional sitcoms because its characters are so far removed from what is depicted as the norm, says Jack Nachbar, professor of popular culture at Bowling Green State University. But in actuality, they're closer to the real norm than anything we have ever seen.[19]

Shows like *The Simpsons* and *Married with Children* are parodies of the ideal modern family, satirizing romantic love, maternal love, and domesticity as well as family togetherness. As one teenager remarked, "They are fun to watch but I sure wouldn't want to have them over for dinner." In contrast, shows like *Seinfeld* and *Murphy Brown* are regarded as mainstream and "with it." In other words, the satirical shows knock down the nuclear family sentiments and values, while the straight, humorous sitcoms reinforce the permeable family sentiments and values.

At the movies, consensual love is a common theme in contemporary films ranging from *Pretty Woman*, the story of a warm-hearted prostitute, to *The Piano,* the story of an unhappily married Victorian woman who bargains away sexual favors to her lover, one by one, to buy back her beloved piano, key by key. In both of these movies, a dash of romantic love complicates an otherwise consensual relationship.

Shared parenting is modeled in movies such as *Three Men and a Baby*, in which three men share the responsibility for looking after an infant. Likewise, the urbanity of contemporary family life is given voice in movies such as *Mermaids*, where two daughters of a single mother travel about the country with her as she moves from job to job and from love affair to love affair. The daughters' reluctant acceptance of this lifestyle is one evidence of the urbanity of postmodern youth.

Finally, the permeable family value of autonomy is glorified in films such as the highly successful *Home Alone*. It tells the story of a boy who is accidentally left behind when his family takes a trip to Europe. He copes magnificently and even outwits two bungling house thieves. This film, which depicts a young man who is self-reliant, self-confident, and extraordinarily competent for a young person his age, was so successful it spawned a sequel, *Home Alone 2*, which was an even greater hit.

The attraction of such films to children is understandable. Children of four or five tend to think that adults are all-knowing, all-powerful, godlike creatures. Once they get to be six or seven, however, children acquire new mental abilities that enable them to check out what adults say and do. When they discover, as they inevitably do, that we don't know one particular thing, they conclude that we don't know anything. And because they know something we don't know, they think that they know everything and we know nothing! I call children's belief that they are brighter than adults "cognitive conceit."[20] Generally children keep this conceit under wraps. It only appears episodically when, for example, they lose a game with an adult and will not play the same game again.

This cognitive conceit explains the pleasure children take in films like *Home Alone*. What is different about these films is not that children enjoy them but that their parents do as well. Films of this genre reinforce in parents the value of autonomy among children—the belief that children are able to take care of themselves from an early age. This belief helps to lessen some of the residual (modern) guilt parents may feel about having to leave their own children home alone. Indeed, the movie's title epitomizes children and youth in the postmodern family much as *It's a Wonderful Life* epitomized family attitudes for young people growing up in the modern era.

In contemporary children's literature, the barriers and taboos under which I and other writers once labored are no longer operative. Today, almost anything goes with respect to children's books. According to *Thursday's Child,* a book published by the American Library Association:

> As the sixties moved into the seventies, the sexual content [of children's books] became more explicit. John Donovan's *I'll Get There: It Better Be Worth the Trip* (1969) contains one suggested, quickly passed over, homosexual incident, but in Isabelle Holland's *The Man without a Face* three years later, there is no doubt about the homosexual relationship. And 1977 saw the publication of a problem novel by Judy Blume, *Forever,* that is as explicit as a sex manual . . .
>
> The matter of the factual explicitness of problem novels is accompanied by unrestrained language. Back in 1959 Karl Bjarnhof, in an adult novel, would not have surprised readers by having one of his youthful characters remark: "But Hamsun . . . He's the one who swears in his books. I don't mind people swearing, but in a book?" By 1973 a child in John Neufeld's *Freddy's Book* could ask the librarian for a "book about f——king." In an article written in 1975 Norma Klein said she would "like to see four-letter words used as frequently in realistic books for children as they are in everyday lives of what I consider respectable and upperclass people."[21]

The new style in children's literature is in keeping with the relaxed standards in films and television with respect to nudity, profanity, sexual activity, and violence. All reflect the new family sentiment of consensual love and urbanity, and the value of autonomy. But unless this new freedom is handled responsibly, it may unnecessarily expose the young to disturbing material for no purpose. Do young children really gain anything worthwhile from listening to profanity or from observing overt violence or sexual activity?

The power of the media messages being sent to children by films, television, and literature pales in comparison with that of children's computerized video games, a medium that did not exist in the modern era. In his book *Video Kids*, Eugene Provenzo Jr. describes the world of Nintendo this way:

> The great majority of the games included in the Nintendo system are based on themes of aggression and violence. In the most common scenario found in the games, an anonymous character performs an act of aggression—typically mediated through some type of technology—against an anonymous enemy. There are no conscientious objectors in the world of video games; there is no sense of community, there are no team players. Each person is out for himself. One must shoot or be shot, consume or be consumed, fight or lose.[22]

In terms of postmodern sentiments, the video-game culture of kids values autonomy (the Mario Brothers hardly qualify as family togetherness) and, in the explicitness of its violent content, presumes the urbanity of its young players.

Like television, video games propagate rather than dispel stereotypes, particularly of women. Provenzo points out that

> women—when they are included at all in the games in the Nintendo system—are often cast as individuals who are acted upon rather than as initiators of action . . . Gender bias and stereotyping are evident throughout . . . [If] video games are an important entryway into the world of computing for children and adolescents, then women are suffering a double injustice: they are being sex-typed, and they are also being discouraged [by the sexist content] from participating in the use of computers, a fact that may put them at a significant disadvantage in terms of their future educational and job potential.[23]

Parents who wish to limit their children's exposure through the media to aggression, violence, profanity, overt sexuality, and stereotyping get very little assistance today from government regulators.

There are no longer censors, such as the Hayes Office, to monitor television and radio broadcasts or to adequately rate films, videos, and computer games. The lack of self-regulation exercised by the media has the effect of undermining the unilateral authority of those parents who might want to exercise it. Even if we don't have a television, our children may be exposed to objectionable material at school and at friends' houses, in malls, and elsewhere.

It is simply impossible to preview every TV show, movie, radio program, or video game. Because we cannot control all that our children see, hear, and play, it is tempting to throw up our hands and do nothing. Although we cannot do everything, we can do something, and this is to talk with our children and teenagers about unexpected encounters with inappropriate violence, sexuality, and profanity. We can also set strict limits on how much time can be spent playing Nintendo and other video games. In discussing television or video game content, however, we have to deal with our children on a level of mutuality, because we can no longer unilaterally protect them from the material. All that we can, and should, do is to try to limit whatever adverse effects these exposures may have.

• *FAMILY SUPPORT IN THE SCHOOLS*

By midcentury, the parent population in America had changed dramatically, and so too did its responsibility for childcare. The proportion of immigrant parents to nativeborn parents had dropped significantly. Today, most parents now have at least a high school education, and postmodern parents do not feel intimidated by the schools. The racial integration of the public schools was, in part at least, a parental initiative. At the same time, the postmodern distrust of grand theories led educators to focus on concrete curriculum objectives rather than on abstract social aims. Parents can relate to these specific goals more easily than to an idealistic educational philosophy.

As a result, postmodern schools have become much more responsive to the needs and demands of parents for childcare, for instilling values, for teaching their children about the effects of tobacco, alcohol, and drugs, and for help in preparing their children for the threats and dangers of the real world. In so doing, the schools reflect and support the sentiments and values of the permeable family in a direct and straightforward fashion.

Consider the sentiment of consensual love. Schools now recognize many different family kinship systems, and the forms children have to fill out provide for nonnuclear family options. Many schools also have support groups for children of divorced families. The schools' mirroring and support of the sentiment of consensual love is most apparent in high school. Sex education is often mandatory, and while premarital sex is not condoned, the message to use protection is very clear. Some high schools now dispense condoms.

There is also direct acceptance and support for the sentiment of shared parenting. Full-day kindergartens, now common in school districts all across the country, speak to the need of working parents to have quality, affordable full-day care for their children. Before- and afterschool programs for children of working parents are also becoming more common, and some school systems even subsidize childcare for children as young as six weeks of age. Schools thus not only acknowledge shared parenting but are playing an ever increasing role in the support of that sentiment.

Schools are also reflecting and bolstering the permeable family sentiment of urbanity. Multicultural and antibias curricula are being introduced at all grade levels, including early childhood.[24] Children are now taught about drug abuse, sexual abuse, and AIDS. Curriculum materials too are more sophisticated. Contemporary history books now detail the violence, cruelty, and destruction that accompanied the conquest of the New World. The important contributions of women and ethnic minorities to our science and culture, as well as to our military triumphs, are now being increasingly recognized.

The value of autonomy is also reflected and reinforced in postmodern education. The current advocacy of a voucher system for parents is a good example. With vouchers parents would have a choice as to the school their children would attend. While there is a good deal of controversy over whether the voucher system works, the concept itself reflects the new emphasis on giving parents more autonomy in the matter of school choice. In some school districts magnet schools have been set up to attract students with varied interests and to attract parents with different ideas about education.

In Cambridge, Massachusetts, for example, students crisscross the city on public school buses in order to attend the elementary school of their parents' choice. When the school day is over, they are bussed to their chosen afterschool program, often in a different elementary school. Sometimes Cambridge parents choose an elementary school in a different neighborhood from their home because of the particular curriculum offered there, but then choose an afterschool program nearer to their home or workplace for convenient pick-up at the end of the day.

Cambridge parents obviously benefit from the willingness of the school system to accommodate their needs for child transportation and flexibility. The children in that city, on the other hand, are not being coddled; they are expected to master the intricacies of the bussing system, and to be at the right place at the right time without direct adult supervision. In a more protective world, children would go home at the end of the school day, or at least remain within the safe, familiar confines of their neighborhood school. In Cambridge (whose neighborhoods in many ways epitomize the lifestyle of the permeable, postmodern family) the needs of busy working parents, from a broad spectrum of socioeconomic and ethnic groups, are afforded top priority, and their children are expected to cope.

The value of autonomy is also reflected in the postmodern educational emphasis on self-esteem, in contrast with the modern focus on personal adjustment. This new orientation goes along with the shift from broad to specific educational goals. The new focus on self-esteem (how the individual child feels about himself) makes it clear that individual achievement takes precedence over social adjustment (concern for what other children and adults feel about the child). While professionals continue to argue over what self-esteem means, and whether it is one thing or many, the term is omnipresent in postmodern discussions of education.[25]

Self-esteem is believed by educational psychologists to be critical for academic achievement and for successful competition in all domains. But the concept also reflects the permeable family value of autonomy and the need of each individual to be able to go it alone if necessary. If children have self-esteem, parents have been led to believe, they will not only do well academically but will also be able to cope with any of life's vicissitudes, including those future challenges which are impossible for any educational system to anticipate. Yet self-esteem, unlike adjustment, focuses first and foremost on the autonomous well-being of the young person, and only secondarily on his or her adaptation to society.

• *PROTECTING CHILDREN'S RIGHTS*

With the movement into the postmodern era, the temper of the laws regarding children and youth have changed in keeping with the new value of individual autonomy that characterizes the permeable family. It also mirrors the new emphasis on constitutional rights engendered by the civil rights and women's movements. The emphasis is no longer on protecting children but rather it is on protecting children's *rights*.

But because there are still many carryovers from the modern era, we can find a great deal of contradiction in the contemporary laws regarding children and youth. Some of these laws are founded on the modern perception of children and youth as in need of protection and security, while others are based on the perception of children and youth as autonomous individuals with adultlike civil rights. Although the Supreme Court has said that children "are possessed of fundamental rights that the state must respect," it is not clear what rights these are and whether, and in what situations, these rights preempt parental rights. According to Philippe Ariès,

> Americans have not made up their minds on the matter of children's rights. In 1967, for example (in re-Gault) the Supreme Court ruled

that juveniles charged with delinquency were entitled to adult rights to due process—right to counsel, right to appeal, and so on. Yet juvenile offenders are still considered special. Thus in Arizona, upon reaching eighteen, a person may have his juvenile court and police records destroyed (even if the crime involved was murder). Other states also have such "Wipe the slate clean" provisions.[26]

Likewise children and youth are still not regarded as fully entitled to the right to protection from cruel and inhuman punishment, at least not in the case of corporal punishment by parents or school authorities.[27] Yet in some cases the Supreme Court has ruled that children have the same rights as do adults. In *Belloti v. Baird,* a state law requiring parental consent for a minor's abortion was successfully challenged. In *Goss v. Lopez* the Court ruled that schools were required to provide students with due process before subjecting them to short-term suspensions. Likewise in *Smith v. Organization of Foster Families for Equality and Reform* the Court ruled that New York City authorities were required to hold a hearing before a child was transferred from one foster home to another.[28]

It is certainly true that in many of these cases the children have benefited from adults' defending their constitutional rights. But many postmodern adults argue in children's behalf because they have accepted the postmodern perceptions of childhood and teenage autonomy, not because of their abiding commitments to the health and welfare of young people. Lawyers themselves are beginning to question this overemphasis on children's rights. Bruce C. Hafen wrote in the *Harvard Law Review:*

> With our loss of confidence in paternalism, however, a subtle but important shift has occurred in the public mind away from commitment to the right of children to be nurtured . . . Similarly, some commentators have argued that children must be "liberated" from minority status or from other age-related legal limitation, sometimes drawing parallels between the inferior statuses of slaves, women and children. The reform movement for children's rights, especially in its approach to group litigation and its reliance on

> constitutional theories, has borrowed extensively from the legal experience in the civil rights movement, risking some uncritical translations of egalitarian concepts that ignore children's lack of capacity and their need to be protected from their own immaturity.[29]

Philippe Ariès concludes, "For better or worse, American children enjoy more adult rights today than they did 20 years ago—and often more adult responsibilities as well."[30]

The contemporary legal system, to the extent that it mirrors the permeable family value of autonomy, may thus deprive children and youth of the protection and security once afforded them by the laws of the modern era. In moving toward the protection of children's rights, rather than the protection of children, the legal system has also moved toward a relationship of mutual rather than of unilateral authority with respect to the young. The value of autonomy is now strengthened by the changed mores of the larger society.

•*HELPING ADULTS COPE*

Unlike the modern helping professions that were largely homogeneous and theory-driven, the helping professions in the postmodern world are heterogeneous and responsive to the special needs of different groups and of different individuals. As a result, postmodern helping professions speak directly, rather than indirectly, to the sentiments and values of the permeable family. In so doing, however, they reflect and reinforce the new imbalance in the family's ability to meet the needs of its members.

The sentiment of consensual love, for example, is now reflected and buttressed by the many helping programs targeted at men and women who have undergone separation, divorce, and remarriage. Compared with the modern era, when the helping professions paid little attention to the marital relationship, it is now a central focus of therapeutic intervention. A few of the current titles of this genre will illustrate this new direction. In their book *Marriage and Marital Therapy,* Thomas Paolino and Barbara McCrady present psychoanalytic, behavioral, and system approaches to the problem of troubled marriages. Other books such as *Families and Family Therapy, The Evaluation and Treatment of Marital Conflict, Divorce and Separation: Context, Causes, and Consequences,* and *Treating the Remarried Family* all address the here-and-now issues of marital dysfunction.[31]

Likewise, the helping professions' acceptance and reinforcement of the sentiment of shared parenting is evidenced in the new attention paid by health professionals to the issues of early education and the importance of quality daycare. A great many research investigations were and are being carried out, and a multitude of books, articles, and conferences now address these issues. For example, the American Association for the Advancement of Science, the nation's foremost scientific organization, sponsored a symposium on the long-term effects of early educational intervention, particularly project Head Start.[32] More recently, the Carnegie Foundation for the Advancement of Teaching published *Ready to Learn: A Mandate for the Nation,* which reports on the benefits of early education and recommends improvements.[33]

The helping professions also reinforce the postmodern value of urbanity. Unlike the modern helping professions, postmodern workers adopt a new, nonjudgmental, nonpathological assessment of nonnuclear family arrangements and lifestyles. Since 1986, for example, the *Diagnostic and Statistical Manual* of the American Psychiatric Association no longer lists homosexuality as a sexual dysfunction.

Finally, the mirroring and reinforcement of the postmodern sentiment of autonomy is omnipresent. Within psychology, the focus on traits such as "competence" and on processes such as "self-actualization" reflect this new emphasis on individual rather than social fulfillment. Similarly, postmodern psychiatry has turned its focus from the ego and social adjustment to the self and its disorders, in particular narcissism.[34]

As the helping professions moved toward more face-to-face treatment procedures and to group therapies, the unilateral authority of the therapist was considerably reduced. Indeed, in the nondirective therapy of Carl Rogers, a pioneer in this domain, the therapist often did little more than reflect the client's (not "patient's") own words and phrases back to him or her. In many ways, therefore, the postmodern helping professions have come to emphasize mutual, rather than unilateral, authority.[35]

Postmodern media, schools, laws, and the helping professions tend, in many ways, to reinforce the sentiments and values of the permeable family. They are also inclined to give more weight to mutual rather than unilateral authority. While these emphases have many exceptions and variations, they appear to reflect the dominant direction of society. As such they also contribute to the new family imbalance. Efforts to redress the family need imbalance will have to involve all of the social institutions that impact on the family.

Parents

5

From Intuition to Technique

How we rear our children is determined as much by our perceptions of ourselves as parents as by our objective knowledge about healthy childrearing. In turn, our perceptions of ourselves as parents are embedded in, and derive from, the educational philosophies of the society in which we live. In modern times, two different educational philosophies, and hence two different perceptions of childrearing, were in constant competition.

One of these philosophies of education derives from the writings of John Locke. Locke started from the perspective of adult society and the need to socialize children to live in that society. He proposed that the mind was a "blank slate" *(tabula rasa)* and that experience or tutelage was all important in its formation.[1] According to this nurture position, children will not spontaneously unfold into responsible, productive, and God-fearing adults. Childrearing cannot be left to nature or to chance but must follow a well-conceived plan to attain the desired result. From this perspective, parenting is a matter of learned technique.

The other broad approach to parenting derives from the philosophy of Jean Jacques Rousseau. Although Rousseau was influenced by Locke, he had a very different outlook on education and hence on childrearing. Rousseau began from the standpoint of children and argued that adults must adapt their childrearing to the child's emerging needs, interests, and abilities. For Rousseau, the mind was part of nature and should be allowed to follow its own predetermined path of development.[2] From this nature perspective, effective parenting is largely a matter of nourishing and safeguarding the child's development and requires nothing more than unlearned intuition.

During the reign of the nuclear family, the perception of parenting as intuition was much more in favor than was the perception of parenting as learned technique. This modern perception was underwritten by the new science of child psychology, which was heavily influenced by Darwinian ideas. The early child psychologists such as James Mark Baldwin, Wilhelm Preyer, James Sully, and Milicent Shinn all took a naturalistic, developmental approach to child growth and behavior. Their work encouraged the perception that parents were best advised to observe their children and to adapt their childrearing to the child's developing needs, abilities, and interests. This intuitive approach to childrearing was further reinforced by the increasingly familiar psychoanalytic ideas that were publicized in both articles and books for parents, written by professionals.[3]

The perception of parenting by intuition was a fitting corollary to the nuclear family sentiments of romantic love, maternal love, and domesticity and the value of togetherness. Romantic love was a liberated, uncontrived emotion that sprang unbidden from the heart. Maternal love was regarded as an instinctual response to one's offspring. Domesticity and togetherness were also seen as naturally emerging feelings in the highly evolved human family. The perception of parenting as an unlearned, intuitive activity was in keeping with these sentiments. In addition, the perception of parental intuitive knowledge also legitimatized the parents' use of unilateral authority.

With the movement into postmodernism and the ascendance of the permeable family, however, the perception of parenting as nurture or technique has become more popular and influential than the perception of parenting as nature or intuition. And this perception has occurred in tandem with a new emphasis by writers in the field of child development. In the 1960s the importance of experience and technique in education and in childrearing became a dominant motif. Noted educators and psychologists such as Benjamin Bloom, J. M. Hunt, and Jerome Bruner were in agreement as to how much could be, and should be, accomplished by the employment of "early intervention" techniques of childrearing and education.[4]

The postmodern perception of parenting as technique was as much a cause as it was an effect of the new emphasis in child psychology. Whatever the causal connections, the perception of parenting as technique was of a piece with the new sentiments of consensual love, shared parenting, and urbanity, together with the family value of autonomy. Consensual love, in contrast to romantic love, involves conscious choice and decisionmaking. Likewise, shared parenting implies that childrearing can be learned and put into practice by nonparental caregivers. Urbanity and autonomy suggest learned sophistication and independence rather than innate domesticity and dependence. The perception of parenting as learned technique also suggests that parents, no less than children, must be learners and in this respect puts them on a par with their offspring. The perception of parenting as technique thus also promotes mutual rather than unilateral authority.

In this chapter we will examine the shift from intuition to technique by looking at the tone, attitude, and aims of the advicegiving literature for parents from before and after midcentury. Then, we will observe how these differences are played out in the advice to parents regarding structure, communication, discipline, and education. What we will find is a change from the general developmental descriptions provided by modern writers to specific directive prescriptions provided by postmodern writers.

It is important to underscore the point, however, that these are only differences in emphasis. I do not mean to suggest that modern parents were entirely dominated by the nature philosophy of education and childrearing, nor that postmodern parents were governed solely by the nurture philosophy.

The Advicegiving Literature

Child-health professionals writing for parents in the modern era were generally supportive and respectful of parents' good sense and intuitive wisdom about children. They took it as their task to provide parents with a summary of the burgeoning information about how children grow and develop, about general norms of development. Wise, well-meaning parents could, it was assumed, easily translate these norms into appropriate practice. In their books, therefore, these writers generally took a reassuring and sympathetic tone. An excellent example can be found in the books of Benjamin Spock:

> Don't take too seriously all that the neighbors say. Don't be overawed by what experts say. Don't be afraid to trust your own common sense. Bringing up your child won't be a complicated job if you take it easy, trust your own instincts, and follow the directions that your doctor gives you. We know for a fact that the natural loving care that kindly parents give their children is a hundred times more valuable than their knowing how to pin a diaper on just right or how to make a formula expertly.[5]

For Spock, as for other modern writers for parents, this supportive tone was coupled with a nonjudgmental attitude taken toward both parents and children. In part, this attitude derives from the strong maturational bent among modern writers.[6] When one looks at children as growing through stages or phases, behavior at one level of development is simply different from that of another stage; it is neither right nor wrong, good nor bad. An infant who is crawling is not wrong because he is not walking; crawling is an appropriate form of locomotion at that stage of development. Valuative judgments are uncalled for from this maturational perspective.

Modern writers were concerned with the whole child and with fostering healthy physical, social, intellectual, and emotional development. They assumed that normative development was healthy development. Parents who encouraged normative development were fostering well-rounded personalities in their children. The risk for this supportive, nonjudgmental, whole-child, how-do-children-grow school of parental advicegiving was that parents would interpret the norms too rigidly and might see their child as deviant if he or she did not follow the developmental guidelines exactly.

It is certainly true, of course, that even during the modern era there were writers of the nurture persuasion, even though they were not in the majority. John B. Watson, writing in the early decades of this century, took a strict technique approach to childrearing. He argued that nurture, not nature, was the major determinant of how individuals turned out. His tone was directive rather than supportive: "The time was when we used to think it took generations to make a well bred person. Now we know parents can do it in a few months' time if they start to cultivate the garden before the weeds begin to grow."[7] Employing the principles of conditioning, parents could even toilet train their children within the first few weeks of life: "It is quite easy to start habits of day time continence (conditional response) when the child is from 3–5 weeks old by putting the chamber to the child (but at this age never on it) each time it is aroused for feeding. It is often surprising how quickly the conditioned response is established if your routine is unremitting and your patience holds out."[8]

During the modern era, Watson's technique approach was the exception rather than the rule. Beginning about midcentury, however, the number of "technique" writers grew larger, while the number of "intuition" writers grew smaller. Modern advicegivers such as Benjamin Spock, T. Berry Brazelton, and Penelope Leach are in the minority today.[9] They have been replaced by writers who tend to be prescriptive in tone, judgmental in attitude, and specific in their aims.

Many of these postmodern advicegivers are not behaviorists in the tradition of either Watson or B. F. Skinner. But their tone remains directive rather than supportive. This is true even for Haim Ginott, who could well be regarded as the father of postmodern parental advicegiving. His crucial point—that parents must distinguish between a child's actions and his person—is echoed in most of the postmodern childrearing literature. Nonetheless, in writing for parents, Ginott's tone is prescriptive, almost accusatory, rather than supportive: "When we call our teenager 'stupid' or 'clumsy' or 'ugly' there are reactions in his body and soul. He reacts with resentment, anger and revenge fantasies. He may then feel guilty about his hostility and ask for punishment by acting up."[10]

Although modern writers often gave parents a list of do's and don't's, they were less ready than postmodern writers to target specific parental behaviors for modification. The focus on technique, however, makes it natural to illustrate correct techniques by contrasting them with incorrect ones:

Correct	*Incorrect*
"Ice cream that is left on the counter will turn to soup."	"Ice cream belongs in the freezer, not on the counter. Where is our head, in the clouds?"
"The dirty dishes belong in the dishwasher, not in the sink."	"How many times do I have to remind you? What do you think this is, a restaurant?"

In the words of Nancy Salamin and Martha Jablow: "If your comment is directed at the deed, rather than the doer, your children won't hear it as a personal attack."[11]

Although this approach makes the valuable distinction between the child and the event, it is still judgmental. There is clearly a right and a wrong way to say things to children. Moreover, the wrong way, as Ginott and his followers suggest, may be damaging to the child. This admonition, that if you say something in the wrong way you may injure your child, is for the most part absent from the modern advicegiving literature. Paradoxically, therefore, while postmodern writers argue that parents should take a nonjudgmental attitude toward children, the experts themselves take a judgmental attitude toward parents. The risk is that parents may become overly concerned about doing things the "right" way and convey this inhibiting and constraining concern to their child.

Postmodern writers for parents have a different and more specific aim in mind than was true for modern parental advicegivers. Whereas modern writers were concerned with normative development of the whole child, postmodern advicegivers seem to have a much more specific target in mind, namely the child's sense of self-esteem. If parents use the right techniques, they will accomplish their specific goals without doing damage or harm to the child's positive sense of himself or herself.

Both the modern and the postmodern advicegivers were concerned with four elements of childrearing: structure, communication, discipline, and education. But as we will see in the sections that follow, their respective approaches were quite different.

Structure

Since the end of the last century, the pendulum of advice to parents regarding how much structure children need for healthy development has swung from restrictive to permissive and back again. Indeed, reviews of the advicegiving literature in *Good Housekeeping, Ladies' Home Journal*, and *Women's Home Companion* from 1890 to 1970 seesaw back and forth over this hundred-year time period.[12] In the 1920s, for example, Watson's behavioristic ideas sometimes led to restrictive childrearing advice, whereas, beginning in the 1930s and 40s, Freudian ideas encouraged more indulgent childrearing counsel.

With the postmodern era, however, a new consensus has emerged that "authoritative" parenting is the most effective and successful mode of control with children. In much-quoted research, the psychologist Diana Baumrind found that parents who are authoritative (who exercise firmness with love) have children who are more self-confident, more considerate of others, and more independent than are children of parents who are either authoritarian (exercise firmness without warmth) or permissive (express warmth without firmness).[13]

• DEVELOPMENTAL NORMS

Regardless of the type of structure they advocated—restrictive or permissive—modern writers provided parents with normative information about child development, and they supported "intuitive" parents in drawing up general, age-appropriate rules and limits. Postmodern writers, in contrast, put much more stress on the use of rules and limits in specific situations and with regard to particular behaviors.

The modern focus on providing parents with child development norms as a basis for exercising structure is illustrated by Selma Fraiberg in her still popular book *The Magic Years:*

> If we understand the process of child development, we see that each developmental phase brings with it its characteristic problems. The parent's methods of helping the child must take into account the child's own development and his mental equipment at any given stage. This means that there is very little point in speaking categorically about "childhood anxieties" or "discipline problems in childhood." The anxieties of the two year old are not the same as the anxieties of the five year old. Even if the same crocodile hides under the bed of one small boy between the ages of two and five, the crocodile of the two year old is not the same beast as the crocodile of the five year old—from the psychological point of view. He's had a chance to grow with the boy and is a lot more complex after three years under the bed than he was the day he first moved in . . . Therefore, a practical book for parents needs to approach the croco-

> dile problem from the point of view of the two year old and again from the view of the five year old.[14]

Two other modern child-health professionals who believed in providing parents with developmental markers as a basis for the exercise of structure were Arnold Gesell and Frances L. Ilg. As a result of their careful observations of children at different levels of development, they were able to provide parents with year-by-year profiles to assess their own child's progress. Gesell and Ilg were careful to emphasize that individual children differ over a wide range, and that parents should not use the profiles in any rigid way:

> Do not be surprised to find that your child does some things that are not even mentioned in this book! We know that every child is an individual and that he travels by his own tailor-made time schedule. Nevertheless, we have given you in the characterizational profiles, the descriptive maturity traits and in the growth gradients, a frame of reference to consult. If you do not use this reference frame too rigidly, it should help to make your child more intelligible; and if he is at all normal, as he probably is, then you will have the reassurance that he is steadily (though not evenly) moving towards higher levels of maturity.[15]

For Fraiberg and for Gesell and Ilg, the important thing was to provide parents normative information about child growth and development. With that information, parents' sound powers of observation and deduction would lead them to the most effective use of parental structure. This modern counsel regarding structure is again nicely expressed by Spock: "Good hearted parents who aren't afraid to be firm when it is necessary can get good results with either moderate strictness or moderate permissiveness."[16]

The tenor of modern childrearing advice placed a great deal of responsibility on parents. Parents were required to closely observe their children to see how they measured up to the "normal" pattern of development. By a process of trial and error, parents had to discover what kind of limit-setting worked best, given their own personality and that of their child. Children, on the other hand, were the beneficiaries of this customized approach to childrearing.

Of course, not all parents had either the time or the inclination to read about child development and to work at devising custom-made rules and limits for their children. For some modern parents, the emphasis on intuitive knowledge was an excuse to do "what comes naturally" and not to worry about what they said, or did, to their children. Moreover, the consumers of the childrearing literature probably constitute a small proportion of the parent population at any given time. In many subcultures within our society, childrearing is determined much more by ethnic mores and customs than it is by the advice of childrearing experts. Nonetheless, the overall societal trends are there, and they do have a ripple effect even on parents who do not consume the childrearing literature directly. For example, when modern parents sent their children to school, children were likely to come into contact with teachers whose methods were informed to some extent by the prevailing literature.

• *HOW-TO PARENTING*

Postmodern parental advicegivers are much more directive regarding how much structure to provide than were the modern childrearing experts. The following excerpt from a 1991 book, *Parent/Teen Breakthrough*, not only specifically directs parents in the use of "correct" techniques but also tells parents what they have been doing wrong:

> During all of your kid's preteen years you've been automatically saying things like "Change your clothes" and "Make sure you do your homework." Suddenly not saying those things leaves a huge gap. Your kid comes home from school and you say, "How are you doing?" He says, "Fine." Now what?
>
> Actually, you don't have to do anything to fill the gap. As you're switching over, the best way to improve your relationship with your teenager might very well be to back off. Instead of controlling, do nothing. Just be available. Say hi. Ask what's up. Ask if your kid

> needs anything when you go shopping. Don't try to force an artificial togetherness. Just be available when your kid comes to you.[17]

Here is another example of this directive, technique-focused, parenting advice regarding structure:

> To do a good job, all people need to know the rules. Like any employee, children too need to know what's expected of them and what they can expect when they follow the rules and what will happen when they don't. Limit-setting will give your children these guidelines . . . When you finish reading this book, you will be able to set and enforce limits like the following, which includes all three components [Limit, Reason, Consequence]:
>
> Limit: Johnny you can play outside in the backyard but you cannot go in the front yard, or on the sidewalk, or out into the street.
>
> Reason: In the backyard you are safe from being hit by a car.
>
> Consequence: If you go out of the backyard, you will have to come into the house and stay in for the rest of the day.[18]

In both of these examples, the issue of human development is minimized. Indeed, in the last excerpt, the child is likened to an employee! Parents are directed to use discipline techniques as if they would be effective regardless of the developmental level of the youngster.

The directive, technique approach to structure is in some ways easier for parents but more difficult for children—just the opposite of the nondirective, intuition approach. The difference is not unlike that between a classroom in which the teacher and the children make their own curriculum materials and one in which the materials come as a commercial package. In creating their own curriculum, the children and the teacher have to work harder, but children learn a lot in an interesting way. "Store-bought" curricula are easier for the teacher but are often dull and uninteresting for children. In the same way, prepackaged structure techniques make it easier for parents and other caregivers, and they provide consistency for children who are continually shunted back and forth between parents, teachers, daycare providers, and others. But this approach deprives children of rules and limits made-to-order for them, and in this respect it contributes to the postmodern need imbalance.

Communication

In the modern era, those who wrote for parents offered only general principles about language development and parent-child communication. Postmodern writers offer, instead, a great many specific techniques and formulas to assist parents in communicating with their children.

•*AGE-APPROPRIATE EXPECTATIONS*

Modern parents were generally told at what ages children could be expected to utter their first word, when they would begin to speak in phrases and sentences, and the age at which they might be expected to use pronouns, adverbs, and prepositions. When parents were given advice about how to communicate with their children, it was often in the most general terms about the kinds of things that ought, and ought not, to be said to children. This information, it was believed, would provide intuitively blessed parents with the guidelines they needed to talk appropriately with their children.

A typical example is provided by the famed English psychologist and educator Susan Isaacs, writing in the 1930s:

> Don't discuss children in front of them, nor in general assume that they won't listen, notice, or understand.
> Don't tease or use sarcasm—laugh with the child, not at him.
> Don't give moral lectures to the small child; if you find yourself doing this, don't be surprised or angry if he is bored.
> Don't assume that the child understands what you are saying to him just because you do.
> Don't lie or evade.[19]

When modern writers did get specific about communication, it was to give parents ways to encourage their children to talk about a subject. In this way parents would have a chance to listen to their children's ideas and to appreciate their level of understanding. Fraiberg provides a good illustration of this type of advice:

> We have seen that at the time the child asks his first questions, and for a long time afterwards, he already has his own notions, his private theories about procreation. These theories are based on his own observations of body functioning which most commonly lead the child to draw analogies from eating and elimination. The facts we give him are beyond his experience, they appear to him as strange or even fantastic, and the educational achievement may be only one theory (ours) superimposed on other theories (his). The result is often further confusion.
>
> It may be very helpful, then, to take the child's private theories into account *before* we introduce him to new facts. "Where does the baby come from, Mama?" "Tell me where you think it comes from, Danny?" Or we can say, "You try to guess and then I'll help you figure it out." In this way we can deal with the child's theories first and then help him look at them too.[20]

In both of these examples, the authors leave a great deal for parents to do. They suggest that parents have to be sensitive to the child's level of development and to gear their communications accordingly, but other than providing a few opening questions or phrases, they do not offer specific verbal examples or models. This advice demands a great deal of time and attention on the part of parents. Children are again the benefactors inasmuch as the resulting communications are likely to be in keeping with their needs and levels of understanding. It is certainly true, of course, that many modern parents did not read this material nor behave in this way.

•*DESCRIPTIVE PHRASES AND "I" MESSAGES*

Modern childrearing experts did not devote more time or space to communication between parents and children than they did to any other topic. In the postmodern childrearing literature, however, communication issues take up most or all of the book. This probably reflects the fact that, in part at least, the permeable family is more egalitarian than the nuclear family, and democracy necessitates more communication. In any case, postmodern writers have provided parents with a bulging thesaurus of sample phrases for communicating effectively with their children.

Ginott was perhaps the first to show that much of our spontaneous, well-intentioned communication with children was not what it seemed. Good-natured labeling, praise, and teasing often carried messages that were the opposite of what the parent intended.[21] At a meeting with parents, reported by his students, Ginott asked:

> "What is it about the language I use with children that is different?" The parents looked at one another blankly. "The language I use," he continued, "does not evaluate. I avoid expressions that judge a child's character or ability. I steer clear of words like stupid, clumsy, bad, and even words like beautiful, good, wonderful, because they are not helpful; they get in a child's way. Instead I use words that describe, I describe what I see, I describe what I feel."
>
> Recently, a little girl in my playroom brought me a painting and asked, "Is it good?" I looked at it and answered, "I see a purple sun, a striped sky, and lots of flowers. It makes me feel as if I were in the country." She smiled and said, "I'm going to make another."[22]

Here Ginott provides not only general principles but also concrete templates of phraseology that parents can use to formulate what to say in similar situations.

Two of Ginott's students, Adele Faber and Elaine Mazlish, have followed Ginott's lead in directing parents in the use of communication techniques with children. In their workshops for parents these authors have parents role-play different situations. A principle they teach is not to deny the child's feelings. In one scenario a participant plays a child who has just had a shot at the doctor's office and who complains: "That doctor nearly killed me with that shot." Then they have the parents play out the role of a parent who denies feelings and one who accepts them. Here are some examples of parental communications that deny feelings:

"Come on, it can't hurt that much."
"You're making a big fuss over nothing."
"Your brother never complains when he has a shot."
"You're acting like a baby."
"Well, you better get used to those shots. After all, you're going to get them every week."

And these are examples the authors give of accepting the child's feelings:

"Sounds as if it really hurts."
"Must have been painful."
"Mmmmm, that bad."
"Sounds like the kind of pain you'd like to wish on your worst enemy."
"It's not easy to get those shots week after week. I bet you'll be glad when they are over."[23]

Another author who has followed Ginott's lead is Thomas Gordon. His well-known Parent Effectiveness Training program is quite specific about the correct language to use:

Keep in mind that praise is usually a statement about others—how *they* look, what *they* said, what *they* did. As such praise will logically come out as *You messages* followed by judgments or evaluations.

"You did a fine job . . ."
"You are so well coordinated . . . "
"Your speech was excellent . . . "
"You have such beautiful skin . . . "

One alternative to praise is a clear message that expresses to another precisely how you feel. Called *I messages,* these are accurate, self-revealing messages that clearly share what is going on inside of you:

"I feel good when . . . "
"I was pleasantly surprised when . . . "
"I was relieved when . . . "
"I enjoyed it so much when . . . "
"I got excited when . . . "

> I messages . . . communicate something about yourself, not evaluations of the other person. This difference is crucial, because evaluations are the very parts of praise that cause so many problems.[24]

While these postmodern techniques and advice are very sound, they tend to ignore what the modern writers emphasized, namely, the child's level of development and conceptual understanding. In many ways, learning the communication techniques described by these authors is easier than engaging in the careful observation of age and individual differences demanded by modern writers. Yet children understand language in different ways at different age levels. A preschooler, for example, who engages in magical thinking might well misinterpret the message "I feel good when you pick up your things" as meaning that she can magically influence her parents' feelings. When the parent is unhappy, the child might feel responsible for that as well.

Ginott and those who have followed him have made a very important contribution to our understanding of the many ways that children can interpret what we say. What they fail to take into account is how children's interpretations of our communications are affected by their level of intellectual development as well as their level of verbal comprehension.

Discipline

Discipline has to do with the ways in which we train children in self-control, character, and orderly behavior. Both modern and postmodern writers for parents are generally opposed to corporal punishment as a means of discipline. The real difference between them is in the directedness and the specificity of their disciplinary advice.

• *MISBEHAVIOR FROM THE CHILD'S POINT OF VIEW*

Modern advicegivers for parents dealt with discipline from a perspective-taking orientation. They believed that if parents were aware of the child's point of view, they would be able to exercise effective and appropriate discipline techniques. The English pediatrician and psychiatrist D. W. Winnicott, writing in 1957, provides a reassuring example of how looking at a child's behavior from the child's perspective suggests a calm and effective course of action.

> After a moment's thought, it will be seen that in an ordinary household, one in which there is no ill person who could be called a thief, actually quite a lot of stealing goes on; only it is not called stealing. A child goes into the larder and takes a bun or two, or helps himself to a lump of sugar out of the cupboard. In a good home no one calls the child who does this a thief . . . It may be necessary for parents to make rules in order to keep the home a going concern. They may have to make a rule that whereas the children can always go and take bread, or perhaps a certain kind of cake, they may not take special cakes, and not eat sugar from the store-cupboard. There is always a certain amount of give and take in these things, and life in a household to some extent consists in the working out of the relation between the parents and the children in these and similar terms.[25]

In the same vein, the educator Dorothy Cohen, writing in 1972 but still in the modern mode, tries to help parents to look at the "misbehavior" of schoolage children from their point of view. She makes it clear that much "misbehavior is an expression of children's development stage rather than evidence of a stiff-necked rebelliousness." She, like Winnicott, assumes that alerting parents to the child's perspective will encourage them to handle difficult situations in a positive and constructive way:

> Children of the middle years are contradictory. They seem so capable and yet so unwilling to do the most obvious things within the adult scheme of orderliness and responsibility. Yet they are struggling with adult values, ideas, knowledge, and skills and are, in fact, learning to be responsible, orderly, organized, and realistic—but among their friends, and to some extent, at school. Home is the last place where they will show this striving, because home, during the middle years, is where children must dispel their parents' illusion that they are babies. They do this by resisting the old conformities . . . Although parents must persist in requiring that the routines of daily life be attended to, it must be with the full awareness that, for the moment, the children will often seem not to be taking much in, and for periods on end may give no sign that they have heard at all.[26]

Both Winnicott and Cohen assume that, once parents understand the child's point of view, their sound intuitions will guide them in taking appropriate action. Taking the child's point of view demands good will, time, and effort on the part of parents. The child is the clear beneficiary. Parents who make the effort to understand their children's point of view are likely to treat children fairly and in an age-appropriate manner. To be sure, not all modern parents did so, and many followed the dictum "Spare the rod, spoil the child." Nonetheless, the dominant theory of discipline—if not the practice—was taking the child's perspective.

• *SAFE-GUARDING SELF-ESTEEM*

The postmodern perception of parenting as a technique has changed the focus of disciplinary advicegiving. Where the modern writers were concerned with helping parents understand the child's actions, postmodern writers are attentive to helping parents modify the child's behavior without damage to the child's self-esteem. Haim Ginott was, again, among the first to offer parents concrete verbal formulas for dealing with discipline situations. The aim of these verbalizations was to correct behavior without harm to the child's sense of self.

> I like descriptive words because they invite a child to work out his own solutions to problems. Here's an example: If a child were to spill a glass of milk, I would say to him, "I see the milk spilled," and I'd hand him a sponge. In this way, I avoid blame and put the emphasis where it belongs—on what needs to be done.
>
> If I were to say instead, "Stupid. You always spill everything. You'll never learn, will you!" we can be sure that the child's total energy would be mobilized for defense instead of solution. You would hear, "Bobby pushed my hand" or "It wasn't me; it was the dog."[27]

Ginott was once confronted by a modern mother, who had a firm belief in the efficacy of love-motivated intuition. She said:

> "Dr. Ginott, what you've been telling us is very interesting. But I've always felt that it is not so important what you said to a child as long as he knows you love him. I believe you can say almost anything. I mean, in the final analysis isn't love what really counts?"
>
> Dr. Ginott replied:
>
> "I do not discount the power of love. Love is wealth. But even with material wealth, we often find that large sums need to be broken down into small currency. In a phone booth, a dime is more serviceable than a fifty dollar bill. For our love to serve our children, we must learn how to break it down into the words that can help them—moment by moment—as when milk spills, or a drawing is offered for approval. And even when we are angry we can still use the kind of words that do not damage or destroy the people we care about."[28]

Ginott is thus concerned with how we handle situations in which, through accident or design, harm or damage has been done. His focus is on the effects of parental communications on their children's perceptions of themselves. He is not concerned with the different ways children at successive age levels might perceive the same situation.

Thomas Gordon has also suggested techniques aimed at altering the children's behavior without injury to their sense of self. Like

Ginott, his focus is not on the child's developmental level but rather on techniques for dealing with discipline situations. He emphasizes not blaming the child and separating the action from the person. He also introduces the notion of problem ownership:

> Whenever a child is doing something that prevents you from getting some need satisfied, think of the behavior as unacceptable since it is causing *you* the problem. It is you who "owns" the problem.
>
> However, should the child be experiencing some type of need deprivation, think of the situation as one in which the child has the problem—that's when the child owns the problem.[29]

Gordon then offers techniques such as finding out what a child needs, making a trade, and using nonconfrontative "I messages" ("When the TV is on so loud, I can't carry on a conversation with your mother").

Both Ginott and Gordon share the belief that advice to parents should be concrete and provide them with verbal formulas that will enable parents to educate the child while contributing to the child's positive sense of self. As in the case of structure and communication, giving parents specific disciplinary techniques makes their job easier than does asking them to take the child's point of view and working out discipline practices accordingly. While postmodern children undoubtedly benefit from parental concern for their self-esteem, they also lose the sense that their parents are trying to understand their individual point of view.

Again, just as many modern parents failed to use the perspective-taking approach, many postmodern parents probably do not use the language techniques suggested by Ginott and others. One problem with the Ginott-type advice is that it does not give parents an outlet for our quite legitimate anger. To tell the truth, as a father I had some trouble finding the words to separate the person from the deed. Usually, when one of my sons broke the rules or a window, I was too angry to speak calmly and objectively. My own solution was to express my feelings, but in an exaggerated, humorous way: "You do that again and you will be grounded so long they will call you Rip Van Winkle II," or "If I hear that word again, I'm going to braid your tongue." In this way, I could express my appropriate annoyance and anger without doing harm to my son's sense of self.

Perspective-taking reflects the unilateral authority generally exercised by modern nuclear parents. The parent, not the child, must understand the other person's point of view and make decisions that take both points of view into account. In the postmodern mode, where language is center stage, the parent is responsible for his or her language but not for the language of the child. This reflects a relation of mutual rather than of unilateral authority.

Early Childhood Education

In the broad sense, education includes everything the child learns in the very process of living and maturing. In the narrow sense, however, education refers to knowledge, values, and skills that children are taught by adults, either parents or teachers. Both modern and postmodern writers for parents generally agree that for children over the age of six or seven, education in the narrow sense is best provided by formal schooling.

Where we do see a sharp difference between modern and postmodern writers, however, is in regard to the education (in the narrow sense) of young children. By and large, modern writers urged parents to educate their young children only in the broad sense. In contrast, many postmodern writers insist that parents should educate young children in the narrow sense—that they teach young children skills such as math, reading, and computers.

• *STRUCTURING THE ENVIRONMENT*

In giving advice to parents of young children, childrearing experts of the modern bent emphasized young children's tremendous curiosity and eagerness to explore their world. Parents had to refrain from providing too much information too fast. Susan Isaacs wrote:

> Our descriptions and explanations are useful when children are older, to supplement their own experience: but they are useless as a substitute for it. We may like explaining, but it is not always the most useful thing for our children. Whatever they can discover by their own effort in exploring and experimenting, they should. And our general aim should be to encourage them to find out as much as possible for themselves, turning to us for help or for information really beyond their own reach. Our best reply to many of their questions would often be "What do you think?" "Shall we try?" "Let's find out" rather than "It is so and so." For if we indulge in the habit of giving information dogmatically every time, the children get into the corresponding habit of asking for it—sometimes because they want to please us, sometimes because our way of being all-wise has made them helpless.[30]

Likewise, Selma Fraiberg described the toddler as a kind of scientist:

> No subject is too commonplace for his study. He analyzes the contents of waste baskets, garbage cans, clothes closets, kitchen cupboards and drawers with a zeal and energy that would do credit to a whole archaeological expedition. In fact, when he has completed these excavations it is impossible to believe that so much debris could be dug up by one small investigator working in solitude with no other aid but his bare hands . . .
>
> He puts us to shame, at times, by his ability to see details which we do not. *He* is the one who will notice that the elf in his picture book is not wearing the feather in cap that he had worn in earlier pictures. It is he who discovers that we have omitted a detail in our retelling of a familiar story.[31]

Modern writers, then, emphasized the young child's spontaneous learning and the need for parents to encourage this learning by asking questions and affording the child a safe environment within which to perform his "scientific investigations." Such nondirective advice places a lot of responsibility on parents, while providing children with a safe and secure, but challenging and exciting, world. Certainly there were many parents in the modern era who "pushed" their young children. Yet the major thrust of childrearing advice was against such "hurrying."

• *STRUCTURING THE CHILD*

Many postmodern writers, by contrast, urge parents to teach academic subjects to their infants and young children. This approach presupposes that children are competent to learn such subjects if only the parent will use the appropriate techniques. Many of these writers take their starting point from Jerome Bruner, who wrote in his 1960s bestseller, *The Process of Education:* "We begin with the hypothesis that any subject can be taught effectively in some intellectually honest way to any child at any stage of development."[32]

In the thirty years since Bruner wrote those famous lines, no one has yet taught young children calculus, astrophysics, or biochemistry. Indeed, we are having a difficult time teaching these subjects to college students! Nonetheless, the idea that young children can, with the right techniques, be taught any subject at any age, and that their intelligence and their self-esteem will be enhanced thereby, has become part of our conventional wisdom. It has contributed to a full library of books offering instructional techniques to parents. Consider: *Help Your Baby Learn; Teach Your Baby to Read; Teach Your Child to Read in Sixty Days; How to Raise a Brighter Child; How to Have a Smarter Baby;* and *Give Your Child a Superior Mind.*[33]

A couple of examples from this subset of postmodern books will help make this directive advice about early instruction a little more concrete. We should perhaps begin with those at the extreme—writers who are encouraging parents to teach their children while they are still in the womb! Susan Ludington-Hoe, a nurse-midwife, suggests in her book *How to Have a Smarter Baby* that parents

> *Stroke* your fetus and say "Stroke, I'm stroking you."
> *Pat* your fetus and say, "Pat, I'm patting you."

Gently Squeeze your fetus and say, "Squeeze, I'm squeezing you."
Rub your fetus and say, "Rub, I'm rubbing you."

If you stroke after your fetus has kicked, you may be teaching him that his activity brings some change in his environment. This is called imitative behavior and is important because he learns that he has some control in the world. Maybe he's even thinking, "When I kick, Mommy pats me and rubs me and talks to me. What power I have, this is marvelous."[34]

But even writers closer to the mainstream are suggesting that we instruct young children in complex academic skills. Seymour Papert, who studied with Jean Piaget, nonetheless believes that even young children can be taught to program computers: "For [some readers,] programming is a complex marketing skill acquired by some mathematically gifted adults. But my experience is very different. I have seen hundreds of elementary school children learn very easily to program, and evidence is accumulating that much younger children can do so as well."[35]

Although Papert, following Bruner, argues that all children can be taught programming, he hedges his bets by setting conditions that will probably never be met:

I am left with two clear impressions: First that all children, under the right conditions, can acquire proficiency with programming that will make it one of their most advanced educational accomplishments. Second, the right conditions are very different from the kind of access to computers that is now becoming established as the norm in our schools. The conditions necessary for the kind of relationships with a computer that I will be writing about in this book require more and freer access to the computer than educational planners currently anticipate. And they require a kind of computer language and a learning environment around that language very different from those the schools are now providing. They even require a kind of computer rather different from those that the schools are using.[36]

Oddly, Papert seems to hark back to the doctrine of "formal discipline," according to which learning Latin and Greek and mathematics, and now programming, improves the mind. There is no evidence for the intelligence-enhancing effects of formal discipline. Moreover, neither children nor adults need to learn to program in order to use computers. What we need, and what is becoming more available, are computer programs for interested young children that are appropriate to their level of mental skill and ability.

Child development researchers are contributing to the pressure to teach young children in more technique-oriented ways. In the second (1991) edition of his textbook entitled *Children's Thinking,* Robert Siegler writes: "In fact young children can learn more than Piaget thought they could and they can benefit more from a greater variety of instructional techniques than Piaget thought they could . . . The findings dovetail with the unsuspected early competence that children have been found to have even without direct training. Not only do children understand more than previously thought, they also can learn more."[37] But like Papert, Siegler immediately offers a caveat: "It is important not to throw out the baby with the bath water, however. Although young children can learn to solve these problems they often find doing so exceptionally difficult."[38]

The conditions and caveats with which academicians balance their arguments for early education are often not heard by those who translate these findings into books for parents. For example, the lead story in the July 1993 issue of *Life* magazine was entitled "Babies Are Smarter than You Think," and on the front cover were the following statements about infants:

> They can add before they can count.
> They can understand a hundred words before they can speak.
> And at three months, their powers of memory are far greater than we ever imagined.[39]

While data have been gathered that can be interpreted this way, the implications are that even very young children not only know a lot more than we gave them credit for but can learn a lot more as well—if we only use the right techniques.

The idea that parenting is a matter of learned technique is certainly reinforced by this kind of writing. Although parents are assured that these techniques will add greatly to the child's intelligence and self-esteem, the evidence for such claims remains to be gathered. Certainly, following the precise, step-by-step instructions provided by Ludington-Hoe or establishing the kind of computer environment described by Papert requires as much time and effort as does providing a setting for children to explore and discover on their own. The difference is that in the technique orientation the parents make the decision as to what the child should learn; in the developmental orientation the needs and interests of the individual child are the deciding factors.

When it comes to early childhood education, therefore, we have to distinguish between using unilateral authority in a direct and in an indirect way. Many of the writers discussed above believe that, with young children, unilateral authority should be used directly, in the sense that the adult decides what the child should learn. In contrast, modern writers (and the majority of professionals in the field of early childhood education) believe that, with young children, unilateral authority should be used indirectly, by preparing the learning environment. Contemporary, high-quality early childhood centers have "interest areas" (reading, science, art, "dress-up," cooking) and allow children choice as to which area to go to and how long to spend there. Put differently, effective early childhood educators exercise their unilateral authority indirectly, by structuring the environment, not the child.

In closing this chapter on parenting, it is important to reemphasize that the balance between intuition and technique is relative rather than absolute. While modern writers were strong on conveying our growing body of knowledge regarding child growth and development to parents, they left the task of translating that information into concrete practices up to parents. Many parents in the modern era could tailor-make their parenting practices, but many others could not. In contrast, postmodern writers often neglect much of the child development literature and focus instead on specific issues and techniques. This is beneficial for those parents who need techniques, but it fails to provide them with the knowledge of child development that gives them an understanding of why techniques succeed or fail. Consequently, when faced with a situation for which no technique has been provided, they may be at a loss.

What would be most beneficial to parents would be books that contain both information about child development and practical techniques growing out of that information. Parents could then reap the double benefits of intuition and technique for their children at every stage of development.

Children

6

From Innocence to Competence

Postmodern children go through the same stages of crawling, walking, talking—and talking back—as did their counterparts growing up a half century ago. Nonetheless, we perceive children today quite differently than we did before midcentury. This change has not come about because of any new, revolutionary research findings about children. Our scientific knowledge about child growth and development has indeed increased over the past few decades, but it only adds fresh details to an outline that was already sketched by the early workers in the field. Our societal perception of children, however, is not a photocopy of our extant knowledge about this age group. Rather, it is always a mirror image of our prevailing family feelings and values. As these change, so too does our perception of children.

In keeping with the sentiments of the nuclear family, adults in the modern era generally saw children as innocent, in need of parental protection and security. The sentiment of romantic love led us to view children as the precious progeny of a romantic union. Likewise, the sentiment of maternal love presupposed a vulnerable child who could not survive without maternal nurturance. Finally, the sentiment of domesticity, together with the value of togetherness, took as given that children were in need of the protection and security that could only be provided in a constant and sheltered home. The perception of innocent children in need of adult protection also reinforced the unilateral authority of modern parents.

Now that we have moved into the postmodern era, we have a new perception of children. Today we see them as competent, as ready and able to deal with any and all of life's vicissitudes. The sentiment of consensual love extends to children, who are deemed able to voluntarily withhold or bestow their affections. Shared parenting, in turn, takes as given that children are competent to accommodate to nonparental caregivers and to out-of-home settings from an early age. The sentiment of urbanity and the value of autonomy presuppose children ready and able to process an unending flow of information and to make sound choices and decisions from an early age. Childhood competence thus also supports the belief in the appropriateness of mutual authority in the permeable family.

Both the modern perception of childhood innocence and the postmodern perception of childhood competence distort reality. Modern children were considerably less innocent than parents and the larger society supposed, and postmodern children are less competent than their parents and the society as a whole would like to believe. In the case of childhood innocence, however, the distortion worked in children's favor. It placed many more demands on parents to provide protection and security than it placed on children to accommodate to the needs of adults.

The postmodern perception of childhood competence, in contrast, has had the opposite effect. It has relieved parents and society in general from much of the responsibility for providing protection and security for children. But it has placed many new demands on children for autonomy and self-reliance. While some of these demands have allowed children to demonstrate formerly unrecognized competencies, many others are age-inappropriate, overwhelming, and stressful. Put differently, the perception of childhood competence has shifted much of the responsibility for child protection and security from parents and society to children themselves.

This societal remake of our image of children is evidenced in the new demands we make on children in the areas of maturity, education, recreation, and safety.

Maturity

Childhood, in the modern era, was seen as a very special period of life that children were entitled to enjoy without adult intrusion. As a consequence, children—at least most of those in the white middle-class majority—experienced few demands for maturity, for coping with the dangers, unpleasantness, and temptations of the real world. With the movement into the postmodern era, and a new image of childhood competence, demands for children to demonstrate maturity are present in abundance.

•*MODERN PERCEPTIONS OF INNOCENCE*

The time period during which we regarded children as innocent and placed few demands for maturity on them has been relatively brief. As Alisdair Roberts describes it:

> Caring and even sentimental attitudes to children gathered strength through the nineteenth century. This movement of opinion was gradual but, on evidence of books written for children, a new spirit emerged in the 1880's. After a long period of moral seriousness, the plain but virtuous child fell out of favor. Instead ringleted heroines, dainty and innocent, gave the upstairs nursery its tone. Among older children playfulness and mischief became acceptable, and their reading (bought by relatives) positively urged them to be madcaps and tomboys. With the dawning recognition that it is possible for children to be too good, we have crossed into the modern world.[1]

This image of childhood as a period during which children should be allowed to be children was mirrored in the literature of the early decades of this century:

> Nowhere is this [distance between childhood and adulthood] more charmingly expressed than in Kenneth Grahame's account of his own childhood, *The Golden Age,* wherein children see themselves as the fortunate ones, and adults as the "Olympians," powerful but misguided. When adults have the power to do otherwise, how can they possibly wish to spend a lovely Sunday going to Church and drinking tea on the lawn instead of climbing trees and digging for hidden treasure? Childhood is the ideal estate. This assumption also is made in other books of the period such as *The Wind in the Willows* (in which the animals are really children), the Nesbit books, and most of all in Barrie's *Peter Pan* (produced first as a play in 1904). It was not that the children in these books wanted to evade maturity and responsibility; it was rather that childhood had its own special character and flavor, that could not be given up without a sense of loss. Childhood was to be prolonged as long as possible.[2]

Because of this perception of childhood innocence, few, if any, demands were made on children to cope with life's dangers and temptations. Indeed, maturity in the sense of precocity tended to be ridiculed as abnormal—"Early ripe, early rot," as the saying went. But childhood innocence weighed heavily on parents. For it was up to parents to protect and shield children so that they could experience and enjoy this very special time in their lives.

Modern child psychiatry and psychology, with their focus on the development of the child and the differences between children at different age levels, reinforced the innocence motif. In the 1946 edition of the *Handbook of Child Psychology* (a periodic compendium of the latest research on child development), data on children's intellectual, social, emotional, and language development are grouped according to specific stages of development: infancy, early childhood, and so on. Development research emphasized both the achievements and limitations of each epoch and thus supported the perception that children, in some respects at least, were more innocent than they would be later.[3]

• *POSTMODERN DEMANDS FOR MATURITY*

The Supreme Court's historic ruling in 1954 in *Brown v. Board of Education* opened the way for school desegregation. But the television and newspaper images of black children in Little Rock, Arkansas, bravely walking to school surrounded by national guardsmen while being cursed and spat on by white adults and their children had an additional consequence. It reinforced the postmodern perception of children as able to act maturely even under enormous stress. In 1964, federal legislation funding Head Start publicly sanctioned the perception that young children are mature enough to profit from out-of-home educational settings.

While both of these events had to do with disadvantaged children, their messages were not lost on advantaged parents. As Marie Winn suggests, this new image encouraged parents to try to prepare children for, rather than protect them from, the dangers and temptations of postmodern life:

> Why, these tough little customers don't require protection and careful nurture! No longer need adults withhold information about the harsh realities of life from children. No longer need they hide the truth about their own weaknesses. Rather, they begin to feel that it is their duty to prepare children for the exigencies of modern life . . . and as they expose children to the formerly secret underside of their lives—adult sexuality, violence, injustice, suffering, fear of death—those former innocents grow tougher, perforce less playful and trusting, more skeptical—in short more like adults.[4]

Some of the postmodern demands on young people for age-appropriate maturity, such as their participation in the Head Start programs, *are* beneficial to children. It is only when these demands presuppose competencies that children do not in fact possess that they place undo stress on children. That postmodern children are having problems dealing with some of the new inappropriate demands for maturity is evidenced by a whole new literature designed to help young people cope with the many new stressors they must now confront. It amounts, in effect, to a kind of bibliotherapy—healing oneself through reading. But bibliotherapy places the responsibility on the reader, namely, the child. As a review in 1989 in the *Washington Post* points out:

> On the top shelf at the local bookstore, the Sesame Street gang stars in a volume about coping with day-care. One shelf below, a happy-go-lucky family of bears offers to teach our four-year-old a cautionary lesson about meeting strangers.
>
> Afraid of the dark? Moving? Pet died? There's a slim, gaily colored book exploring each of these subjects.
>
> Welcome to the neurotic new world of children's literature. The benign land of *Cat in the Hat* and Mother Goose is being elbowed aside by self-help volumes for the preschool set. The children's sections of most stores are crammed with a startling array of books aimed at child-sized anxieties. A chain outlet we visited recently had little books dealing with the fear of flying, bed-wetting, security blankets, making friends, eating junk food, cleaning up messy rooms, going home when asked, waiting turns, telling the truth and many others.[5]

Literature for older children is also geared to teaching them about topics from which, at an earlier time, adults thought they should be shielded. Here is a description of a children's book called *Losing Uncle Tim:*

> Daniel is a little boy who adored his Uncle Tim. He remembers him as "more fun than any other grown-up I knew." They used to go for long walks in the woods, and tried to outwit each other in hard fought battles of checkers. Then one winter Uncle Tim began to stay home and sleep a lot, and Daniel's mother told him the awful truth: Uncle Tim had AIDS.
>
> Daniel's sad and fearful reaction to Uncle Tim's worsening condition and his eventual acceptance of his death are the story of *Losing Uncle Tim,* a book that was written for an audience of six-year-old

> readers. With its vivid and poignant treatment of AIDS, *Losing Uncle Tim*, by Mary Kate Jordan, is but one example of the stark new realism of children's books.[6]

The bibliotherapy and new realism in children's literature may be, in part at least, a needed correction to the overidealized literature for children of the modern era. And certainly for young people who are experiencing some of the painful realities depicted in these books, this literature may be beneficial. But too often distressing material is presented out of context, to children who have not experienced death, disease, or divorce. When such material is conveyed to children without regard to their needs, expressed interest, or ability to comprehend, it simply makes them anxious for no purpose. Discussions with children of such topics as AIDS and abuse are likely to be more therapeutic for parents than they are for children.

For example, a father once asked me about the following problem. His eight-year-old son had been very attached to his grandmother. The grandmother suffered from terminal cancer and had taken her own life. What the father wanted to know was whether or not he should tell his son about the manner of his grandmother's death. He wanted very much to tell his son that his grandmother had committed suicide, but his wife was against it and that is why he asked my advice. He was sure that if he did not tell his son, someone else would, and he wanted the boy to hear it from him.

I assured him that it was unlikely that anyone would discuss the grandmother's suicide with the boy. I also suggested that he let his son mourn his grandmother and that the discussion about how she died be left until he was older and in a better position, emotionally and intellectually, to understand his grandmother's action. Although I did not say this, it was clear to me that the father was upset about the suicide and wanted to alleviate his own distress by sharing it with his son.

Many modern parents, like many postmodern parents, have unwittingly shared unhappy information with their children to lower their own anxieties rather than to lessen the child's. Yet it is also true that the postmodern perception of child competence is more conducive to this type of sharing than is the perception of childhood innocence. Certainly when children have painful experiences (witnessing an accident, the death of a grandparent), it is essential to talk with them about these experiences, not once but many times. It is only when frightening or painful material is presented "out of the blue," without reference to any lived experience, that it is inappropriate and makes children anxious to no purpose.

Education

The educational demands made on children during the first half of this century were quite different from those being made on school children today. Modern schools were child-centered in the sense that educational demands on young people were tailored to their developing abilities and interests rather than to a predetermined course of study laid down by a remote educational authority. In contrast, postmodern schools are curriculum-centered in the sense that the educational demands made on children are primarily based on subject matter, rather than child-development, considerations. Child-centered education was hard work for teachers but beneficial for children. Curriculum-centered education is often easier for teachers but may confront children with inordinate pressure.

Again this is a relative imbalance. Not everything about modern education was optimal. Many modern teachers took child-centeredness as an excuse not to set limits and to be rather laissez-faire regarding academic standards. Modern teachers were also unaware of the important postmodern distinction between the child and his actions. I recall that as a kindergartener (during the modern era, you can be sure) I made a collage on a large piece of red construction paper. When I was done, I decided to make it even more attractive by taking my scissors and rounding the corners. My teacher, who had looked favorably on my efforts up till then, took one look at my finished product and proclaimed, "You've ruined it!"

Many contemporary teachers, by contrast, do an extraordinary job of tailoring their teaching to the individual needs of kids, despite very large classes and children who speak many different languages and come from varied backgrounds. But in general, the postmodern emphasis on curriculum and achievement gives much more weight to grades and test performance than to what children know and understand.

• *PROGRESSIVE EDUCATION*

John Dewey idealized education as the bedrock of democracy and saw it as an extension of the home and as furthering the wishes and hopes of parents: "What the best and wisest parent wants for his own child, that must the community want for all of its children. Any other ideal for our schools is narrow and unlovely; acted upon, it destroys democracy. All that society has accomplished for itself is put, through the agency of the school, at the disposal of its future members."[7]

Since the "best and wisest" modern parents wanted to protect their children and provide them with age-appropriate demands for achievement, this is what the schools had to provide as well. An excellent example of this child-centered philosophy translated into practice was provided by the Fairhope School, which Dewey and his daughter described in their book *Schools of Tomorrow:*

> She calls her methods of education "organic" because they follow the natural growth of the pupil. The school aims to provide for the child the occupations and activities necessary at each stage of development for his unfolding at this stage. Therefore, she insists that general development, instead of amount of information acquired, shall control the classification of pupils. Division into groups is made where children naturally divide themselves. These groups are called "life classes" instead of grades. The first life class ends between the 8th and 9th years; the second between the eleventh and twelfth, and since an even more marked change of interests and tastes occurs at the period of adolescence, there are distinct high school classes.

> The work within the group is arranged to give the pupils the experiences which are needed at that age for the development of their bodies, their minds and their spirits.[8]

In the *Elementary School Journal* of 1946, Dorothy Stewart's review of the preceding decades of research in her article "Children's Preferences in Types of Assignments" also reflects the progressive philosophy:

> As educators began to understand the importance of the child as an individual, education underwent many changes. Projects, units and centers of interest were introduced with the idea of capturing the child's attention and of relating the study to his experience in living. Materials were simplified to meet the child's needs and the fact that not all children within a given grade were working at the same rate of speed was taken into account.[9]

Other research studies reported in this journal around that time bear titles which reflect their child-centered emphasis. "The Content of Children's Letters" and "Relating Reading to Individual Differences" are two examples.[10]

After the launching of the Soviet satellite Sputnik in 1957, the developmental emphasis as exemplified in the Fairhope School and in the articles in the *Elementary School Journal* came under attack. Child-centered progressive education came to be looked upon as "permissive" and coddling and in need of much more rigor and discipline. By the 1960s American education was largely curriculum- rather than child-centered.

Despite the criticism leveled against them, many progressive schools did a respectable job of educating the young. Modern education required both teachers and parents to put forth the effort to make age-appropriate curricular demands on children. The result of this unpressured schooling was solid academic achievement without undue emotional distress. Indeed, the demise of child-centered education is correlated with (but is certainly not the sole cause of) the decline in the academic achievement of postmodern children and youth.

• CURRICULUM-CENTERED PHILOSOPHY

In the 1950s the revelations of the civil rights movement challenged Dewey's ideal of education as a democratizing institution. The new data made it clear that our educational system was far from democratic and did not provide equal educational opportunity to all children. Moreover, the soul-searching set off by the launching of Sputnik, and the wide dissemination of books such as Rudolf Flesch's *Why Johnny Can't Read*, gave the impression that our schools, despite their solid achievements, were not only undemocratic but were soft and ineffective as well.[11]

If John Dewey was the leading proponent of modern, child-centered education, Jerome Bruner was perhaps the most vocal advocate of postmodern curriculum-centered education. Bruner clearly acknowledged the role of child development in education, but he believed that one could bypass developmental limitations with the right methods: "What I have said suggests that mental growth is in very considerable measure dependent upon growth from the outside in—a mastering of techniques that are embodied in the culture and that are passed on in a contingent dialogue by agents of the culture."[12]

Bruner argued that the most appropriate people to pass on these techniques to children were the experts in each discipline. In keeping with this proposition, the curriculum reform movement of the 1960s was led by university professors appalled at the datedness and inaccuracy of much of the material being taught in the schools. Supported by the National Science Foundation, the Ford Foundation, and other groups, a number of renowned scholars (for example, Max Beberman in math and Jerrold Zacharias in physics) set about writing new curricula for the schools. The result was a set of new up-to-date math, science, and language textbooks and teaching methods. Summer workshops for teachers were organized to train them in the use of the new curriculum materials and practices.

These academicians knew their subject matter, but they did not know children. And though they may have worked with teachers and students of child development, the resulting curricula gave little evidence of such collaboration. If progressive education made too few intellectual demands on children, the new curricula made too many. The new math, for example, tried to teach young children variable-base arithmetic. While children were still having trouble with base-ten place values, they were expected to understand place values for base two. In biology, the Science Curriculum Improvement Study attempted to teach basic biological concepts like that of the "organism" in the early elementary grades. While the organism concept seemed elementary to the scientists, it was not a simple idea for children to grasp.

By the mid-1970s, it was clear that the new curricula had failed and that children were doing worse than they had done during the progressive, child-centered era. The result was the "Back to Basics" movement in education. The language of the Back to Basics movement suggested that the poor performance of young people was a product of modern child-centered permissiveness (rather than postmodern curriculum-centered inappropriateness) and that the new movement was going to "get tough" on kids. Actually, it got easier! Schools went back to teacher-written curricula that were child-centered and age-appropriate. And children started to do better!

But before that quiet revolution could take hold, a new international challenge emerged. This was the growing economic and industrial potential of Japan and the threat that America might lose its economic preeminence. That threat has increased with the forthcoming economic union of Europe and the growing industrialization of the Pacific rim. As a result, we are now undergoing still another educational reform movement stimulated by the poor showing of our students in comparison with those of other countries and by the decline of math and language SAT scores over the last twenty years. Again, we are hearing calls for more rigorous science and math programs and national standards. Unfortunately, many of the "new" educational initiatives are based on the same misconceptions as the curriculum reform movement of the 1960s.

The curriculum orientation of the last thirty years is again reflected in articles in the *Elementary School Journal*. In 1990 Nuthall and Alton-Lee described the research over the preceding thirty years in this way: "Research in teaching and classroom learning has changed from an enthusiasm for objective descriptive studies through correlational and experimental paradigms to ethnographic and interpretative studies closely related to the personal experience of teachers."[13]

A couple of representative titles of research studies reflect the postmodern emphasis on curriculum and instruction rather than child development: "Geography, Curriculum and Instruction in Three Fourth Grade Classrooms" and "Kindergarten Pupil and Teacher Behavior during Standardized Achievement Testing."[14] In the modern era there would not have been any standardized achievement testing of kindergarten children to write about! Indeed, the imposition of standardized testing on young children is another example of the new and largely inappropriate educational demands made on children. Young children are competent in many ways, but not in the taking of standardized tests.

As a result of this curricular emphasis and early introduction of standardized testing, many children are failing unnecessarily. Nationally, we now hold back some 10 to 20 percent of our children for a second year in kindergarten, and in some communities the percentage is as high as 50 percent! Children who are retained or who are put in transition classes may feel that they have failed; as one child of five who was not yet reading told me, "I guess I must be a flop in life." It is heartrending to see children who think of themselves as having failed the system, when in fact it is the system that has failed them.

Curriculum is important, but so too is child development. What we need so badly are curricula that are up-to-date *and* developmentally appropriate for the intended age groups. It makes little sense to spend a month teaching decimal fractions to fourth-grade pupils when they can be taught in a week, and better understood and retained, by sixth-grade students. Child-centeredness does not mean lack of rigor or standards; it does mean finding the best match between curricula and children's developing interests and abilities.

Recreation

When children were seen as innocent, and childhood was considered a very special time, young people were often left alone to pursue their own forms of recreation. Perhaps with the exception of Little League, modern children experienced few adult demands for "winning" or competition. Now that we see children as competent, adults have increasingly taken charge of young people's recreational activities, and postmodern children are often under considerable pressure to compete and to win. Because such competitive recreational activities more often reflect adult, rather than child, needs, they add to children's stress and contribute to the new family imbalance.

• *CHILD-INITIATED PLAY*

In the modern era, when children were regarded as innocent, they were left largely to their own devices. As innocents they could hardly do harm to one another, after all. On their own, children perpetuated a rich culture, with legal rules and a system of justice reminiscent of preliterate society. Iona and Peter Opie, writing in 1959, expressed this appreciation of the culture of childhood:

> The school child, in his primitive community, conducts his business with his fellows by ritual declaration. His affidavits, promissory notes, claims, deeds of conveyance, receipts and notices of resignation are verbal, and are sealed by the utterance of ancient words which are recognized and considered binding by the whole com-

> munity . . . Of Barbarian simplicity, the schoolchild code enjoins that the prior assertion of ownership in the prescribed form shall take the place of litigation; that not even the deliberately swindled has redress if the bargain has been concluded by a bond word. Further, it will be noticed that the gesture with which the significance of the language is stressed, for example, spitting, crossing fingers, and touching cold iron, are gestures which have become an accepted part of ritual since times long before our own.[15]

In addition children had to learn the superstitions ("Step on a crack, break your mother's back"), incantations ("Rain, rain, go away, come again another day"), riddles ("Why did the tomato blush? She saw the salad dressing"), skipping rhymes ("Jelly on the plate, Jelly on the plate"), and games (hide and seek, cops and robbers) that made up another part of the culture of childhood. These verbal formulas and games were the child's entrance ticket to the culture of childhood, but they served other purposes as well:

> These rhymes are more than playthings to children. They seem to be one of their ways of communicating with each other. Language is still new to them, and they find difficulty in expressing themselves. When on their own they burst into rhyme, of no recognizable relevance, as a cover in unexpected situations, to pass off an awkward meeting, to fill a silence, to hide a deeply felt emotion, or in a gasp of excitement. And through these quaint ready-made formulas the ridiculousness of life is underlined, the absurdity of the adult world and their teachers proclaimed, danger and death marked, and the curiosity of language itself savored.[16]

To be sure, this culture placed demands on children. Yet these were age-appropriate demands because they were created by the children themselves. Children often competed fiercely with one another, but there were no adult egos involved. The biggest problem for adults was staying out of the children's world. And when they did get involved, as in the national and regional marble tournaments of the 1950s, it was a child's, not an adult's, game that was being played.

This is an idealized picture of innocence, of course. Many modern children, particularly those of immigrants and minorities, often worked from an early age or helped their parents with a family business or with taking care of younger brothers and sisters. Yet even these children participated in the language and lore of childhood to some extent. And, although they were treated as competent in some regards, even as translators of the culture to their parents, they were still looked upon and dealt with as children in most other respects.

•*ADULT-SUPERVISED COMPETITION*

Now that we have moved into the postmodern era and see children as competent, our attitude toward their recreation has changed as well. In part, to be sure, this change was effected by the change in our environment. Fifty years ago it was possible to tell children to go out and play, even in urban areas. Today, many urban and suburban communities are no longer safe for children. Certainly, one reason that we have more adult-organized recreational activities for children today is that such activities provide adult supervision and safety in an increasingly crime-prone environment.

But our new perception of child competence has helped bring about this change. For example, we could still bring young people together under adult supervision and still leave them to engage in their own play and games. But we do not. We now have more than two million children in Little League, less than a million in Pop Warner football, many millions in soccer and hockey, and hundreds of thousands in individual competitive sports such as swimming, tennis, and ice skating.

While some of these sports programs are well run and ensure that all children have an equal opportunity to play, to take turns at different positions, and to enjoy the sport, this is not always the case. The postmodern perception of childhood competence seems to have provided some parents with a new outlet for meeting their own needs without sufficient attention to those of their children. Catherine Shisslak, a professor of psychology and family medicine, put the problem this way: "The worst psychological problems in children's sports are caused by parental pressure, particularly when parents use the child as a projection of what they wanted to achieve but couldn't . . . I've seen parents using a child's participation in sports as a way of getting away from their miserable lives. I've seen mothers traipsing around the country to gymnastics meets with their daughters so they don't have to deal with their own bad marriages. Unconsciously, the child gets the message that she has to do this to keep Mom or Dad happy."[17] James Santomier, an expert on physical education and sports, describes some of the parental pressures he observed when he attended his son's swimming meet: "Between races parents would make offers of money, bicycles, if their child won or beat a record. That's how parents transform what should be natural and fun into work. And that's why there's a whole generation of people who, when they stop competing, don't continue physical activity."[18]

The perception of child athletic competence puts children under stress in other ways as well. They may permanently injure themselves. Pat McInally, in a newspaper column giving advice to young athletes, had this to say about Little League pitchers throwing curve balls:

> Physically, a young person's elbow is not fully developed in most cases until 17 or 18 years of age. Children's elbows, when X-rayed, appear to be broken up because the bones are not united. The cracks will eventually fill up with calcium, but it takes many years.
>
> Kids throwing curve balls could cripple themselves. The elbow should not be put under the strain used when throwing these pitches. In addition to damaging the bones that are not yet united, it is possible to stretch the ligaments in the elbow as well. These have very little elasticity at any age and certainly not in the Little League years. They're not prepared for the work load that many young pitchers ask them to carry.[19]

The National Injury Surveillance System of the Consumer Product Safety Commission has estimated the injury rate per 100,000 5–14-

year-old children per year to be 454 for football, 359 for baseball, 280 for basketball, 108 for soccer, 102 for wrestling, 101 for gymnastics, and 907 for bicycling. Injury was defined as a visit to an emergency room of a participating hospital. The number of bike injuries reflects the fact that children still fail to wear protective gear such as helmets.[20]

In the postmodern era, then, many of the recreational demands made on children come from adults and may put them at risk both psychologically and physically. In effect, the new perception of children's athletic competence has given some parents and coaches, however unwittingly, a venue for satisfying some of their own unmet needs through their involvement in children's sports activities. To be sure, some young people, particularly those who are athletically talented, may gain a great deal from participation in team sports. Many other youngsters, however, may find it a very stressful, unhappy, and unrewarding experience.

As in the case of early childhood education, the recreational demands on young people in the modern and the postmodern era seem to contradict the shift from unilateral to mutual authority. In the modern era, participation in the culture of childhood, the making and breaking of rules, modification of rhymes and riddles taught children mutual respect, at least for one another. With the postmodern era and prevalence of organized team sports coached by adults, the emphasis is on unilateral rather than mutual authority.

The contradiction is again resolved when we introduce the distinction made in the last chapter between direct and indirect unilateral authority. In the modern era, parents—and adult society generally—exercised unilateral authority indirectly, by providing an environment that was safe for children to play in, to acquire the language and lore of childhood, and to make and to break their own rules. Indirect adult-child unilateral authority encouraged child-to-child mutuality. Today, in the postmodern world, however, adults exercise unilateral authority directly in having children play adult games under adult supervision. The exercise of direct unilateral authority thus encourages child-adult mutuality in the sense that children are participating in adult rather than childhood games. While it is certainly true that the environment is less safe today than it was in the modern world, it is still possible for adults to monitor recreational areas while children are permitted to follow their own play and cultural imperatives.

Safety

The issue of children's safety is complex. The environment outside the home today is much less safe for children, from many different perspectives, than was the modern environment. And a number of safety issues, including drugs and AIDS, have emerged in the postmodern world that were not major concerns in the modern world. And finally, the issue of safety touches upon feminist issues, because women as well as children were victimized by the nuclear family myth which denied that harm could come to women and children within the haven of the home.

Nonetheless, some of the patterns visible in the domains of maturity, education, and recreation can also be observed in the area of children's safety. When children were seen as innocent, it was largely the parents' responsibility to look after their well-being and to teach them the skills necessary for self-protection. Now that children are seen as competent, the young are increasingly being asked to protect themselves, and nonparents are teaching them skills of self-defense. Overall, this shift puts more safety responsibility on children and less on parents and other adults.

This difference can be illustrated by the way the issue of child abuse was treated in the modern era in comparison with the manner in which it is treated today. Although child abuse can be verbal, physical, or sexual, I will limit this discussion to sexual abuse.

• *CHILD ABUSE IN THE NUCLEAR FAMILY*

During the late modern era, child abuse was believed to be largely, if not exclusively, limited to sexually perverted individuals. It did not occur in nuclear families, according to the myth. Even Freud, in his mature years, may have been a victim of this widely held belief. As a young researcher, Freud had believed his patients when they told him of childhood seduction, and he gave graphic depictions of the need imbalance of those incestuous relationships:

> All the peculiar circumstances under which the ill matched pair continue their love relation: the adult—who cannot escape his share of the mutual dependence inherent in a sexual relationship, and yet is imbued with complete authority and the right of punishment, and can exchange the one role for the other to the unbridled gratification of his moods; the child—helpless victim of this capriciousness, prematurely awakened to every kind of sensation and exposed to every kind of disappointment, often interrupted in the sexual activities assigned to him by his imperfect control of his natural needs—all these grotesque, yet tragic, incongruities become stamped upon the further development of the person concerned and his neurosis, manifesting themselves in innumerable lasting consequences which deserve to be carefully traced out.[21]

But later Freud rejected this interpretation and contended that his patients had fantasized these attacks because of their own infantile sexual desires for the parent of the opposite sex:

> Under the pressure of the technical procedure which I used at that time, the majority of my patients reproduced from their childhood scenes in which they were sexually seduced by some grown-up person. With female patients the part of the seducer was almost always the father. I believed these stories and consequently supposed that I had discovered the roots of subsequent neurosis in these experiences of sexual seduction in childhood. My confidence was strengthened by a few cases in which relations of this kind with a father, an uncle or elder brother had continued up to an age when memory could be trusted . . . When, however, I was at last obliged to recognize that these scenes of seduction had never taken place and that they were only phantasies which my patients had made

up or which I myself had perhaps forced upon them, I was for some time completely at a loss.[22]

Freud did not remain at a loss for long. To account for these "screen memories," he created a new theory of infantile sexuality that became the foundation of psychoanalysis. The imagined scenes of seduction could now be traced to the child's oedipal wishes for the parent of the opposite sex.

Perhaps Freud gave up the seduction theory because the evidence for infantile sexuality was more compelling. In part, however unconsciously, he may have given it up because it was so socially unacceptable. At a time when the nuclear family was ascendant, it was hard to believe that parents or other relatives might sexually abuse young children.[23]

Freud's ideas on infantile sexuality were eventually widely accepted. The result was that many health professionals ignored evidence of abuse in children and dismissed adult patients' tortured recollections of such abuse as only screen memories. The sentiments of the nuclear family, then, together with Freud's rejection of the seduction theory, were not helpful to either children or adults. It prevented those in the helping professions from recognizing and protecting children from adults who were doing them harm. But it also prevented adults who had been abused from getting the help they so badly needed.

At a more general level, however, the theory of infantile sexuality led modern parents to regard child molestation as limited to sexual perverts outside the family who needed to be apprehended and treated. And they saw it as their responsibility to make sure that this happened. In taking it upon themselves to protect children from sexual abuse, modern parents gave additional evidence of the old imbalance. To illustrate, in the April 1957 issue of the *Ladies' Home Journal* an article describes how parents in Omaha, Nebraska, banded together to provide better protection for their children against sex offenders. The stimulus for this action was the experience of a mother who had encouraged another mother to bring charges against a sex offender.

> "This is no place for a child," Mrs. E. C. Torgerson thought as she looked around the police courtroom at the bums, petty criminals and drunks slouched on the wooden benches. Had she done right after all in persuading the little girl's mother to press charges?
>
> Mrs. Torgerson was chairman of the Juvenile Protection Committee of the Omaha, Nebraska, P.T.A. council. She thought of her own little Susan as she watched the eight-year-old walk uncertainly toward the judge and face the defendant—a man accused of indecent exposure and trying to pick up the child in his car. Mrs. Torgerson strained to hear the murmured testimony of the six witnesses—neighbors who had seen the man in the car. Then she heard very audibly the judge's verdict: "Case dismissed—failure of proof."[24]

It was at that point that Mrs. Torgerson energized her committee and, after two years of hard work, they not only got the laws changed but forced judges "no longer qualified" to resign. They were also influential in the establishment of a psychiatric clinic to deal with these offenders.

While psychologists of this era offered suggestions to children as to how to protect themselves from child abuse, these suggestions most often directed young people to go to an adult for help. In one article Alice Sowers, then director of the Family Life Institute at the University of Oklahoma, encouraged parents to instruct their children to report suspicious actions of strangers to parents, teachers, a policeman, or some other older person. Here are some of her suggested guidelines for children:

> Any stranger who asks you to go anywhere with him—be polite but firm; say "No."
>
> Any stranger who invites your friends to go with him—write down the license number of the stranger's car. No pencil handy? Scratch with a stone on pavement or in the dust.
>
> Any stranger who tries to talk with you in a movie theater—tell the usher.
>
> Any stranger who tries to touch you at the movies—tell the usher.

> Any stranger who talks to you, offers you candy or toys, invites you to get into a car with him, or bothers you in any way—report him at once to the first older person you see.[25]

These instructions were directed toward older children (Who would be in a movie theater unaccompanied and who could write down a license number?), and they encouraged the child to look to an adult in authority for protection. In the activities of the PTA group and in the advice given to children, the demands for children to protect themselves were softened by instructions to seek help from adults.

Parents, and adults generally, were expected to be the major protectors of children's safety. Whatever demands for self-protection they made on children were always age-appropriate and were tied to dealing with strangers and to looking to adults for help. With respect to child sexual abuse, therefore, children were protected from those outside the home, but not from those within it. At the same time, modern parents took much more responsibility for protecting children from abuse by nonfamily members than is true today. It provides another example of the unilateral authority exercised by modern parents.

•*SELF-PROTECTION IN THE PERMEABLE FAMILY*

One of the postmodern challenges to the presupposition that the home was a safe place for children came from the growing incidence in the 1960s of the "battered child syndrome." It was discovered, for example, that the hairline fractures commonly observed in the X-rays of children were not as accidental as they were often reported to be. Many of these fractures had been willfully inflicted. The American Humane Society detected 662 of such cases in just a single year.[26]

Only in the 1980s, however, was the widespread sexual abuse of children documented and publicized by the media. During this same period, the books of the psychoanalyst Alice Miller became bestsellers. Her argument was the reverse of Freud's. Miller wrote that her patients, often psychiatrists in training, did indeed fabricate screen memories. But these concocted memories of parental "goodness" served to disguise the painful abuse and mistreatment they had actually experienced at the hands of their parents.[27]

Stimulated by these new facts and conceptualizations, a large number of programs have been developed to help prevent or at least identify such abuse. What is postmodern about these programs is that they presume children competent enough to learn self-defense techniques. The majority of programs to prevent child abuse have been designed for elementary school children, but some have been devised for preschoolers. Most of these programs aim at both primary prevention (to keep the abuse from occurring) and detection (disclosure of abuse). These programs vary in the number and length of presentation, and in formats that include slides, movies, discussions, and role-playing as well as written material such as comic books.

Many of these programs attempt to teach children difficult concepts such as "good" touching and "bad" touching or "comfortable" and "uncomfortable." But these discriminations are sometimes difficult to make, even for an adult. And some of the verbal techniques children learn to defend against abuse can be misapplied. A six-year-old who had gone through a child abuse prevention program at school responded to her mother's request that he wash his hands for dinner by saying, "You are not in charge of my person!"

Another child, whose mother spent an hour with her reading a book about never going with strangers, asked her daughter, "Do you understand, do you understand?" To which the daughter replied, "Yes, I understand, I understand, but what is a stranger?" The concept of a stranger is very difficult for a young child. Another child, told not to play outside alone, was happily playing by himself in the yard. The following conversation began with the mother shouting: "I told you not to play outside by yourself."

"It's okay, Mom, I'll know the bad man when I see him."

"How will you know him?"

"Well, he'll have a bandage on his head."

"He'll have a bandage on his head?"

"Yes, you said he was sick in the head."

Sometimes the results can be more serious. Some children may become so worried that they misidentify healthy adult hugs and pats. The result is that these programs may do more harm than good. The psychologists N. D. Reppucci and J. J. Haugaard conclude, after a comprehensive review of these programs and the research as to their effectiveness:

> Without . . . more thorough investigations of ongoing prevention programs, we cannot be sure whether preventive programs are working, nor can we be sure that they cause more good than harm. This harm may come in two forms. As mentioned, the programs may adversely affect a child's positive relationships with meaningful people in his or her life or cause the child undue worry or fear at least in the short run. However, it may also be that these programs can actually place some children at a greater risk for sexual abuse if we incorrectly assume that children are protected because of these programs . . .
>
> The fear is that parents, teachers and others who work with children will abdicate their responsibility to protect to the abuse prevention programs.[28]

Like the postmodern school curricula, sexual abuse curricula often ignore the child's needs, interests, and abilities and are more reflective of adults' need to teach than of children's need and readiness to learn. But they also reflect the postmodern perception of child competence and the assumption that the properly taught child can protect herself. Reppucci and Haugaard refute this assumption:

> The complexity of the process that a child must go through to repel or report abuse, the variety of abuse situations that a child may encounter, and the short duration of most prevention programs virtually ensure that a child cannot be assumed to be protected

> simply because of participation in a program. Adults must be encouraged to continue and to increase their protective efforts rather than be reassured that children are learning to be self-protective.[29]

In the modern nuclear family, children's need for protection against sexual abuse in the home was denied by the theory of infantile sexuality and the concept of screen memories. Now, in the postmodern world, children are denied protection against sexual abuse inside and outside the home by the perception of child competence and the mistaken belief in young people's ability to defend themselves against those who would do them harm. With respect to sexual abuse, therefore, children are as much victims of an imbalance in the postmodern world as they were in the modern era.

There is a difference, however, and that is in parental and societal attitudes. In the modern era parents believed it was their responsibility to protect children against abuse, and they often made concerted efforts to do so. The idea that sexual abuse might occur in the home was simply outside the realm of possibility, given the idealized nuclear family. Postmodern parents and postmodern adult society in general are less willing to take responsibility for protecting children but are more willing that children learn to protect themselves. Although postmodern parents engage in such instruction out of genuine concern and with the best of intentions, it may do more to reduce their own apprehension than to serve as a protection for their children.

Although it may go against our postmodern sensibilities, we need to change direction. It is our responsibility as parents, teachers, and health professionals to learn the signs of child abuse, to learn the procedural and legal steps that need to be taken to stop abuse, and to punish the offender. That is to say, programs to prevent child abuse are being directed to the wrong audience. They should be for adults, not for children.

The shift from the perception of the child as innocent to the perception of the child as competent has greatly increased the demands on contemporary children for maturity, for participating in competitive sports, for early academic achievement, and for protecting themselves against adults who might do them harm. While children might be able to cope with any one of these demands taken singly, taken together they often exceed children's adaptive capacity. In addition, because these demands often serve adult needs more than they do the needs of children, they contribute to the new imbalance.

Adolescents

7

From Immaturity to Sophistication

We looked upon adolescence, during the modern era, as a stage of life devoted to preparing the young person for the dangers and demands of the outside world. This image of adolescence as a period of social, emotional, and behavioral immaturity was consistent with the protective nuclear family sentiments that had also given us the notion of childhood innocence. It was consistent, too, with the exercise of unilateral authority, since bewildered, temperamental teenagers obviously needed the clear guidance and direction that only more mature adults could provide.

Now that we have moved into the postmodern era, the modern saga of adolescent immaturity is out of date. It is no longer a fitting sequel to the tale of a competent childhood. In its stead, a new perception has been created: teenage sophistication. We now look upon adolescents as worldly-wise in matters of sex, drugs, music, computers, and consumerism. The teen years are no longer seen as a period of training for adult life; they are considered to be, rather, a *different form* of adult life, with its own unique indices of maturity. Postmodern adolescents are seen as different from, but not necessarily less knowledgeable or sophisticated than, adults. The logical result has been a sharing of authority between parents and teenagers.

Like the contrasting perceptions of childhood innocence and childhood competence, the perceptions of both adolescent immaturity and adolescent sophistication distort the realities of this age group. Young people were never as immature as the sentiments of the nuclear family made them out to be. In the modern era, adolescents knew much more about the facts of life than their parents or the larger society was willing to acknowledge. Similarly, postmodern youth are in many ways less sophisticated than parents and the adult society might wish. Many young adolescents are really not prepared, without parental support, to withstand the peer group pressures to become sexually active, to use drugs, to "drop out."

The following description of adolescence, written in 1965 just as the nuclear family was beginning its decline, presents a very modern, as opposed to postmodern, image of teenage immaturity and confusion:

> The adolescent presumably is engaged in a struggle to emancipate himself from his parents. He therefore resists and rebels against any restrictions and controls they impose upon his behavior. To facilitate the process of emancipation, he transfers his dependency to the peer group, whose values are typically in conflict with those of his parents. Since his behavior is now largely under the control of peer group members, he begins to adopt idiosyncratic clothing, mannerisms, lingo and other forms of peer-group fad behavior. Because of the conflicting values and pressures to which the adolescent is exposed, he is ambivalent, frightened and unpredictable.[1]

This image of adolescent immaturity was, on the whole, more beneficial to adolescents than is our contemporary image of adolescent sophistication. Because they did not expect teenagers to behave like adults, modern parents tolerated teenage awkwardness, rebelliousness, mood swings, and social gaffes. But at the same time they felt a responsibility to provide the guidelines and standards that adolescents needed to establish their own limits and values and to eventually grow up. Thus, in the modern era, parents of teenagers provided both firm authority and affectionate acceptance, which together encouraged their children to take the risks of confrontation in the service of self-discovery.

This exercise of authority with ongoing consideration of what was best for the young, combined with unending patience and good will, was very demanding of modern parents. The perception of adolescent immaturity, therefore, lent its weight to the old imbalance. The postmodern perception of adolescent sophistication, in contrast, has weighted the balance in the other direction. While adolescents are quite sophisticated in some respects, they are quite naive in others. Yet the perception of adolescent sophistication has led parents, and adult society in general, to abandon many of the value- and limit-setting responsibilities that modern adults felt it their duty to perform. There is also much less tolerance for personal and social lapses among teenagers. As a consequence, postmodern adolescents must now find their own values and standards in an often critical and disapproving adult environment. Postmodern parents, in contrast, often feel liberated once their children have become adolescents and can fend for themselves.

To be sure, I have overdrawn this contrast to make a point. Many modern adolescents, particularly those of immigrant parents, took on adult responsibilities from an early age. Likewise, many contemporary adolescents have parents who fit the modern mold. Nonetheless, if we look at society as a whole, we can discern a major shift in how parents and other adults regard teenagers. This change in our perception of adolescence can be seen in each of the transition demands that we associate with development during the teenage years: psychological, sexual, occupational, and cultural.

Psychological Demands

During the modern era we looked upon the adolescent's psychological progress toward adulthood as uniquely marked by "storm and stress" associated with an "identity crisis"—the inevitable personality upheaval that resulted from giving up a secure, innocent childhood for the cares and responsibilities of grown-up life. No other period of life was comparable to the metamorphosis a teenager had to undergo. In the postmodern era, by contrast, we regard adolescence as not unlike any other of life's difficult transition periods. Because of this different perception of what teenagers experience, the psychological demands we place on young people differ considerably now from those of the modern period.

• *THE MODERN MORATORIUM*

The modern perception of adolescent immaturity was established by G. Stanley Hall, who published his classic two-volume work on adolescence in 1904. Hall advocated the biological theory of recapitulation, according to which individual development recapitulates the development of the human species. In many ways, Hall saw adolescence as comparable to the Renaissance period of human history.

> Adolescence is a new birth, for the higher and more completely human traits are now born. The qualities of body and soul that now emerge are far newer. The child comes from, and harks back to, a remote past: the adolescent is neo-atavistic, and in him the later acquisitions of the race slowly become prepotent. Development is less gradual and more saltatory, suggestive of some ancient period of storm and stress when old moorings were broken and a higher level attained.[2]

Hall marshaled a tremendous amount of biological, sociological, anthropological, as well as psychological data to advance his view of adolescence. Although many of his descriptions of youth, like those of Aristotle, still ring true, the theory of recapitulation has been long discarded. While there well may be parallels between the development of individuals and the species, there could hardly be causal connections between the two developments. The history of society is far too varied and complex to be preprogrammed into the genetic endowment of single individuals.

If Hall provided the scholarly foundation for the modern perception of adolescent immaturity, it was the psychoanalyst Erik Erikson who made it a popular theme of late modern culture. For Erikson, adolescence was a period devoted to the construction of a sense of personal identity that would bring together all the disparate senses of self (as son or daughter, brother or sister, student, athlete, friend, enemy, and so on) into a unified working identity. The sense of personal identity provides both continuity with the past and guidance and direction for the future. To accomplish this enormous task, young people require a moratorium, a kind of sabbatical from grown-up responsibilities and pressures to make important decisions about their lives.[3]

In Erikson's view, the attainment of a sense of personal identity presents the young person with a crisis, because a failure to construct such an identity would leave an adolescent with a sense of role diffusion, of not knowing who or what he was. The result would be a need to constantly look to others for guidance, direction, and decisionmaking. While a certain amount of role diffusion is necessary to avoid personality constriction, a healthy resolution of the crisis leaves the adolescent with a sense of identity that is much stronger than the sense of role diffusion. In describing adolescence as a period of identity formation that requires a psychosocial moratorium, Erikson gave us fresh insight into the significance of adolescent immaturity for healthy emotional development.

The modern perception of adolescence as a psychologically difficult formative period was widespread in the popular mind. It was a major theme of the modern literature dealing with youth. The questing, coming-of-age modern adolescent was delineated by Hermann Hesse in *Siddhartha,* by Mark Twain in *Huckleberry Finn,* by J. D. Salinger in *The Catcher in the Rye,* and by John Knowles in *A Separate Peace.* In all of these portrayals, an adult world of standards and values is the environment in which the adolescent can test out who and what she is. The importance of this adult envelope is emphasized in Erikson's description of the needs of a teenager seeking an identity:

> The evidence in young lives of the search for something and somebody to be true to can be seen in a variety of pursuits more or less

> sanctioned by society. It is often hidden in a bewildering combination of shifting devotion and sudden perversity, sometimes more devotedly perverse, sometimes more perversely devoted. Yet in all youth's seeming shiftiness, a seeking after some durability in change can be detected, whether in the accuracy of scientific and technical method or in the sincerity of obedience; in the veracity of historical and fictional accounts or the fairness of rules of the game; in the authenticity of artistic production and the high fidelity of reproduction, or in the genuineness of convictions and the reliability of commitments.[4]

In the ideal modern world, adults provided the authenticity, fairness, veracity, and reliability against which adolescents could forge their identity. And though the formation of identity was difficult for young people, it was also hard on their parents. It was the parents who had to provide youth not only with role models but also with a hiatus from financial and other responsibilities, so that teenagers would have the leisure to fashion an identity. And it was the parents who had to confront young people's often acrimonious, self-defining challenges and tests of parental and societal authority. Although modern adolescents might not have seen it that way, the modern world's provision of a discrete period of life devoted solely to identity formation benefited them at the expense of wear and tear on their parents.

• *THE POSTMODERN PASSAGE*

The psychological demands made on postmodern youth are far different from those made on modern adolescents. While modern adolescents could be psychologically shielded within the confines of the nuclear family and only gradually exposed to the harsh realities of the outside world, such shielding is no longer possible in the permeable family. From an early age, postmodern children must deal with the barrage of information and images conveyed by television and with the realities of permeable family life. Serious identity formation, seen as a toughening of one's psyche to resist the demands of the harsh outside world, can no longer be postponed until adolescence; it must begin in early childhood.

So, too, must the separation from parents begin earlier. In many ways, the tight emotional bonds of the nuclear family made a rebellion against the parents a necessary step toward independence and autonomy. In the postmodern permeable family, where children often have lived for a good part of their life in single-parent homes or stepfamilies where togetherness is less highly valued—or less often achieved—and who have often spent many of their waking hours since infancy with childcaregivers who are not their parents, there is much less conflict between parents and their adolescents than was reported in the modern era.

The conflict of the nuclear family was not a myth but was rather a product of much tighter family emotional ties than is true of the family today. These looser emotional ties may also help explain the fact that more than 50 percent of 20–24-year-olds continue to live with their parents today, as opposed to only 40 percent thirty years ago.[5] While these statistics undoubtedly mirror a changed economic situation, they also, in part at least, reflect an easier, less emotionally constrained relationship between parents and their young adult offspring.

The theoretical basis for the postmodern view of adolescence comes from a number of psychiatrists who have challenged the modern perception of youthful immaturity and identity formation. Daniel and Judith Offer, for example, have argued that adolescence is no longer, if it ever was, an especially conflictual stage in the life cycle. These researchers studied a group of young men over an eight-year period—from their entrance into high school to their completion of college. They found no evidence to support the idea that postmodern adolescents experience more conflict and "storm and stress" than do either children or adults. In addition, these investigators contend that their data do not support the idea that adolescence is a period uniquely important for personality development.[6]

Other psychiatrists are contesting the idea that adolescents must construct a sense of personal identity in order to move successfully into young adulthood. For example, Robert J. Lifton has argued that, in the contemporary world, it is psychologically healthy to postpone vocational choices until young adulthood and beyond. In his view, given the rapidly changing postmodern economic scene, a continued openness to vocational options is psychologically healthier, and more adaptive, than a closed or completed vocational identity. In the postmodern world, the most successful adolescents will be those prepared to move through several vocational roles in the course of their working lives.[7] One could also argue that contemporary youth must also be open to adopting new kinship roles (half-brother, stepdaughter, stepgrandson) created by permeable family life.

Finally, Heinz Kohut disputes the notion that it is the postmodern adolescent's identity "crisis" that is the cause of adolescent emotional distress:

> The psychopathological events of the late adolescence described by Erikson—I would call them the vicissitudes of self-cohesion in the transitional period between adolescence and adulthood—should therefore neither be considered as occupying a uniquely significant developmental position, nor should they be explained primarily as due to the demands of this particular period. (These stresses constitute only the precipitating external circumstances.) But an adolescent's crumbling self-experience should in each individual instance be investigated in depth—no less than those equally frequent and important cases of self-fragmentation which occur during other periods of transition which have overtaxed the solidity and resilience of the nucleus of the self.[8]

According to these child development specialists, therefore, the psychological transition demands on postmodern adolescents are no greater, and no less, than those made at other passage points in the life cycle. Transitions are stressful, but no more stressful in adolescence than, say, at midlife. Adolescence is not of unique importance in personality formation. Identity crises, if they occur, are individual matters, not the norm. Implicit in these depictions of postmodern young people is the idea that adolescents are, after all, really not that much different from adults. These portrayals of adolescence do not emphasize, as Erikson did, adolescents' special need for adult-modeled values such as authenticity, commitment, and truth. For these psychiatrists, such values are required throughout life and not just during adolescence.

In many ways, therefore, the views of the experts reinforce the perception of adolescent sophistication that the permeable family lifestyle has created in parents. It depicts an age group whose members are as prepared to meet the demands of the adolescent transition as they will be to meet the many transitions of adulthood. It is also, in a number of respects, a much more accurate portrait of contemporary teenagers than is the modern depiction of adolescent storm and stress and of identity crises. The postmodern portrayal is more photographic, more tied to the wide range of individual differences among teenagers than was the modern, idealized painting of this age group.

Yet, this said, it is also true that in many respects the adolescent transition *is* unique. Unlike adulthood, it is a period of extremely rapid physical, emotional, psychological, and social growth. This period of rapid growth leads to a metamorphosis unlike any transition that occurs in adulthood. Adult transitions take place within a relatively fixed firmament of physique, mental ability, and established social roles. Adolescent transitions do not. Even though young people are now exposed to demands for identity formation from an early age, they still need time in adolescence to adjust to their new body configuration, their new emotions, their new thinking abilities, and their new patterns of social interaction.

Accordingly, young people as a group still need a protected time within which to adjust to all of the transformations they have experienced. In addition, they still require the security of adult role models because during a period of rapid psychological and physical change it is difficult to find internal direction. Adults have to provide guidelines. Different adolescents will use the same adult limits, standards, and values in different ways, just as they will use the same food to grow to different heights and body configurations. But the psychological nourishment of adult authenticity, fairness, and commitment, like nutritional nourishment, is essential.

Unfortunately, the perception of adolescence as an age period coextensive with adulthood, and of adolescents as sophisticated, leads many adults to neglect to provide teenagers with either a protected time period or a protective envelope of adult values. Adolescents are expected to find such a covering on their own. The perception of adolescent sophistication makes life psychologically harder and more stressful for adolescents. It also makes life harder for those "old-fashioned" parents and adults who want to provide young people with the values and limits they need. For those adults who do not see this as their duty, however, the image of adolescent sophistication is a convenient way out.

Sexual Demands

The shift from modern to postmodern assumptions about adolescence is perhaps most evident in the domain of sexuality. Modern adolescents were seen by adults as sexually immature, while postmodern adolescents are seen as sexually sophisticated. The perception of teenage immaturity carried with it few demands for sexual activity and in fact discouraged it. In contrast, adults' perception of teenage sophistication assumes sexual activity and even seems to accept it, if reluctantly.

The statistics tell the tale. In 1953 Kinsey reported that about 10 percent of adolescent girls and 25 percent of adolescent boys had engaged in sexual intercourse.[9] When Kinsey's figures are compared with more recent statistics, the extent of change is startling:

> Since 1970, there have been six national surveys documenting sexual activity [among adolescents] . . . The incidence of sexual activity

> increased dramatically from 1971 to the late 1980's in both younger and older age cohorts of adolescents. In 1988, by age 19, 76 percent of white females, 85 percent of white males, 83 percent of black females, and 96 percent of black males had coitus at least once.[10]

This extraordinary increase in the number of sexually active adolescents gives evidence of the enormous demands to become sexually active made on postmodern teenagers. But these new transition demands are not simply a reflection of changed peer group mores. They also derive from the changed portrayals of adolescent sexual activity in films, on television programs, and in rock music lyrics. The necessary, if reluctant, acceptance by parents and schools of postmodern sexually active teens, while not a demand for sexual activity, is not a prohibition either.

•*MODERN MORES*

The modern perception of adolescent emotional immaturity made no demands on adolescents for sexual activity and was even an argument against it; it assumed that young people were emotionally unready for such intimacies. Teenage girls who were sexually active were looked upon as "tramps" and were socially ostracized. "Nice" girls were afraid of ruining their "reputations." Sexually active boys were also not especially highly regarded, although a "boys-will-be-boys" attitude among adults made occasional lapses forgivable. Thus, peer pressure among modern teenagers was against becoming sexually active.

Of course, modern adolescents were not exempt from the sexual drives of puberty. To satisfy the need for some physical intimacy without "going all the way," teenagers set up their own rules and codes of "petting" to limit their sexual activity. When I was an adolescent, we boys recognized certain zones through which couples progressed. "Above the neck" was the first zone and meant kissing and nuzzling. "Below the neck and above the waist" was the second zone. It meant touching a girl's breast, usually with her clothing on. The next step—a major one reserved for couples who had known one another awhile—was the "bare feel." Couples seldom touched one another below the waist, and rarely before they were high school seniors. Older adolescents and young adults often performed mutual masturbation, but intercourse was reserved for engaged or married partners.

Adolescents' own codes of behavior were augmented by adult proscriptions and chaperoning. The adult view of the modern teenager's sexuality are reflected in the Gesell, Ilg, and Ames 1956 manual for parents of adolescents, *Youth: The Years from Ten to Sixteen.* Here is their description of the "typical" sixteen-year-old boy:

> The boys who have become interested in girls have become even more interested, and some now show less desire for the more peripheral stimulation of nude pictures or lurid literature. But some are finding it difficult to control their sex impulses, and they masturbate frequently, seek erotic stimulation in pictures, read too easily procured sex novels (leaving corners of special pages turned down). Many seem to find increasing stimulation from rhythmic sources—music, dancing, their own movements. And daydreams seem to have become an even more potent source of arousal than at fifteen.[11]

As far as boy-girl interactions, Gesell and colleagues report these findings:

> Physical contacts with girls, mostly in the form of kissing and petting, are becoming increasingly common. Fourteen-year-old girls report they have "trouble" with these older boys, and sixteen-year-old girls become very adept at distracting them when these boys impulsively make advances. With the kind of social freedom given to young people today, it is unfortunate that some boys are not yet mature and moral enough to justify this freedom. They need the self-control, the sense of responsibility and the imagination to foresee the dangers of injudicious petting.[12]

The modern demands made on adolescents—by themselves, by their peers, and by adults—to control their sexual impulses worked a hardship on those young people who were sexually mature and experiencing normal sexual desires. At the same time, the social support for adolescents to postpone sexual intercourse protected many young people from too early intimacies and from the risks of pregnancy and venereal disease. Parents, on the other hand, were constrained to shield and protect their adolescents from sexually provocative material and to closely chaperon their heterosexual activities. On balance, therefore, the perception of adolescent sexual immaturity made heavier demands on parents and other adults than it did on adolescents themselves.

•*POSTMODERN PEER PRESSURE*

In the postmodern era, we have come to see youths as sophisticated and knowledgeable in sexual matters. Social institutions, particularly the media but increasingly the law (in lowering the age for statutory rape) and the schools (in providing sex education and distributing condoms) reflect and reinforce this perception. Adolescents tend to see themselves in this way as well. Indeed, the modern peer group prohibitions against becoming sexually active have now been reversed. No longer are teenagers who are sexually active regarded as "low lifes." Indeed, one fifteen-year-old girl told me recently that there was so much peer pressure to become sexually active that she was going to do it "just to get it over with."

The perception of adolescent sophistication impacts even upon those adolescents who choose not to become sexually active. For example, peer group pressure is such that they are forced to accept and condone the suggestive language and behavior of their sexually active peers, even if it makes them uncomfortable. And young people just moving into adolescence have to cope with the overt sexuality in MTV, films, and audiotapes targeted specifically at them. Many of the song lyrics written for the preteen and young adolescent audience are replete with graphic sexual references. My eleven-year-old niece and her girlfriend compiled, at my request, the following list of sexually explicit songs they were familiar with.

"I Just Want to Make Love to You" (Foghat)
"Let's Talk about Sex" (Salt n Pepa)
"I Wanna Sex You Up" (Color Me Bad)
"I Want Your Sex" (George Michael)
"Do Me" (Bell Biv Devoe)

Despite their sexual activity and their constant exposure to sexually explicit materials, postmodern adolescents often appear as naive about sexual matters as their peers in the modern era. Interview studies make it clear that a great many postmodern adolescents remain surprisingly uninformed with respect to a number of the basic facts about sexuality:

> A sixteen-year-old girl remarked, "I wasn't ready for it being so *real.* Because in movies they don't get sweaty and—you know—all this awkward stuff. Like maybe not being that easy to get in, him not finding the right place, it kind of hurting." Most of the boys who had intercourse said they wished they had a book of instructions. "All the time I was thinking about doing it, I was worrying, *'How do you do it?'*"
>
> A surprising number of boys feared that there was something wrong with them because they did not know how a male's body functions sexually. A few, for example, thought that they suffered from impotence when they lost an erection, and many, because they did not know how long it normally takes a male to reach orgasm, believed they were premature ejaculators.[13]

High school counselors tell me many similar stories. Some adolescents believe, for example, that they will not get pregnant if they engage in intercourse standing up. Despite sex education courses and the abundance of sexual material available in so many different media, contemporary adolescents often have the same mistaken ideas about sexuality as did their modern counterparts.

The postmodern demands and expectations that adolescents become sexually active at an early age puts a lot of stress on these young people. I met with a group of thirteen- and fourteen-year-old boys on Cape Cod who bragged about their sexual exploits. They also believed that you didn't have to go with a girl "for more than a month" before you had intercourse. When I talked to some of these boys alone, however, they revealed that they were still virgins but were afraid to admit it to their peers. Like the young woman described earlier, these young men felt tremendous peer group pressure to become sexually active.

The pervasive assumption that sexual activity is appropriate behavior for today's sophisticated adolescents—a view that is now reflected in and reinforced by the media, the schools, and the legal system—makes parenting difficult for those mothers and fathers who want to resist this assumption. There is little, if any, social support for parents who want to shield their teenagers from the pervasive sexuality of our society. These parents do what they can but feel that they are fighting a losing battle. Other parents accept sexually active teens as a necessary evil and cope the best they can. Still other parents welcome the sexual activity of young people and may even abet it by allowing early dating, early use of cosmetics, and the wearing of suggestive clothing. While sexual activity among teens is hard on many parents, it probably is harder on teens, who are at risk for emotional problems as well as for pregnancy and life-threatening disease.

The appearance of AIDS has created a new source of anxiety and concern about teenage sexuality that did not exist in the modern era. Of all age groups, teenagers are most at risk for contracting sexually transmitted diseases (STDs). They are least likely to use contraceptives and, if they do make an effort, most likely to use them irregularly and improperly. Although only 2 percent of AIDS victims so far have been in the 13–21 age group, health professionals recognize that many AIDS victims contracted the disease as adolescents. There is a real danger of increasing numbers of HIV-positive teenagers.

As yet, the appearance of AIDS has not had a major impact on teenage sexual activity. It has, however, made both parents and schools more aware of the need for effective sex information and education. In my work with adolescents, I have found that scare tactics have, if anything, the opposite effect of what was intended. What does work is to have teenagers who themselves contracted an STD or became pregnant speak to other teenagers. Recently, I met a young man who travels about the country talking to students about AIDS. He himself became sexually active when he was fourteen, in part, he says, seeking affection after losing both parents. He is HIV-positive and speaks eloquently of his earlier sense of invulnerability and his current sense of dread. To hear this from a peer has a powerful impact on many adolescents.

Occupational Demands

The way we perceive adolescents also determines the demands we make, and the expectations we have, with regard to their employment. During the modern era, when adults looked upon adolescents as immature, they saw work as a way of teaching young people some of the values, standards, and habits necessary to make a successful transition to adulthood. Employers felt responsible for training the young people they hired. Because adolescents benefited from this training and because it demanded time, energy, and patience on the part of adults, it contributed to the old imbalance.

Today, parents doubt that sophisticated young people have much to learn from being employed, particularly in fast-food emporia. Many employers, moreover, no longer feel responsibility to train, except in the most superficial way, the young people on their payroll. If young people want to learn anything from their work experience, they have to do it on their own. Because postmodern work experience often benefits the employer more than the adolescent, it contributes to the new imbalance.

• *THE MODERN WORK ETHIC*

The belief that supervised work has many positive benefits for youth is clear in this description from the 1950s:

> Part-time work still plays an important part in the lives of many adolescents and increasing numbers are holding jobs. In a typical town high school in 1953 to 1954, about one-fourth of the freshmen and one-half of the seniors were holding jobs. They were doing work as clerks, salesmen, typists, apprentice cooks, electricians, garage assistants, laborers, servants in homes and clubs, stock boys, machine operators, nurses' aides.

The adult commitment to the training of young people during the modern era was illustrated by the work experience programs, according to Ruth Strang: "The work experience program enables the high school student to do part-time work under supervision, and thus to extract the maximum value from it. The 'four-four plan' developed in the Oakland, California, school system during wartime made it possible for students to spend four hours in school and four hours on the job. The work experience was treated like an elective subject and was supervised jointly by the school and by the employers."[14]

When I was an adolescent, I had a job in a drugstore and learned not only how to handle the soda fountain and make sandwiches but also how to push slow-moving items! When business was quiet, I helped the pharmacist count pills and fill bottles with cough syrup and glycerin. To be sure, I did typical adolescent things like adding an extra scoop of ice cream to the malted milks I made for friends, but overall I was given considerable responsibility for handling money and dealing with customers.

In addition to the skills I learned, there were benefits of a more personal kind. Part of the value of adolescent work came from the fact that we young people were expected to contribute a portion of our earnings to the family to help pay the bills. This made us feel that we were assuming financial responsibility for ourselves (parents would give us back a portion for spending money) and easing some of the financial burden borne by our parents. Although the financial contribution made by adolescents was of benefit to their parents, what young people gained in the way of enhanced self-respect, responsibility, and maturity often far outweighed the monetary assistance accrued by their parents.

• THE POSTMODERN PAYBACK

Now that we regard adolescence as a form of adulthood, we no longer look upon youthwork as having the benefits it had for young people as late as the 1950s. And it doesn't. In their comprehensive study in the 1980s, Greenberger and Steinberg found that the majority of adolescents now work in fast-food restaurants and have little opportunity to learn useful skills or attitudes from their work experience:

> The average young person spends less than 10 percent of his or her time on the job—only about five minutes of every hour—in activities such as reading, writing and arithmetic. More than one fourth of the typical adolescent's time on the job is spent in one of two activities: cleaning things or carrying things. Most jobs are characterized by little task variety, highly routinized activity and the constant repetition of fairly uninteresting tasks.[15]

Postmodern youthworkers are not gaining the workaday skills and habits that modern youthworkers did. Nor are they gaining the personal benefits that come from contributing their earnings to the family:

> By far the majority of working young people do not contribute much of their earnings to their families: 82 percent allocate none or "only a little" to help defray the costs of housing, groceries, and other expenses of living. Youth from less economically advantaged circumstances probably contribute more than others. For example, only 58 percent of black youth in this survey reported that they did not give any of their earnings, or gave only a little of their paycheck, to their family, compared with 87 percent of white youth. Nonetheless, the proportion of earnings going to youngsters' families certainly is not staggering. For the sample as a whole, only 8.4 percent reported allocating half or more of their paycheck to helping the

family (5.5 percent of the whites and 21.5 percent of the blacks); and only 1.1 percent reported turning over their entire paycheck for this purpose (0.7 percent of the whites and 3.2 percent of the blacks).[16]

In modern families, where togetherness was the reigning value, contributing one's paycheck for the benefit of the family made good sense. When autonomy is the governing value, however, parents would be embarrassed to ask, and their offspring would be affronted to be asked, to contribute to the family income. Accordingly, postmodern youth often do not acquire either work skills or a sense of personal responsibility and maturity from working. In the postmodern era, work is largely a way for adolescents to earn money to spend on themselves.

While the occupational demands on youth are less today than in the modern era, the benefits they derive are also fewer. Indeed, the loss to youth of the positive benefits of work experience is far greater than the loss to the family of young people's financial contribution.

Cultural Demands

Few art forms or fashions, during most of the modern era, could be ascribed to a unique youth culture. As a consequence, up to the mid-1950s there were few cultural demands on the young, beyond simply imitating the behavior of adults. Adults, therefore, had the responsibility of providing exemplary cultural models for young people to emulate. Young people, however, perversely chose the least healthy adult behaviors to emulate. Modern youth, eager to appear grown up, often engaged in smoking and drinking to demonstrate their maturity. Nonetheless, to the extent that adolescents had only to imitate adults, whereas adults had to be concerned about their impact upon the young, the perception of adolescent immaturity tilted the family balance in favor of adolescents.

In the postmodern world, however, young people, partly as a result of their new image of sophistication, have developed a culture of their own. Beginning in the 1950s, rock music was a uniquely youthful artform that effectively alienated adults from youth and its emerging culture. This new culture was unique not only in its music but in language, dress, and behavior. Having their own culture, however, put new demands on adolescents—for keeping up, for being creative. Adults, on the other hand, were freed from the responsibility of being the only role models for the young. Accordingly, the emergence of a new youth culture increased the cultural demands on youth while relieving adults from many of their cultural transmission responsibilities.

• *THE MODERN IMITATION OF ADULTS*

Salinger's hero, Holden Caulfield, provides a particularly intense portrait of an adolescent who is attempting to imitate adult behavior as a way of meeting the demand for maturity and sophistication:

> In case you don't live in New York, the Wicker Bar is in this sort of swanky hotel. I used to go there quite a lot, but I don't anymore. I gradually cut it out. It's one of those places that are supposed to be very sophisticated and all, and the phonies are coming out of the window. They used to have these two French babes, Tina and Janine, come out and play the piano and sing about three times a week. One of them played the piano—strictly lousy—and the other one sang, and most of the songs were either pretty dirty or in French.[17]

The anthropologist Margaret Mead—attempting to explain why some societies develop a separate youth culture, while in others young people imitate their elders—considered the determining factor to be the rate of technological change. She argued that in postfigurative cultures, where change was slow, all knowledge, values, and skills were acquired from the society's elders. Such societies were rich in tradition and ritual, and youth were inculcated with a respect for age and authority. In such societies there was no place for an original youth culture.

When the pace of technological change increases, however, the culture becomes cofigurative. In these cultures, young people often become more skilled in the new technologies than are parents and other adults. According to Mead, American society was cofigurative until at least midcentury. Modern adolescents, for example, who grew up with cars were more proficient in their use than adults who grew up before the automobile was invented and mass-produced. Nonetheless, there were still many skills and values that modern youth had to acquire from adults. Mead describes the derivative nature of youth culture in modern cofigurative societies this way: "There are societies in which approbation by the elders is decisive for the acceptance of new behavior; that is, the young look not to their peers, but to their elders for final approval and change."[18]

While cofigurative, or modern, societies permit some social learning from peers, moving into adulthood is mainly a matter of modeling adult behavior. In such societies adults have considerable responsibilities for training the young in the skills, values, and traditions of the society and for transmitting the culture.

• THE POSTMODERN YOUTH CULTURE

Now that we have moved into the postmodern era, the cultural transition demands on the young have become much more onerous. According to Mead's terminology, postmodern society has to be regarded as prefigurative. In such societies technological change is so rapid that the young must devote most of their energy to learning new knowledge, skills, and values, and they have little time left to learn the lessons of the past. The knowledge and skills of elders are often outdated and of little practical value. As a result, the young have little respect and veneration for parents in particular, or for adult society in general. In a transition period such as ours, parents may wish to play a cofigurative role, but their offspring will have none of it. Mead epitomizes this generational conflict in the following presumed dialogue: "Cofigurative parents are wont to say, 'You know, I have been young and you have never been old.' Prefigurative youth are likely to reply, 'You have never been young in the world I am young in and never can be.'"

As we become more postmodern, however, we increasingly abandon our cofigurative claims to superiority over youth— in vocational knowledge (insofar as we admit that we have no better idea than they do what will be demanded by the twenty-first century), in skills (particularly those pertaining to electronic and computerized entertainment and education), and values (since many adults see themselves as a confusing combination of modern and postmodern mores).

We no longer expect or encourage young people to imitate our broader adult culture. Rather, we expect them to create one of their own. Such expectations place new cultural demands on youth. Youth can no longer take adult culture as the model for their language, dress, or music. Rather, they must look to the tutelage of their own youth subculture. And this adolescent subculture is quite different from adult society—in its recreation (such as skateboarding), its hang-outs (often video arcades), and its ritualistic practices (from head shaving to neon-colored hair dyeing to body piercing).[19]

That is to say, beginning in the late 1950s, together with the emergence of the permeable family and the perception of the competent child, a new youth culture catering to sophisticated adolescents was created. Popular music spearheaded its emergence. In the previous era adolescents had listened to the same music as their parents. To be sure, "bobby soxers" came in droves to "swoon" to Frank Sinatra. But the songs he sang were written for adults and extolled adult values.

What happened in the late 1950s, as we all know, was the emergence of a new musical style—a fusion of country-western and rhythm and blues that came to be known as rock 'n' roll. Rock 'n' roll immediately separated youth, who loved it, from adults, who hated it. Popular music, which had once catered to adults, now found a new and eager audience, adolescents. When rock music became the mainstay of the new youth culture, it was transformed from a form of entertainment into "a dialogue between young people [which] in its lyrics as well as in the emotional power of its beat and texture . . . provides the quality of identification which comes from knowing [that one's] most urgent concerns and anxieties are understood by others."[20]

Popular music thus helped young people achieve a culture of their own that had all of the elements of a true culture, including: (1) the establishment of common norms and values, (2) a specific language not shared by the larger culture, (3) a common style of behavior, including fads, (4) standards specifying correct dress and grooming, (5) a feeling of "ingroupness," and (6) the filling of specific needs left unattended by the larger society.[21]

The availability of a unique youth culture, along with other aspects of the presumed adolescent sophistication, misleads adults into believing that adolescents no longer want, or need, adult-defined limits, values, and standards. Yet these are just the areas in which the youth culture is severely limited. Youth culture offers guidance in matters of taste, clothing, music, language, and entertainment. Yet in regard to manners and morals it offers little more than searing attacks on the status quo. When parents and other adults who work with adolescents assume that the youth culture provides all that young people need in the way of moral direction, they effectively leave young people in a moral vacuum.

On Our Own

The overall result, therefore, of the postmodern perception of adolescent sophistication is that young people are left to find their own way to adulthood. While many adolescents discover, in one way or another, a path to maturity, their adultness often does not feel real or authentic to them. The "thirty-something" generation is the first to move into maturity under the new imbalance, and the problems this generation experienced is suggested in a number of films and TV sitcoms, as described in the *New York Times:*

> It is a truism among Baby Boomers that none of them ever feels grown up. Their parents may have guarded such a feeling as a dirty little secret, but this generation refuses to be quiet about it. The idea provides the nagging uneasiness beneath *The Big Chill*, the bedrock assumption of television's *Thirty Something* and the most astute features of *Big*. In recent years films from *Star Wars* to *Who Framed Roger Rabbit?* have catered to this childish side of a huge potential audience.[22]

The presence of a youth culture has also rearranged the battle lines of the intergenerational conflict. Where once these lines were between adolescents and adults who were over thirty, it is now between succeeding generations, currently between the Baby Boomers and the following generation that Howe and Strauss call "Thirteeners"—America's thirteenth generation.[23] Whereas the Boomers grew up in a cofigurative society in which they still took some values from the elders and retained some respect for societal tradition, this has not been true for the twenty-something group which has grown up in a prefigurative world.

One consequence of this new independent youth culture is a reversal of the traditional generational conflict. In the modern era youth could attack the older generation after which it had modeled itself. As they matured, the younger generation discovered that the older generation had not practiced the values and the morals that it had preached. Hence the motto: "Don't trust anyone over thirty." But in the postmodern world, the young—the Thirteeners—have not modeled themselves after the Boomers. Moreover, the Boomers are now attacking the younger generation for not having "the right stuff," after having left them to find that commodity pretty much on their own.

> We of the rising generation have to work this problem out all alone . . . I doubt if any generation was ever thrown quite so much on its own resources as ours is . . . The rising generation has a very real feeling of coming straight up against a stone wall of diminishing

> opportunity. I do not see how it can be denied that practical opportunity is less for this generation than it has been in those preceding it.[24]

In summary, the perception of adolescent immaturity, though it may have done a disservice to adolescents in some respects, nevertheless reinforced the unilateral authority of parents and adults. This authority guaranteed that adults would play a responsible role in helping young people meet the psychological, sexual, occupational, and cultural demands of their transition to adulthood. For the postmodern generation, however, the perception of adolescent sophistication has encouraged mutual authority between young people, parents, and other adults. As a result, postmodern adolescents have much less support from the older generation in meeting the demands of the transition to a secure adulthood. And this despite the fact that the demands for today's adolescents are much more difficult to satisfy than were those of the modern era.

If all this were not enough, even if youth navigate the passage into adulthood without a major disaster, once they get there, the possibility of attaining a standard of living comparable to that of earlier generations has diminished considerably. This is the economic yardstick of the new imbalance.

Diagnosing Disorder

8

From Sex to Stress

Since the early decades of this century, individuals have often turned to the "helping professions" when life's emotional burdens seemed unbearable or when problems inside and outside the family seemed unsolvable. The kind of help that was offered, however, was—and still is—very much a function of the prevailing worldview. During the modern period, the concepts of emotional wellness and mental disorder were quite different from those of the postmodern era, but each set of ideas in its own way has contributed to an imbalance in the family's ability to meet the needs of all its members.

An outstanding achievement of the modern era was the description of insanity as a disease or illness. Talking about mental disorder as an illness was an enlightened advance over the premodern attribution of demonic possession to psychologically troubled individuals. Once the insane were described in medical terms, as psychologically ill people, they were given medical treatment, not exorcised, exiled, or killed. Asylums for the mentally unsound and a medical specialty for their treatment—psychiatry—were the direct consequences of the modern, medical discourse of mental illness.

Although the disease account of mental illness was first introduced with respect to the insane, it was eventually extended to include the less severe emotional disorders—the psychoneuroses. Sigmund Freud altered the course of psychiatry when he demonstrated the linkage between the psychoneuroses and repressed infantile sexuality.[1] The language of mental illness, together with psychoanalytic language, led those in the helping professions to trace all adult neurotic problems to childhood sexual trauma. Preventive mental health measures, therefore, were primarily directed at parents' childrearing practices.

Since the 1950s the disease discourse of psychoneurotic disturbance, and the Freudian psychosexual terminology, have been challenged on a number of counts.[2] The illness terminology suggests that neurotic disturbance originates, and remains encapsulated, within the individual. Yet we now recognize that even the most emotionally healthy individuals can become impaired when exposed to unceasing and inordinate demands for adaptation. Psychological disturbance is understood as a product of the *interaction* of the individual and environmental circumstances, and is not reducible to the dynamics of the individual personality.

In accord with this new understanding of neurotic behavior, people who in another time would have been considered ill are now thought to be merely dysfunctional.[3] And the source of this dysfunction is not repressed sexuality but stress.[4] This does not mean that the postmodern helping professions have completely rejected all of Freud's theories and concepts. Freud's discussions of the unconscious, of the nature of dreams, and of the ego's defenses are still widely accepted and used. What has been laid aside is the disease discourse of neuroses, which suggested that emotional disturbance has a particular locus that can be excised by psychotherapy.

In contrast, the postmodern discourse of dysfunction suggests that neurotic behavior can be understood, in part at least, in terms of the stressors operating on the individual or family in question. Accordingly, the attention of postmodern preventive interventions has shifted from being concerned with childrearing practices to providing intervention programs for families, and stress reduction and management techniques for adults.

The modern preventive efforts directed at childrearing benefited children, insofar as they focused attention on improving parenting practices, but adults suffered from having their real-life issues ignored. Postmodern preventive efforts geared to adult stressors pay relatively little attention to stress experienced by children and youth. The modern psychosexual discourse thus strengthened the old imbalance, just as the postmodern stress discourse buttresses the new imbalance.

Modern Freudian Psychotherapy

Beginning with Freud's analysis of the psychoneuroses, the basic themes of modernity—progress, universality, and regularity—were woven into the modern discourse of mental disorder. Like Newton, Darwin, and many other scientists before him, Freud sought an underlying universal principle or law that would explain the many surface variations he saw in the behavior of emotionally disturbed patients. He hoped to classify those disorders into a regular pattern, and to help his patients progress toward a new state of improved well-being.

•PROGRESS AND DEVELOPMENTAL ARREST

In his essay "Infantile Sexuality," Freud described in minute detail the ways in which a disturbance of infantile sexuality was translated into the symptoms of neuroses—anxiety, phobias, obsessive/compulsive behavior—and interfered with normal, healthy development (that is, progress). A patient's neurotic symptoms also revealed the stage of infantile sexual development at which the disturbance or trauma had occurred. For example, in the case of obsessive/compulsive character disorder—a neurosis characterized by the repeated intrusion of an irrational thought into a person's mind, producing anxiety and a compulsion to act either to neutralize the thought or to realize it—Freud linked the symptoms to a "fixation" at the anal (two-year-old) level of psychosexual development.[5]

This developmental arrest, or fixation, model of mental illness has been used to account for all types of psychological symptoms and even for juvenile delinquency. Here is an example:

> Theoretical considerations tend to support the thesis that female delinquency is often precipitated by a strong regressive pull to the pre-oedipal mother and the panic which such surrender implies. As we can readily see there are two solutions available to the girl who is faced with an oedipal failure or disappointment which she is unable to surmount. She either regresses in her object relationship to the mother or she maintains an illusory oedipal situation with the sole aim to resist aggression. This defensive struggle is manifested in the compulsive need to create in reality a relationship in which she is needed and wanted by a sexual partner. These constellations represent the paradigmatic precondition for female delinquency.[6]

The Freudian theory of emotional illness as a matter of arrested progress in infancy and early childhood dominated psychiatric and psychological thinking for the first half of this century.

• *UNIVERSALITY AND NEUROTIC GERMS*

To a large extent, modern medicine was built upon the "germ" theory of disease. A particular disease, no matter where or when it appeared, was always caused by the same underlying pathological "germ." In the same way, modern theories of the psychoneuroses started from the assumption that a particular neurotic syndrome, no matter when or where it occurred, was generated by the same underlying diseased universal psychological "complex." Freud believed that it was the child's complex of infantile sexual impulses that became infected. The potential for complexes themselves (such as the oedipal complex) was universal: "It is also our belief that they are the common property of all men, a part of the human constitution, and merely exaggerated in the case of neurotics."[7]

Alfred Adler also traced adult neuroses to a diseased universal underlying infantile complex, albeit a different one from that proposed by Freud. He wrote: "All children have an inherent sense or feeling of inferiority which stimulates the imagination and incites attempts to dissipate the psychological inferiority by bettering the situation. A bettering of one's situation results in a lessening of the feeling of inferiority. From a psychological point of view, it can be regarded as a compensation."[8]

Melanie Klein offered still another, competing, theory that traced child and adult neuroses to diseased universal infantile masturbatory fantasies:

> In a paper read before the Salzburg Congress in 1924, I put forward the thesis that behind every form of play-activity lies a process of discharge of masturbatory phantasies, operating in the form of a continuous motive for play; that this process, acting as a repetition compulsion, constitutes a fundamental mechanism in children's play and in all subsequent sublimations; and that inhibitions in play and work spring from an unduly strong repression of those phantasies, and with them of the whole imaginative life of the child.[9]

The modern belief in diseased infantile complexes as the underlying "germs" of neurotic illness meant that all adult psychological disturbances originated in the patient's childhood. As a result, clinicians often misdiagnosed those dysfunctions that were in fact attributable to the person's immediate life circumstances. Many modern men and women spent a good many years in therapy "working through" their diseased infantile complexes while the stressors of their workplace, their family responsibilities, and their adult love relationships went unexamined and unremedied.

This centering on disturbances of universal complexes sometimes worked against modern children as well. I once evaluated a child who was suffering from an acute anxiety attack as a result of his parents' impending divorce. The child was literally immobilized by anxiety. The first diagnostic work-up, done in a very psychoanalytically oriented clinic, dwelt exclusively upon the child's oedipal problems. This work-up totally ignored the child's very real fears and anxieties: Where was he going to live? Who was going to look after him? Would he ever see his father again? And so on. These anxieties had nothing to do with the boy's infantile sexuality and everything to do with his feelings of insecurity and vulnerability engendered by his parents' divorce.

Overall, however, the modern reduction of psychological disorders to diseased underlying universal infantile complexes worked a greater hardship on adults than it did on children, if for no other reason than that a larger number of modern adults than modern children went into psychotherapy.

• *REGULARITY AND HEALTH*

In the Freudian scheme, all individuals have the predisposing complexes of mental illness, but they only become infected by "precipitating" causes—irregular accidental surface events, such as the child's viewing the "primal scene." This conception of irregular surface events as infecting underlying predisposing complexes is perhaps best illustrated in Freud's dream theory. In Freud's view, every dream is occasioned by some event that occurred during the preceding day, "the day residue," which excites the deep-seated complexes and gives shape to the dream.[10]

But accidental surface events can also infect a deep and abiding predisposing emotional complex and cause it to develop into a neurosis. This chain of events is illustrated in Freud's case of Little Hans. One of Freud's colleagues had a five-year-old son, Hans, who developed a horse phobia. The parents had kept detailed records of the child's activities and of their conversations with him. On the basis of these records, Freud concluded that the phobia was a projection of the boy's fear of his father (a fear generated by Hans's oedipal wish to do away with the father and to possess the mother) onto a horse. This phobia was precipitated by the following accidental surface event:

> It was at this stage of the analysis that he recalled the event, insignificant in itself, which immediately preceded the outbreak of the

> illness and may no doubt be regarded as the exciting [precipitating] cause of the outbreak. He went for a walk with his mother and saw a bus-horse fall down and kick about with its feet. This made a great impression on him. He was terrified, and thought the horse was dead; and from that time on thought that all horses would fall down . . . Nevertheless, his fear of horses persisted: nor was it clear through what chain of associations the horse's falling down stirred up his unconscious wishes.[11]

The case of Little Hans has become a classic in its thorough description of a young boy's sexual life and how it stimulated his intellectual curiosity and fueled his anxieties. Freud did not present this case to introduce any new ideas but merely as further evidence for his theory of infantile sexuality. Yet it clearly reveals Freud's modern approach to causality. In his view, irregular surface events have meaning and lawful significance only to the extent that they, in one way or another, tie up with a deep-seated regular complex. Modern "depth" psychology thus turned clinical attention away from the many ongoing powerful and irregular surface events (such as physical and sexual abuse) that were often both the predisposing *and* the precipitating causes of adult and child psychological dysfunction.

Transition Theories and Therapies

In modern psychotherapy, treatment was centered on the individual's arrested development, complexes, and precipitating events. As Salvador Minuchin nicely describes,

> The traditional [modern] techniques of mental health grew out of a fascination with individual dynamics. This preoccupation dominated the field and led therapists to concentrate on exploring the intrapsychic. Of necessity, the resulting treatment techniques focused exclusively on the individual, apart from his surroundings. An artificial "boundary" was drawn between the individual and his

> social context . . . As the patient was treated in isolation, the data encountered were inevitably restricted to the way he alone felt and thought about what was happening to him . . . The very richness of the data available discouraged other approaches. As a result, the individual came to be seen as the site of pathology.[12]

One of the first workers to challenge this illness model of mental disturbance was Harry Stack Sullivan, perhaps America's most original psychiatrist. Although Sullivan accepted many of Freud's ideas, such as the unconscious, he rejected others. Sullivan was actually quite postmodern in that he regarded emotional disturbance not as a disease but as a disruption of communication caused by anxiety. He also recognized the interactive nature of psychotherapy and introduced the term "participant observer" to describe the therapist's role in the treatment process. Sullivan was also interested in the other social sciences and incorporated conceptions from cultural anthropology, linguistics, and psychological field theory into his own "interpersonal theory of psychiatry."[13]

Much of Sullivan's work was published posthumously by colleagues and students, from his lectures and working papers. Not so the ideas of his contemporary, and in some ways rival, Karen Horney. Like Sullivan, Horney came to challenge many of Freud's theses, including his account of feminine psychology. She did this in a number of books written for the general public as well as for practitioners.[14]

Horney also looked at neuroses from an interpersonal, rather than an individual, perspective:

> Neuroses thus present a peculiar kind of struggle for life under difficult conditions. Their very essence consists of disturbances in the relations to self and others, and conflicts arising on these grounds. The shift in emphasis as to the factors considered relevant in neuroses enlarges considerably the task of analytic therapy. The aim of therapy is then not to help the patient gain mastery over his instincts, but to lessen his anxiety to such an extent that he can dispense with his "neurotic trends." Beyond this aim there looms

> an entirely new therapeutic goal, which is to restore the individual to himself, to help him regain his spontaneity and find his center of gravity in himself.[15]

Both Horney and Sullivan continued to regard themselves as psychoanalysts even though they had broken with Freud in many respects. They were often called Neo-Freudians.

Perhaps the most well-known of the Neo-Freudians is Erik Erikson. Erikson shared many of Sullivan's and Horney's interests in the social sciences as well as their belief in the interpersonal and social dimensions of emotional disturbance. Erikson, however, moved much farther than either Sullivan or Horney toward an original, and comprehensive, theory of personality development and emotional disturbance.

Erikson's challenge to the illness model and to Freudian theory were first presented in his book *Childhood and Society*. In that work, Erikson provided a comprehensive psychosocial theory of human development that covered the entire life cycle. Although Erikson presented his theory as building upon the Freudian system, it was, in fact, a heretical departure.[16]

First of all, Erikson postulated the existence of a self or identity that was present from birth and that was conflict-free. In the Freudian scheme, the adaptive structure of the personality, the ego, only emerged when the id (the seat of instinctual impulse and desire) was unable to satisfy itself through fantasy alone (for example, an infant who fantasized the breast would receive no nourishment until she made some effort—exerted her ego—to attract the attention of the mother). Other analysts had already argued that certain ego functions were conflict-free, but Erikson went much further in proposing, in effect, a superordinate sense of identity, or *self*, as part of our inborn equipment.[17]

Second, and this is what makes Erikson's work postmodern, he described the stages of adult, as well as of child, development. None of the modern stage theorists, from Freud, Gesell, and Piaget to

Sullivan and Horney, had done that. In addition, although Erikson contended that there are distinct adult stages of development, he also argued that the social propensities for these adult stages are present from the start of life. For example, although fully realized generativity (commitment to the next generation) is characteristic of an adult stage of development, even children can be generative when, say, they are thoughtful of a younger child or an infant.

Still a third innovation was Erikson's contention that the evolution of the sense of identity, or self, came about in a series of critical periods. According to the critical-periods argument, development is not entirely preformed or predetermined but is epigenetic, affected by the experiences the individual encounters at each successive stage of development. Erikson argued that we inherit our human social potential as a set of bipolar opposites. Although these opposites are all present from birth, each pair has a particular period in the life cycle when the balance between the opposites is most easily set. A healthy balance is one in which the positive potential outweighs the negative potential. A certain amount of mistrust, for example, is a healthy counterpoise to an overweening sense of trust.

Moreover, Erikson also argued that even if one emerged from the critical period with the negative potential outweighing the positive, the balance could still be shifted in the healthy direction by events later in life. To illustrate, the preschool child has the potential to attain either a strong sense of initiative that outweighs a sense of guilt, or the opposite. A child who is prevented from exploring and manipulating the environment, or who is reprimanded for doing so, will be likely to develop a sense of guilt that is stronger than his or her sense of initiative. If, however, during the next period of development the child is supported in attaining a sense of industry that is much stronger than his sense of inferiority, this can act back upon, and strengthen, his sense of initiative.

A final break from the Freudian paradigm, and another step toward postmodernism, was Erikson's insistence that adult life experiences could be as devastating as childhood experiences for the individual's mental health. Erikson wrote about war veterans whose emotional disturbance was traceable to the conflict in values and belief they experienced while fighting and killing for their country. He also described the conflicts experienced by American Indians forced to reconcile their pride in their heritage and rich culture with the white man's image of them as savages. Adolescent Indians encountering this conflict for the first time often engaged in self-destructive, pathological behavior. Childhood experiences were not the only ones that could generate conflict and cause severe emotional disturbance.

Despite these postmodern innovations, Erikson remained modern in his contention that his stages were progressive and universal and that irregular surface events could trigger buried complexes and conflicts. Nonetheless, Erikson, like Sullivan and Horney, provided a liberating example for other health professionals who felt constrained by the Freudian conceptions of instinctual drives. Increasingly, the psychosexual discourse of emotional disturbance was challenged by other transitional theories that employed the language of social interactions.

A few examples will illustrate these transitional discourses. Eric Berne introduced his theory of Transactional Analysis (TA) and described the different "games people play." In Berne's view there are three social interactive positions: that of the child, the parent, and the adult. An individual who always tries to play the adult may be as dysfunctional as an individual who always takes the position of the child. Psychological well-being requires the individual to be flexible enough to shift to the position most appropriate to the immediate circumstances. The new social interaction narratives were also evident in a number of holistic psychologies and group approaches such as Gestalt therapy. Although such therapies retained some Freudian elements, they nonetheless emphasized the importance of social interaction in the causation and treatment of emotional disturbance.[18]

These transitional approaches to the understanding and treatment of psychological dysfunction were effective in moving us away from the disease metaphor, the psychosexual language of emotional disturbance, and an exclusive focus on the early childhood of the individual. Yet they remained modern in that they presupposed unidirectional progress and universal dynamics. It was only with the introduction of the concept of stress that a completely postmodern language became available for talking about the causes of psychological dysfunction.

Stress in the Postmodern Worldview

The stress conception incorporates the postmodern ideas of difference, particularity, and irregularity. And although it has a medical dimension, it takes into account environmental as well as physiological contributions to psychological dysfunction.

The stress concept was introduced by the physiologist Hans Selye, who devoted his long career to the elucidation of this syndrome. Selye was led to the discovery of the stress phenomenon while working as a young physician in Prague. He was intrigued by the observation that patients suffering from many different illnesses nonetheless all showed some symptoms in common. Conventional medical wisdom ignored these general symptoms and insisted that they were secondary to the unique primary symptoms that differentiated each illness. That is to say, traditional medicine looked at illnesses as separate and distinct without recognizing that they could still be connected in a kind of clinical *pastiche,* a general condition of what Selye described as "just being sick."[19]

Selye distinguished between stress in the broad sense and stress in the narrow sense. In its broadest connotation, stress is coextensive with life and amounts to the continuous process of responding to the "normal" internal demands made by our bodies and minds as well as to external demands made by people and events in our life space. Used broadly, stress is another term for the process of living; from this perspective, there can be no life without stress. In the narrow sense, however, stress refers to the response to extraordinary demands for adaptation. This is the way in which we use the term stress in our everyday conversations. Selye labeled the events that stress us in the narrow sense "stressors."

The concepts of stress and stressors have brought our understanding of psychological dysfunction into the postmodern world. In the modern conception, a mentally ill person is an individual with a disease; in the postmodern conception, a psychologically dysfunctional person is an individual overwhelmed by stress. Unfortunately, however, Selye elaborated his stress theory almost exclusively with respect to adults, to the neglect of the stressors encountered by children and youth. As a result, stress was—and unfortunately to a large extent still is—regarded as a syndrome limited to adults. The relative neglect of the stress experienced by children and youth contributes to the new imbalance.

• *DIFFERENCE AND DYSFUNCTION*

From a stress perspective, people experiencing psychological dysfunction lack the ability to cope with the stressors they are confronting. This inadequacy is a joint function of the coping strategies that individuals have at their disposal and the intensity of the stressors that are in play. Dysfunction can, therefore, be the result of many different combinations of coping strategies and environmental stressors. Overwhelming stressors may inundate an individual whose coping strategies are more than adequate in most circumstances. On the other hand, mild stressors may immobilize an individual with weak coping skills. Dysfunction, therefore, is not a matter of arrested progress but a reflection of many different patterns of stressors and coping abilities; it is a product of person/environment interaction.

During the modern era, emotional disturbance also had a social component, but the direction of causality was always regarded as unilateral: the child's pathology was seen as a direct consequence of parental actions. Mothers in particular were blamed for any disorders that developed in their children, ranging from autism to the unpreparedness of many men for service in World War II. In the 1960s, however, investigators began to point out that many times an infant's behavior can shape that of the mother as well as the reverse. Studies have shown, for example, that irritable babies may develop less secure attachments than nonirritable infants. While these infant effects upon caregiving relationships can be improved by support and training for the caregiver, they do provide evidence for mutual causality in determining the kind of relationship that exists between a child and a parent.[20]

• *PARTICULARITY AND COPING STRATEGIES*

Viewed from a stress perspective, psychological dysfunction is always particular, a unique reflection of the individual's coping skills and the press of environmental stressors. While each of us acquires our basic coping strategies in childhood, and while these reflect both training and predisposing temperament, there are no universal strategies or stressors. The stress response is always an individual matter; what is a stressor to one person is not necessarily a stressor to another. For one individual, competition in the workplace is a heady stimulus to overachieve, whereas for another it is the cause of constant anxiety and concern. Moreover, as adults, we can learn new techniques of stress management; we are not necessarily locked into our early coping styles. Each case of psychological dysfunction, therefore, must be treated in its own terms and not as a manifestation of one or another universal complex.

A case in point is the syndrome that in the modern era was called hyperactivity and was believed to be (universally) caused by minimal brain dysfunction. In the 1960s this explanation was challenged, and a much more differentiated concept, attention-deficit hyperactivity disorder (ADHD), has been substituted.[21] The syndrome is characterized by inattention, impulsivity, and considerable activity at inappropriate times and places. We now recognize that different children can show one or more symptoms of this disorder and that the cause may range from the physiological to the psychological to the social, or any combination of these factors. There is no universal diseased complex underlying ADHD. Unfortunately, the very complexity of the syndrome enhances the likelihood that children will be misdiagnosed.

•SURFACE EVENTS AND STRESS EFFECTS

Selye argued that it is often the everyday, regularly irregular, extraordinary demands for adaptation that do the most harm. This has led to an examination of the conditions under which we work and the demands made upon us by our daily interactions with family, friends, and others.

Adults have been well served by this new emphasis on the stresses of everyday life, but pressured children and youth have not. Adults regard the life demands made upon them as necessarily more stressful than those experienced by the young. We would, we believe, readily exchange the pressures we feel in the workplace for the school demands, peer pressure, athletic competition, rapid physiological changes, and emotional vicissitudes experienced by children and youth. As a result of this attitude among adults, children and youth are not offered the services of the helping professions to the same extent that adults are, nor are other stress-reducing techniques made available to them.

Postmodern Helping Procedures

When adults seek help with stress and psychological dysfunction, they are likely to encounter two types of interventions: programs aimed at "lifestyle" changes on the one hand, and "family therapy" on the other.

•LIFESTYLE CHANGES

Once psychological dysfunctions came to be understood in stress terms, preventive as well as treatment emphasis shifted to the interaction of the individual with the environment. How we live our everyday lives is as significant as our early childhood experiences for effective psychological functioning. The importance of regular exercise, diet, and time off for recreation are all acknowledged as critical for mental as well as psychological well-being.

At the same time, new syndromes associated with dysfunctional lifestyles have been identified. The "workaholic" is an individual whose symptoms can be directly traced to his or her lifestyle. Other dysfunctional lifestyles that have been identified center on the addictions, whether to drugs, alcohol, or gambling. Addictive lifestyles affect all family members, who may become involved in a pattern of codependency. In such families, members who are not addicted nonetheless engage in a systematic denial of the addiction and, in a dysfunctional way, become dependent upon the addicted person for bad treatment and abuse. Their behavior "enables" the person to continue to pursue his or her addiction. Treatment programs often aim at helping family members alter these codependencies and enabling behaviors.[22]

• *FAMILY THERAPY*

Codependency is only one of many destructive patterns of family interaction that therapists in the 1960s began to identify. The postmodern liberation from the disease approach to emotional problems led to a variety of new therapies, including structural, strategic, experiential, systemic, Bowenian, ecological, and brief therapy. As Minuchin, an innovator in the field of family therapy, points out, many family therapists develop their own approaches to helping dysfunctional families.[23] In their diversity and in their emphasis upon the embeddedness and contextual nature of psychological dysfunction, these workers reflect the postmodern conceptions of difference, particularity, and irregularity. Moreover, each has created his or her own minidiscourse to describe family systems. One of the most influential of these family therapists is Virginia Satir:

> In my years as a family therapist, I have found that four aspects of family life keep popping up:

> The feelings and ideas one has about oneself, which I call *self-worth.*
> The ways people use to work out meaning with one another, which I call *communication.*
> The *rules* people use for how they should feel and act, which eventually develop into what I call the *family system.*
> The way people relate to other people and institutions outside the family, which I call the *link to society.*[24]

In her theory of family interaction and dysfunction Satir reflects the postmodern emphasis on the embeddedness of the individual's problem in the family and in the social context within which that family lives. She finds that dysfunctional behavior derives not from infantile complexes but from problems in each of the four elements described above:

> No matter what kind of problem first led a family into my office—whether an unfaithful wife or depressed husband, a delinquent daughter or a schizophrenic son—I soon found that the prescription was the same. To relieve their family pain, some way had to be found to change these four factors. In all of the troubled families I noticed that:
>
> Self-worth was low.
> Communication was indirect, vague, and not really honest.
> Rules were rigid, inhuman, nonnegotiable, and everlasting.
> The family's link to society was fearful, placating, and blaming.[25]

Although Satir argues that families all over the world deal with these issues, the content is different for each family. Help must, therefore, be tailored to the particular constellation of low self-worth, indirect communication, rigid rules, and impaired links to society that hold for that particular family.

More recently, family workers have begun to extend their contextual approach even further to accommodate cultural and ethnic contexts as well. In their work with Hispanic families, the psychologists

Szapocznik and Kurtines have shown how cultural and family dynamics interact to produce dysfunction. On the basis of those insights they have developed intervention strategies to enhance family members' intercultural skills.[26]

In postmodern family therapy, the emphasis on mutuality among family members and between family members and the therapist often means that children are treated on a par with adults. But by ignoring children's level of development, these systems approaches to the family may place undue expectations and pressures on children to interact in adult ways. The shift from a modern emphasis on sexuality to a postmodern emphasis on stress as the cause of psychological disturbance has been beneficial to contemporary adults, who are no longer treated like dependent children by the therapist. But troubled children and youth are no better served by the postmodern psychotherapeutic community than they were by modern treatment practices. At least during the modern era they were treated in a developmentally appropriate fashion.

Although the lifestyle and family approaches have won widespread acceptance, much clinical work of the modern variety is still practiced. And in some cases it may be the theory and treatment that is most indicated. Today, however, a psychotherapeutic approach based on Freudian ideas is but one among many theories and treatments available to clinicians and their clients. It is the diversity of approaches and discourses of dysfunction that gives contemporary helping professions their postmodern imprint.

Stress among Youth

9

The New Morbidity

The family need imbalance is also a stress imbalance. During the modern era, when the old imbalance was in play, adults suffered greater stress than children and youth. Today, now that the new imbalance reigns, children and youth are under greater stress than adults. We can observe this shift from the old to the new stress imbalance on three different scales: development, normality, and space.

On the scale of development, the stages of childhood were weighted more heavily in the modern era, whereas the stages of adulthood tip the scales today. Likewise, in the modern era children and youth were accorded a greater latitude of acceptable behavior than were adults, while today just the reverse obtains. Finally, prior to midcentury, children and youth had access to relatively more space than did adults, whereas in the last decades of the century, most available space is owned by adults.

When young people's developmental needs for protection and nurture are ignored, when their human differences in growth rates and behavior are deemed deviant, and when they are given little or no space to live and to grow, they are stressed. Young people who are stressed often do what adults do: they engage in actions that are destructive to themselves, to others, or to both. The consequences of these self/other punishing practices are increasingly evident, and have been given a new name, the "new morbidity."

Shrinking Childhood, Expanding Adulthood

In the modern lexicon of the family, the developmental stages of childhood and adolescence were celebrated, while growth in adulthood went relatively unnoticed and unremarked upon. In the 1930s and 1940s, as we have seen, Arnold Gesell and his colleagues provided a language for the day-to-day actions of children at each year of development, and in the 1950s the psychologist Robert J. Havighurst introduced the notion of "developmental tasks." A developmental task is one that arises at a particular period of life and must be mastered if the young person is to move on successfully to the next stage of life. These tasks may be posed by the child's physical maturation, cultural pressures, or the child's own striving. Havighurst outlined specific tasks for each stage of child development, such as learning to talk and taking solid food in infancy and attaining independence in adolescence. He did not, however, describe specific developmental tasks for adults.[1]

Also in the 1950s, the famed Swiss psychologist Jean Piaget offered a new set of terms to describe the stages of intellectual development from infancy through adolescence. According to Piaget, during the first two years of life the child is at the sensorimotor stage and operates according to the logic of action. From about the age of two to about the age of six or seven the child is at the preoperational stage and acquires language and functional logic (a hole is to dig!). Beginning at about the age of six or seven the child acquires concrete operations that enable him or her to engage in syllogistic reasoning and to operate according to rules. Finally, in adolescence, the young person acquires formal operations that allow him or her to engage in abstract thinking and to employ propositional logic. For Piaget, the formal operations attained in adolescence were the peak of intellectual development and power.[2]

A related emphasis came from the modern literature of intelligence testing. Like Piaget's qualitative language, this quantitative measuring focused on the intellectual growth of children and youth to the exclusion of intellectual development in adults. In her analysis of a longitudinal study of gifted individuals, Nancy Bayley reported that intelligence reached a peak around age eighteen, stayed at that level to age thirty, and began to decline after that.[3] David Wechsler, creator of the widely used Wechsler Intelligence Scales for children and adults, wrote in 1958: "Beginning with the investigation by Galton in 1883 . . . nearly all studies dealing with the age factor in adult performance have shown that most human abilities . . . decline progressively after reaching a peak somewhere between ages 18 and 25."[4]

In the modern era, therefore, adulthood was characterized by the language of stasis and the necessary decline of intellectual power and physical vigor. Retirement for men and the "empty nest" for women were all that nuclear family parents had to look forward to after their children were grown. For women in particular, the failure to speak of adulthood as a period of continued personal growth and development contributed to the rise of the feminist movement. Betty Friedan pointed to the inadequacies of this modern discourse for adult women when she wrote:

> If I am right, the problem that has no name stirring in the minds of so many American women today is not a matter of loss of femininity or too much education or the demands of domesticity. It is far more important than anyone recognizes. It is the key to these other new and old problems which have been torturing women and their husbands and children, and puzzling their doctors and educators for years. It may well be the key to our future as a nation and a culture. We can no longer ignore that voice within women that says, "I want something more than my husband, and my children and my home."[5]

Emphasis on the successive stages of childhood was beneficial for children, because their parents, thanks to developmental language, had age-appropriate expectations for their offspring. To be sure, not all modern parents knew or cared about these age norms. Nonetheless, their existence created a social climate conducive to the protection of all children. On the other hand, the failure to provide a way to talk about adult development was destructive for the majority of both women and men.

Just the reverse is true in these postmodern times. The postmodern perceptions of childhood competence and teenage sophistication have all but eradicated the modernist concern with child-developmental stages. The terms used by Freud, Gesell, Piaget, and Erikson, among others, have been eclipsed by the discussion of *a*developmental techniques advocated by Ginott, Thomas, and others.

Granted, the contemporary research literature on child development abounds with studies that seem to demonstrate that infants and children are much more competent than Piaget or Gesell gave them credit for being. The latest revision of one of the leading contemporary texts in child development is quite critical of Piaget's stage approach to development:

> As we have seen, Piaget's theory and observations have received considerable criticism on the basis of recent evidence. Many children seem to be more cognitively advanced for their age than Piaget's theory would suggest. The current findings in infant conditionability and perceptual ability . . . suggest that the infant may know more than Piaget discerned . . . The cognitive abilities in preoperational and concrete operational children also appear to have been underestimated by Piaget.[6]

This excerpt reflects the discomfort many postmodern child psychologists experience with a philosophy that highlights the systematic differences between children at successive age levels. Indeed, a major thrust of contemporary child development theory and research is to demonstrate how competent children really are.[7]

At the same time that the developmental stages of children and youth are being underplayed and minimized, many innovative theories celebrating the stages of adulthood have been introduced and are being widely disseminated. The earliest of these have to be regarded as transitional languages in the sense that they extended the assumptions of progress, universality, and regularity to adult development. Variously described as "self-enhancement," "ego enhancement," "self-actualization," or "existential" theories, these theories all assume a universal, biological forward thrust to life that follows a regular course. As Carl Rogers, a leading spokesperson for this discourse, wrote: "The organism has one basic tendency and striving—to actualize, maintain and enhance the experiencing organism."[8]

Abraham Maslow, another spokesperson for this transitional, self-realization approach to adult development, argued for a "needs hierarchy" such that higher-order needs could only be realized after lower-order needs were fulfilled. From lowest to highest, our needs are for: food and water; safety and security; love and affection; self-esteem and self-actualization. Self-actualized adults sometimes have "peak experiences" that, for a brief time, present the individual with the very best of human existence.[9]

More recently, a new set of terminologies regarding adult development has been introduced that is truly postmodern. In lieu of a universal, progressive urge for self-realization, these discourses describe a series of stages of adult development that are not necessarily progressive, universal, or regular. What these positions share in common is the idea that adulthood is not a constant period but rather one that is full of change for both better and worse.

The psychiatrist Daniel Levinson and his colleagues, who have studied the development of adult men, are quite postmodern in *not* assuming that the stages they observed among men would automatically hold for women. Levinson and his colleagues offer the following language to describe the "seasons of a man's life":

> We identify four overlapping eras in the life cycle, each lasting some twenty-five years. The eras provide a view of the individual from a

> distance. Each era is distinguished by its overall character of living which has biological, psychological and social aspects. The eras form the skeletal structure of the life cycle. Once we have understood the nature of an era from the perspective of the total life cycle, we can examine more specific processes and events as they unfold within it.[10]

Levinson's work was the starting point for Gail Sheehy's more popular book *Passages.*[11]

A somewhat different postmodern description of adult development has been contributed by the psychiatrist Judith Viorst. In her view, our transit through life is best seen as a series of "necessary losses," the title of her book. She describes losses at four different periods of life:

> The losses entailed by moving away from the body and being of our mother and gradually becoming a separate self.
> The losses involved in facing limitations on our power for the human realities of imperfect connections.
> The losses of relinquishing our dreams of ideal relationships for the human realities of imperfect connections.
> And the losses, the multiple losses, of the second half of life, of our final losing, leaving and letting go.[12]

Viorst, like Levinson, recognizes wide individual differences in the course of adult development and the fact that growth is not always positive and "self-actualizing."

The postmodern recognition of adult development has been acknowledged by social science in the creation of a new discipline, "lifespan developmental psychology."[13] It explores intellectual, social, and emotional growth from birth to death. (Geriatric medicine, a new discipline in health care, is concerned with aging adults.)

One outcome of this new lifespan perspective in psychology is a revised portrayal of intellectual growth in adulthood. Lifespan developmental psychologists now distinguish between "fluid" and "crystallized" intelligence. Crystallized intelligence includes our vocabulary, our general fund of information, our understanding of similarities and differences, and our capacity to make reasoned judgments. In contrast, fluid intelligence has to do with our general intellectual power, our ability to engage in productive relational thinking and problem solving. While fluid intelligence may decline with age, crystallized intelligence continues to grow throughout the adult years. Intelligence defined as knowledge and skill continues to increase until at least age sixty.[14] Put differently, the pragmatics of intelligence—good judgment about important but uncertain matters of life—is likely to increase with age.[15]

In many ways, therefore, the postmodern discourse of adulthood is quite different from that used to portray modern men and women. Whereas the modern descriptive language of grown men and women was one of stasis followed by decline, the postmodern discourse of adulthood is one of change and vitality. By contrast, the language now used to describe children and youth suggests a static, fully completed maturity. This postmodern reversal in the narratives of development serves the needs of adults, but it puts new stresses on children and adolescents, who must cope with age-inappropriate demands.

Shrinking Normality, Expanding Options

In modern psychiatry, mental illness was diagnosed by observing the individual's abnormal and irregular behaviors. But during that same period, children and youth were allowed a wide range of acceptable irregularity before they were labeled abnormal. Mischievousness in children and "gaucheness" in adolescence were to be expected and were regarded as developmentally appropriate. Only the most extreme deviations from the norms of child and adolescent behavior were termed aberrant. Within this broad discourse of normality, much of the troublesome language and behavior of children and youth was described as what it was—an expression of time-limited youthful exuberance and impulsivity.

Gesell and his colleagues voiced the discourse of leniency in this way:

> Sometimes, of course, the child's behavior is so unexpected and contradictory that it is very difficult to understand. He may even seem to go backward when the growth gradients demand that he should go forward. In such a situation, whether it arises at home or at school, it is especially important to interpret the problem in terms of development. It must be remembered that the mind does not grow on a straight and even front. The course of development is uneven (in some children more so than others). It zigzags, and sometimes it spirals backward in a way that suggests retreat and regression . . . Development is like a stream, it carves the best possible channel, it flows onward, it reaches a goal.[16]

In the early 1960s, when I first began working as a psychologist for a juvenile court in Colorado, I was permitted to interview and test young people before they had been officially filed upon and their names put permanently on record. Usually I got a pretty good idea as to whether or not the young person was involved in a one-time escapade or had more serious problems. In the former cases, the judge and probation officer would see the teenagers in chambers and, after impressing upon them the serious consequences of another transgression, would release them without ever putting their name on the court roster. In about 99 percent of cases, we never saw the adolescent again. In the modern era, a one-time skirmish with "the law" was recognized as being within the range of normality for adolescents.

If modern children and youth were allowed considerable irregularity in their behavior before they were labeled emotionally disturbed or delinquent, their parents and other adults, in contrast, were expected to behave within a narrow range of social proscriptions. Nonnuclear kinship systems such as single-parent families, families in which two parents work, and remarried families were, in the modern era, regarded as deviant and abnormal. Even modern parents who, for whatever reasons, did not attend PTA meetings or school functions were looked down upon. Moreover, teachers and librarians were also held to strict codes of behavior dictated by the fact that they had responsibility for the young and were expected to set a good example. These strict codes of conduct were often frustrating and demoralizing for both men and women. They accounted for much of the unhappiness of those modern adults who were deemed outside the narrow confines of acceptable social behavior.

In the postmodern era, at the same time that we have abandoned the language of child development, we have also narrowed the range of normality within which the young can function. This became very clear to me as I reflected upon my experience in public schools over the past quarter century. When I took my first job, as a school psychologist, I was relatively inexperienced. I once asked a second-grade teacher whether a young man, who kept bouncing around the classroom, talking to his friends, and teasing the girls, might not have a behavior problem. "No," she replied smiling, "He's just all boy!" Today when I see a second-grader behaving in the same way, I am likely to be told, by the special needs teacher, that he has an attention-deficit hyperactivity disorder (ADHD) and needs to be placed on Ritalin (a drug widely used with hyperactive children). We are too ready today to lump high-spirited children with those whose behavior is truly a result of psychological dysfunction.

Postmodern educational practices contribute to this narrowed discourse of normality. Within elementary education the phrase "special needs" was introduced to encompass all children who deviated from the norm in mental ability, physical health, and personality. While the label of special needs was meant to be nondiscriminatory and nonpejorative, it has narrowed the range of normality by lumping all children with special needs into a single group. Moreover, this discourse ignores the fact that all children have special needs, and provides a good example of how the postmodern emphasis upon difference can sometimes do a disservice to our common humanness.

With respect to high school students, the narrowed range of normality for postmodern youth has been described in another way. In the 1980s an extensive report entitled "Work, Family and Citizenship" discussed in detail the problem of the "forgotten half"—the 20 million high school students who do not go on to college. Most high schools, the report concluded, are geared exclusively toward college-bound youngsters. As a consequence, high schools do not prepare noncollege-bound students for the real world of work. In communities where there are vocational high schools, the students attending such schools are often derided as "vokies" (a derogatory diminutive of vocational education). High schools, by limiting their curriculum to academic subjects, have narrowed the range of occupations that are considered "normal" for postmodern youth.[17]

The new laws aimed at protecting children's rights that came into effect in the mid-1960s also changed what was considered legally normal for young people and what was not. In some states the age of consent for the determination of statutory rape has been lowered. Lowering the age for statutory rape in effect narrows the age range of normality for virginity. Likewise, after the passage of these new laws, court psychologists could no longer interview or test adolescents, as I had been doing before, without first filing upon them. Once these laws were passed, before I could interview or test a young person I had to officially label the adolescent as a suspected felon or worse. While this new approach protects the adolescent's right to due process, it also denies that young person a second chance and a beneficial learning experience. In fact it often turns them in the opposite direction. As one young man told me, who had been unnecessarily filed upon, "Well, you have the name so I guess you play the game!"

At the same time that we have narrowed the discourse of normality for children and youth, we have expanded it greatly for adults. During the modern era, unmarried couples cohabiting, divorced couples, single parents, blended families, and gay lifestyles were all spoken of as deviant. Today, all of these arrangements are considered socially acceptable adult behavior. This expansion of adult normality has been beneficial for adults, who now have many more options and freedoms than they did during the modern era. Narrowing the range of normality for children and adolescents, however, has been a disaster. It has led to stressful labeling of all too many young people as deviant who, in another era, would be regarded as well within the range of normality.

Shrinking Child Spaces, Expanding Adult Arenas

In *The Hurried Child* I argued that postmodern children, unlike modern children, were not given the time to enjoy the pleasures, as well as the pains and frustrations, unique to childhood.[18] But it is not just time that has been collapsed for postmodern young people; their space has been curtailed as well. In the late modern world, space for children and adolescents was a high priority. In many middle-income homes, the "finished basement" was set aside as a place exclusively for the use of children. Children from all socioeconomic levels were allowed to "go out and play" in their backyards, streets, and neighborhoods. Vacant lots were available for use as playing fields, and many communities supported public playgrounds and even paid athletic directors to issue community-owned equipment and to provide instruction and coaching.

Likewise, adolescents spoke of drugstores, malt shops, drive-ins, and large movie theaters as their "spots." In junior and senior high schools, debating clubs, gardening clubs, stamp-collecting clubs, 4-H clubs, and many other groups were provided space in the schools. Groups like Explorer and Sea Scouts were often accommodated in church basements.

In contrast, spaces for adults in the modern era were relatively constricted. For men, there were professional baseball and football games, golf courses, and bowling alleys. For women, there were "downtown" department stores and small local shops. Most other activities centered around schools and churches. Travel was usually limited to automobiles, and there were many fewer motels, hotels, and resorts than today. Foreign travel was available only to the wealthy few who could afford expensive air fares. Compared with adults today, modern adults had access to much less geographical space.

Along with the shrinking stages of child development and the shrinking concept of normality for postmodern children and youth, we see a shrinking of the spaces available to young people. In some homes, the basement, once the exclusive province of middle-income children, has been replaced by the kitchen/family-room complex—a relaxation and recreational area for the whole family. In many families where both parents are professionals, one finds two studies or home offices where additional playspace might have been. A library or music room, a workshop or exercise room, maybe an in-home artist's studio or greenhouse, not to mention a room or small apartment for an *au pair*—all of these kinds of spaces within many middle-class homes have been allocated during the postmodern period to the needs of adults rather than children. Moreover, children who are cramped indoors can no longer just go out and play. Most of our communities are not safe today, and open, unspoiled spaces for roaming and exploring are not available to urban and suburban kids.

In this postmodern era, conversations with children and youth about space almost always turn to discussions of safety. Children and youth are warned about what neighborhoods and areas they should not venture into. For young people in large cities, sometimes no place is safe.

A couple of years ago I gave some lectures at the 92nd Street Y in Manhattan. Walking to the building, I noticed that many stores had yellow placards in the windows. When I inquired about them, I was told that they were symbols that the stores were "safe havens." If children are accosted at a bus stop or elsewhere, they can rush to these places for protection. Around that same time, I gave a talk in a small town in the province of Alberta, Canada. After my presentation, I had a little time before we drove back to Edmonton, where I would catch my plane. I took a walk through the town, which had only one main street. In the course of my walk, I encountered a young man of eight years or so. As he approached me, he smiled and said "Good morning." As a Bostonian, my instantaneous reaction was that this child was retarded! No "normal" child in Boston would address a stranger on the street; it is considered unsafe. But this young man grew up hearing that public spaces are safe, and that people in them can be trusted.

In a 1991 report, Ernest Boyer of the Carnegie Foundation for the Advancement of Teaching, wrote:

> When Carnegie researchers surveyed fifth- and eighth-graders several years ago, more than half agreed that "there are not a lot of good places to play in the neighborhood." One out of five said drugs are a problem. In another national survey of children, over half reported that they had been "bothered" by an older person while playing outside. In no community—city, suburb, town or country—did a majority say that their neighborhood was "very good." A kindergarten teacher in Madison, Wisconsin, responding to our survey, said, "Many of my children come to school worried about the violent events they experienced in their neighborhoods."[19]

If the postmodern world has dedicated little public space to meeting the needs of children, it has devoted even less to meeting the needs of adolescents. The places that young people once could call their own are no longer welcoming. Afterschool clubs have all but disappeared as teachers have little time to devote to them. Although shopping malls have become popular with adolescents, storeowners do not always welcome teenagers. Likewise, corner drugstores have been replaced by chain-store pharmacies that do not cater to young people. Movie theaters have been downsized so that they too no longer provide a large area that will accommodate a youthful crowd or balconies that provide some privacy for kissing and handholding. Many housing developments, restaurants, and adult amusement areas exclude children and youth.

In contrast, many new spaces have opened up for adults. Bike and jogging paths, health clubs, marinas, golf courses, and ski resorts have proliferated. Shopping malls are omnipresent, and there has been a large increase in resort hotels, restaurants, cruise ships, and comedy clubs. The advent of jet travel, the universality of cars, and the expanding network of interstate highways has further broadened the geographic and recreational options of adults with even moderate incomes. To be sure, children who travel with their parents also benefit from this expansion. Nevertheless, in the final tally of spaces, postmodern children are doing much worse than their parents did as children, and much worse than their parents are doing as adults. The lack of space to play, work, and just "hang out" is extraordinarily stressful for children and adolescents alike.

The New Morbidity

Postmodern parents, harried and stressed out themselves, have become convinced that the stress on young people today is relatively minor, and that in any case mature children and sophisticated teenagers can handle it. In fact, as we have seen, children today are under much greater stresses than were children a generation or two ago, in part because the world is a more dangerous and complicated place to grow up in, and in part because their need to be protected, nurtured, and guided has been neglected. Adults who are subjected to stress beyond their ability to cope eventually become dysfunctional in some way. If we accept the discourse of stress, we must at least entertain the hypothesis that children and youth will react in a similar way. Young people whose needs for support and security have not been met, who have been falsely labeled as deviant, and who have no place to go are under stress. But what is the evidence that their long-term well-being is being threatened? Are children and teenagers in fact doing badly?

The phrase "new morbidity" was introduced by the pediatrician Robert J. Haggarty and his colleagues, who were examining data regarding the health and well-being of youth over the last half century. They observed that fifty years ago the leading cause of death among children and youth (the old morbidity) was disease. Fortunately, many of the diseases that once accounted for the majority of deaths among young people, such as tuberculosis and polio, have now been conquered by medical science.[20] Today, however, postmodern psychological and social pressures—what I have called the new imbalance—not physical disease, account for most of the deaths and illness among children and youth. And it is these stress-related illnesses and deaths that constitute the new postmodern morbidity.[21]

Although the new morbidity was originally formulated with respect to adolescent health, there is now a new morbidity at younger age levels as well. On every measure that we have, children and youth today are doing less well than they did hardly a quarter century ago. On tests of strength, endurance, and general muscle tone, young people today perform less well than did young people of comparable age even ten years ago. There has been a 50 percent increase in obesity in children and youth over the past twenty years. "Competent" children left on their own are spending too many hours in front of the television eating junk food.[22] Many of our curriculum-focused schools, in an effort to cut costs or to increase time spent on academic work, have eliminated recess. In such schools there is not time during the school day for young people to get up, run about, and play. Many schools have also eliminated hot meals cooked on the premises, in favor of reheated, unappetizing plastic-wrapped processed foods trucked in on carts. Other schools have eliminated lunch periods altogether: children are given ten minutes to eat lunch at their desk between periods. When children get home and turn on the TV, they are the targets for advertising that promotes high-calorie, high-fat foods low in nutritional content.

In the realm of academic achievement, we are also seeing the effects of the new imbalance. The postmodern perception of children as competent and teenagers as sophisticated has resulted in pushing advanced curricula down ever further into the lower grades. A teacher of high school chemistry at a private prep school told me that, thanks to parental pressure, he is now required to accept freshmen in a course he once taught exclusively for seniors. Although some of the brightest of the young students make it, many others do not. He says that the unsuccessful students, young men as well as young women, often break into tears of frustration.

At the same time that the curriculum is being pushed downward, however, students are not expected to do much homework, and even high school students spend more time watching television than they spend preparing schoolwork.[23] Forty percent of high school students watch television four to six hours a day, while hardly more than 10 percent spend more than two hours a day doing homework. The results are appalling. Recent surveys show that almost 50 percent of American adolescents are unable to perform such quantitative literacy tasks as balancing a checkbook or such document literacy tasks as reading a map. International comparisons are embarrassing. Eighth-grade American students place thirteenth in mathematics skills when compared with children from countries such as Korea, Switzerland, Canada, and Ireland.[24]

Scholastic Aptitude Test scores (SATs) for verbal aptitude among American youth have fallen almost fifty points since the late 1950s.[25] Yet paradoxically, most students at all socioeconomic levels feel under enormous pressure to achieve academically. Somehow, the stress they feel never gets translated into more time and effort devoted to schoolwork, nor into improved test scores.

The effects of the new imbalance is perhaps most striking in the area of substance abuse. Many young people deal with stress in the same way that many adults do, namely, by using substances such as alcohol or other drugs. The use of drugs by children and youth is a good index of the new imbalance and the pressures young people are experiencing. Substance abuse has increased markedly, and the percentage of students using drugs by the sixth grade has *tripled* since 1975.[26] Children often begin their acquaintance with alcohol by drinking wine coolers, next progress to beer and wine, and then to hard liquor. Many young people have little awareness of the alcoholic contents of what they are drinking or its effects.[27]

We now know that some people have a genetic predisposition to alcoholism. We also know that teenagers' bodies process alcohol differently than do adult bodies. This difference is such that a teenager with a predisposition to alcoholism can become addicted in a matter of months, whereas it might take years had the person started drinking at a later age. We now have more than two million alcoholic teenagers in this country.[28] It is truly heartrending to listen to a young woman, aged beyond her years, tell me that she has to have a beer as soon as she gets out of bed in the morning, or she can't function.

Besides sometimes leading to addiction, substance abuse contributes in other ways to the new morbidity. Alcohol-related accidents are the leading cause of death for Americans between fifteen and twenty-four years old, either as passengers or drivers.[29] The time pattern of these accidents is very telling. Most of these car crashes occur on Friday and Saturday nights between 9 p.m. and 4 a.m. in the morning. Although a number of programs have been initiated at the high school and community levels to prevent drinking and driving, the number of accidents continues at a high rate.

Suicide rates for teenagers have doubled since 1968. Overall, 10 percent of adolescent boys and 18 percent of adolescent girls have attempted suicide. Recent surveys suggest that one in five teenagers has contemplated suicide. Although the figures are low in absolute terms, there has also been a doubling of the suicide rate among elementary school-age children over the past twenty years.[30] As a clinician who once worked with courageous child cancer patients eager for every moment of life, I feel outrage when I hear a battered five-year-old say "I don't want to live anymore."

The United States has the highest teenage pregnancy rates of any Western country, twice that of England, the next highest country.[31] About one million teenage girls get pregnant each year. Close to half of these young women carry their babies to term. Yet, because the pelvic girdle of young teenage girls has not yet reached full size and because in many instances they do not get the prenatal care they need, both the young mother and the infant are often at considerable health risk.

And the age of teenage girls becoming pregnant is declining, in part a result of the increased sexual activity of young teenagers. Only about 33 percent of teenagers use contraceptives, and then they may use them irregularly. In addition, the sooner a teenage girl becomes sexually active after attaining menstruation, the more likely she is to become accidentally pregnant. The percentage of teenagers who are sexually active, the early age at which they become active, and their failure to use protection all contribute to the high rate of teenage pregnancy. It is estimated that at least 25 percent of all young women of fourteen years of age in the United States will be pregnant at least once before they leave the teen years.[32]

The incidence of sexually transmitted diseases among young people has reached epidemic proportions. According to data from office-based, for-fee services, the number of visits of women age fifteen to nineteen years old increased for both genital warts and herpes. For genital herpes the increase went from 15,000 in 1966 to 125,000 in 1988. For genital warts the numbers were 50,000 in 1966 and 300,000 in 1988.[33] Some 2.5 million teenagers have had a sexually transmitted disease and one in four sexually active teenagers will contract an STD before leaving high school. Although teenagers are most concerned about contracting AIDS, only about one percent of reported AIDS cases are adolescents. Adolescents are much more likely to contract chlamydia (the most common form of STD and one which causes high rates of infertility in women), genital warts, herpes, gonorrhea, and syphilis than they are to contract the HIV virus. On the other hand, adolescents may be the most vulnerable group for contracting AIDS in the future.

Unfortunately, many supposedly "sophisticated" teenagers subscribe to erroneous ideas (such as the "quick withdrawal" method) about what measures will prevent sexually transmitted diseases. Even with accurate information, many teenagers still believe in the personal fable of their own invulnerability.[34] That is to say, during the early adolescent years, teenagers tend to think that they are special and unique and that they are cloaked in a shield of invulnerability that will prevent them from the harm that may well come to others.

Teenage crime is also on the increase and is another cause of stress among young people. When I met with a group of middle school students who were graduating and getting ready for high school, they surprised me with their concerns. I had supposed they would be worried about the work, about the academic pressure and the lack of the security of a "home room" from which to leave and return. Yet what the young people were most afraid of was the violence in the high school, the fear of being beat up or sexually assaulted. And I have heard the same fears expressed by young people living in the suburbs as well as in the cities.

And violence there is. Homicides in the fifteen- to nineteen-year-old age group increased by 75 percent between 1985 and 1990. Youths sixteen to nineteen suffer the highest assault-with-weapon rate, followed by those age twelve to fifteen. The violence has grown so bold that now young people are assaulted at school. In Massachusetts recently, a young man was shot to death while he was sitting in a social studies classroom. Every day 135,000 American students bring guns to school.[35] In addition to violent crime, it is estimated that millions of lesser crimes, such as theft and assault, are committed in our schools each year. The number of teenagers fourteen to seventeen years old arrested per year has increased nearly thirty-fold since 1950.

These terrible effects of the new imbalance are receiving increasing attention from both individuals and groups. In her book *When the Bough Breaks,* Sylvia Ann Hewlett documents the new morbidity with many case histories. She begins her book with this sweeping description of the effects of the new imbalance, although she does not use that phrase:

> Across the face of America, children are failing to flourish. Rich kids, middle-class kids, poor kids—all deal with risk and neglect on a scale unimagined in previous generations. Problems of poverty, divorce, out-of-wedlock births, absentee parents, latchkey kids, violence, and drugs are no longer confined to the ghetto. They reach deep into the mainstream, they belong to "us" as well as to "them." Child

neglect has become endemic in our society, and childhood is now "far more precarious and less safe" for millions of America's children. In the words of a 1990 National Commission, "never before has one generation of American children been less healthy, less cared for, or less prepared for life than their parents were at the same age." According to an index that measures the social health of children and youth, the well-being of children has declined dramatically over the last twenty years. In 1970 the index stood at 68; by 1987 it had plummeted to 37.[36]

Similar dismal reports have been made with respect to the education of youth:

> In 1987, nearly 1 million young people will leave the nation's public schools without graduating. Most of them will be deficient in basic skills, marginally literate and virtually unemployable. Another 700,000 will merely mark time in school and receive diplomas that will be as deficient in meaningful skills and work habits as most dropouts.
>
> Currently, fewer than 50 percent of high school seniors read at levels considered adequate for carrying out even moderately complex tasks, and 80 percent have inadequate writing skills. In a recent international study comparing mathematics skills in twenty nations, U.S. youngsters made a mediocre showing at best. Not only are our schools failing to develop basic skills, they are also failing to develop the higher-order skills needed for the new information age.[37]

These frightening statistics speak to the negative impact of the new imbalance upon children and youth in postmodern society. As we have seen, the need imbalances that are producing these dysfunctional behaviors originate in the family, the media, the schools, the legal system, and even the helping professions. We are dealing with a large-scale social phenomenon that will not be remedied by simple measures or by quick fixes. Drug and sex education is important, but it does not get at the root cause of drug abuse and reckless sexual activity. Reducing the amount of indiscriminate violence on television and in films will not in itself reduce the violence in our streets. To attack these problems effectively, we have to make changes in all of the institutions that impact upon the family.

There is some evidence that the extent of the damage being done to our children and youth is finally impelling us to action. In the next chapter I will describe a new family form that is emerging, in keeping with changes in other social institutions—a kind of family that is beginning to redress the postmodern imbalance. Only when all of the institutions that impact upon the family, as well as the family itself, begin to pay more attention to the needs of children and youth will we see a decline in the new morbidity.

A New Balance

10

The Vital Family

Adherents of the modern nuclear family have difficulty seeing any of the positive contributions made by the postmodern permeable family, and champions of the postmodern family have just as much trouble acknowledging any of the virtues of the modern family. On the modern side, for example, one respected scholar of the family, David Popenoe, argues, as I have here, that the current state of the American family is a serious problem, particularly for children and youth. The family has a set number of functions, according to Popenoe, and as these are given up, the family must necessarily decline in importance for child life.[1]

What this analysis does not take into account is an overall function that the family has always performed and that it continues to perform today, namely, preparing its members for life in the larger society. Granted, families are not doing as good a job as they may once have done, but this is as much a matter of rapid social change as it is a matter of family decline. Families change as society changes; when that change is rapid, it may be hard for the family to keep pace, and dislocations may result.

Adherents of the permeable family are equally negative about the nuclear family. While writers like Judith Stacey do not deny that "far too many children today suffer serious deprivations or that most children and [their relatives] could benefit from massive infusions of the loving attention that Ozzie and Harriet families have come to represent," she considers the plight of children and youth today to be a failure of social policy, not of the family. The emergence of the postmodern family is, for her, a positive rather than a negative development.

> I believe that no positivist definition of the family, however revisionist, is viable. Anthropological and historical studies convince me that the family is not an institution, but an ideological, symbolic construct that has a history and a politics . . . This concept has been employed primarily to signify a heterosexual, conjugal, nuclear, domestic unit, ideally with one male primary breadwinner and a female primary homemaker, and their dependent offspring. This unitary, normative definition of legitimate domestic arrangements is what my book identifies as ephemeral and with little regret, because of the race, class, gender, and sexual diversity it has occluded and the inequities it has exacerbated.[2]

In many ways, these two writers reflect the values of the old and the new imbalance that have been the major theme of this book. Popenoe regards the old imbalance, wherein society was child-centered and adult needs were subordinated to those of the young, as preferable to the new imbalance. Stacey regards the new imbalance, wherein the adult concerns of race, class, and gender diversity are voiced and supported, as superior to the old imbalance. My own position, argued throughout this book, is that there is much to value, and much to deplore, in both nuclear and permeable families. It really is not a matter of *either* permeable *or* nuclear but rather how we can combine the best of both. In my view, we are moving—stumbling might be a better verb—toward this type of integration.

Within any given historical period, there will be as many family forms as there are major societal upheavals. In America during the early modern era, the extended family predominated because the majority of families lived on farms and because, among other things, leaving home and settling elsewhere was more difficult than it is today. The industrial revolution brought families to the city and permanently altered the structure of family life. The nuclear family was the end result of that late modern adaptation.

We are seeing something similar today. The permeable family should perhaps be understood as an early adaptation to the changes that have been labeled postmodern. As we move further along, continuing changes in society are forcing the permeable family to alter itself more rapidly than was true for the transformation from extended to nuclear family. As a social movement, postmodernism aims at revising and modifying some of the exaggerations, idealizations, and conceits of the modern era. It has, nonetheless, created dislocations of its own that are bringing about some of their own self-corrections.

It is within the context of the ongoing, self-corrective character of postmodernism that still another family form is emerging, one we might call the vital family. *A family is vital to the extent that it energizes and nurtures the abilities and talents of both children and their parents.* In so doing, it redresses the new imbalance by weighing the needs of children and youth more evenly with those of parents and other adults. The vital family still takes many different kinship forms, from the traditional nuclear pattern to that of single parents, adoptive families, blended families, and more. What distinguishes the vital family is its emphasis on lifespan human development—its recognition that both children and adults undergo continuous change and growth—and its adaptive melding of unilateral and mutual authority.

Sentiments of the Vital Family

It seems fair to say that in the 1980s we experienced still a third sexual revolution brought about by AIDS. This disease has now been reported in all parts of the world. The World Health Organization (WHO) estimates that as of mid-1993, worldwide, over 13 million young people and adults have become infected with HIV, the virus causing the disease. The majority have contracted this illness through sexual intercourse, but at least a million children have contracted the disease prenatally. Over 1.5 million cases of AIDS have been reported in North America and Western Europe. To date, some 2 million HIV-infected adults have developed AIDS, and most of them have died.[3]

Researchers now recognize that HIV may act directly as well as indirectly on the immune system and that there may be a family of viruses and not just one. Moreover, some drugs (such as AZT) that were thought to stave off the disease have not been proven very effective. It does not appear that there will be a preventive vaccine or drug cure anytime soon.[4]

The prevalence of AIDS has brought about a significant change in sexual behavior, particularly casual sex, and in attitudes toward consensual love. But other factors have also contributed to this modification. Many young people whose parents have divorced are worried that their relationships might end in a similar manner. They are becoming more cautious about getting married, because they see the step as more serious than a mere social contract. That is one reason the age of marriage has increased to about twenty-five for young women and twenty-seven for young men.

Some of the more recent television programs and films portray families that have stuck together when things got rough, rather than splitting apart. Among books, the phenomenal success of M. Scott Peck's *The Road Less Traveled,* which advocates the rewards of putting in the time and effort needed to make relationships work, points toward a new appreciation of commitment.[5] Peck argues that relationships are not made in heaven, nor by a contractual arrangement, but by an ongoing effort to confront and resolve differences, to communicate openly, and to accept and support each partner's continuing growth and development.

This form of love might be called *committed love.* Many young people who have experienced the trauma of their parents' divorce want a more abiding relationship for themselves and are more likely to commit themselves to the marital vows than was true for people who married when consensual love was a fresh and very attractive idea, and before the AIDS epidemic erupted. Not all committed relationships will be abiding, of course, but these couples at least start out with the understanding that lasting relationships have to be worked at and are neither inherently given nor contractually guaranteed.

Committed love also brings together the unilateral aspects of romantic love with the mutual aspects of consensual love. That is to say, romantic love was often unilateral in the sense that it often involved the one-sided idealization of one partner by the other. With consensual love both individuals are on an equal footing. When a couple moves to committed love, however, the unilateral and mutual love relations are subsumed under a higher-order relationship. There is a willingness to subordinate the "I" and the "Me" to the "We" and the "Us."

This higher-order commitment does not exclude, but rather incorporates, the other types of relationship. It remains unilateral in some respects: maybe one partner makes all the decisions about maintaining the family automobiles, and the other makes all of the decisions about grocery shopping and weekly menus. But the relationship continues to be mutual in that both have a say in deciding what kind of car to buy and whom to invite over for a dinner party. Committed love thus incorporates and builds upon both unilateral and mutual authority relationships; the result is what might be called *appropriate authority.* Each person exercises unilateral authority in certain areas, depending on the individual interests and talents of the two people involved. But they make many mutual decisions together, about issues both large and small.

The permeable family sentiment of shared parenting also seems to be undergoing a transformation. During the early years of the women's movement, many mothers felt political and social pressure to go to work even when they might have personally preferred to stay home with their young children. Now that many of the battles to widen the opportunities of women have been joined, if not won, there is less pressure to pursue a career just for the sake of being a role model. Symbols and appearances seem less important to young women today. Many college women who subscribe to the values of the women's movement do not regard themselves as "feminists."[6]

One consequence of the successes of the women's movement is what might be called the sentiment of *authentic parenting*. Now that working or staying home, or some combination of the two, are all seen as socially acceptable and worthwhile options, parents can be themselves, rather than what they believe they should be. Many new mothers have told me that when their baby was born it was like a "hurricane" or an "earthquake." They did not know what had happened to them. They were wildly, desperately, in love. It tore them apart when they had to be separated from their babies, and the infants were constantly in their thoughts. When the sentiment of shared parenting was the ideal, many mothers denied this attachment and continued working. Today, many more mothers accept this romance and are willing to take a year or two off to be with their babies. They no longer feel they are deserting their gender in so doing.

Fathers are beginning to engage in authentic parenting as well. Now that the first wave of shared parenting is over, fathers no longer have to make a "show" of their parenting activities as public proof of their postmodern male sensitivity. Young fathers today seem much more relaxed in their role as caregivers. They are trying less to prove something to others (and to themselves) than they are taking pleasure in the childcare itself.

It must be said, however, that authentic parenting is producing its own stresses for some marriages. A number of couples I have spoken with who had their first child, or children, in their late thirties were in considerable conflict. Their wish to be authentic parents was competing with their equally authentic commitment to career goals and ambitions.

Authentic parenting, like commitment, integrates unilateral and mutual authority. In the nuclear family, unilateral authority was generally the rule, whereas in the permeable family, mutual authority is most common. Granted that both types of authority are more effective when administered with love, how are the two to be apportioned? While there are no absolute guidelines, in general, authentic parents use unilateral authority when it comes to manners, morals, and values, and they employ mutual authority when it comes to matters of taste, preference, and style. For example, parents need to teach children when to say "please," "thank you," and so on. Manners cannot be left to mutual authority. In the same way, children have to be taught not to hit other children nor to take their candy or toys. On the other hand, as children mature they should be given freedom of choice in matters of taste and preference. At the dinner table, or when eating out, a child's choice of food should be respected. Likewise, children should help decide which musical instrument they would like to play. Authentic parents, therefore, use authority appropriately and in the context of a loving, caring, and accepting relationship.

Other societal changes are also moving us beyond the permeable sentiment of urbanity. The sentiment of urbanity made us more sensitive to the diversity and heterogeneity of our society and the need to value, rather than discourage, these differences. The multicultural curricula in our schools, provisions for people with disabilities, and the close-captioned presentations on television for the hearing impaired are but a few examples of how the sentiment of urbanity, as expressed in the acceptance of diversity, is echoed in the larger society. While urbanity has sensitized us to differences, we now need to begin to integrate these differences through a new sentiment of *community*. In a sense, the community is a larger family to which all its members owe a certain amount of loyalty and commitment. The sense of community recognizes that, despite our ethnic, racial, and socioeconomic differences, we share common goals, aspirations, and responsibilities with other families.

There are a number of social evidences of a new community sentiment. Across America, many schools have made community service an important part of their curriculum. While in some states community service is an extracurricular activity, in others it has become part of the requirements for graduation. Maryland, for example, has mandated that all school districts offer credit for volunteer service. In Vermont, high school students may use community service to fulfill the requirement to complete a research or citizenship project. In cities like Detroit and Atlanta, time spent in community service is a prerequisite for graduation. Nationally, some fifty Youth Corps programs enable young people to acquire skills that will enhance their employability while at the same time providing useful community service.[7]

Communities are also reaching out to the less fortunate, with programs for teenage mothers, for addicted mothers, and for parents with children at risk. In Boston, for example, a program called New Day serves pregnant women and new mothers who are, or were, addicted. In addition to providing childcare and parenting instruction, the program also provides treatment for substance abuse. Project Even Start offers literacy instruction for parents and children for whom English is a second language. Other publicly funded groups assist parents in finding appropriate placements for their children with special needs. Many communities also have clearing centers that help parents find quality childcare.

Parents show their sense of community in many different ways. In a number of cities and suburbs around the country, "mother clubs" have been formed to provide support and share experience and information. Likewise, the mother who heads a cub scout group, or the father who coaches soccer or Little League, is a commonplace example of the sentiment of community. Often these parents have their own children in the group and thus provide a sports program both for their own children and for other youngsters from the neighborhood. It is a nice example of how parents can combine a service to their children with a service to the larger community. Other parents, and increasingly grandparents, are volunteering as teacher aides and individual tutors. A sense of community also often emerges among parents whose children attend the same childcare facility over several years. Many parents befriend the parents of their children's friends and continue to socialize outside the school environment.

Postmodern communities are not just geographic. There are now electronic communities with nationwide bulletin boards and message centers. Via the Internet, Compuserve, Prodigy, and other information systems, individuals far removed from one another can communicate on a daily basis. Unfortunately, some people become so addicted to these electronic communities that they distance themselves from their nearby human communities. There are also radio communities with a proliferation of call-in shows, from the responsible and informative *Talk of the Nation* on National Public Radio to the shows which give voice to communities of prejudice and insularity. Like all communities, these new high-tech gathering places have both their positive and negative sides. What they all demonstrate, however, is our deep-seated human need for a sense of community.

To be sure, the vital sentiment of community is far less widespread than it needs to be, but it is becoming more socially "in" than rugged autonomy. The sentiment of community is also in keeping with the use of appropriate authority. Community involvement allows for both mutual and unilateral authority. Working cooperatively on fund drives for community projects is clearly a mutual endeavor. On the other hand, if a community decides, as a number have decided, to institute a curfew for young people, the whole community cooperates, even though individual families may not agree with the policy.

Values of the Vital Family

The nuclear family value of togetherness in some ways emphasized the dependence of family members on one another. In contrast, the permeable family sentiment of autonomy underlined the independence of family members. Thanks to the new sentiments of committed love, authentic parenting, and community, a new recognition is emerging of our *interdependence,* both as family members and as members of the larger community. The value of interdependence embodies the values of dependence and independence but goes beyond them in its appreciation that neither is possible without an abiding interdependence.

The value of interdependence is increasingly being accepted and put into play in the larger society. Among the helping professions one sees a growing recognition that the one-sided "self-actualization" and "looking out for Number One" mentality may be dysfunctional for the individual as well as for society.[8] Likewise, in industry, the classical input-process-output (IPO) model (which assumed autonomous units for design, manufacturing, and marketing) is being replaced by computer-driven horizontal *workflow* models that take as given that these units are necessarily interdependent. In companies where such models obtain, every member of the organization can operate as both a "customer" and a "performer," depending upon the transaction. According to the *Economist:* "Workflow has . . . given IBM intriguing insights into the integrity, trust and morale of employees. And, whereas IPO methods had helped individuals feel responsible (by setting out their job descriptions and so on), workflow encourages all employees to take initiatives and co-ordinate their actions themselves."[9]

Similar horizontal models of management are being introduced into our schools. The major initiatives of this kind are the School Development Program, begun by James Comer, a Yale psychiatrist, with more than 150 schools; the Accelerated Schools Program, introduced by Henry Levin, a Stanford educator and economist, with about 300 schools; and the Coalition for Essential Schools, led by Theodore Sizer, dean of education at Brown University, with about 200 schools. All of these programs emphasize the individuality of schools, and the need for parents, teachers, and administrators to break down traditional role barriers to arrive at common goals and to share authority.[10] Our strong national tendency toward individualism is still powerful and valuable, but economics, if nothing else, is forcing us to balance individualism with cooperation.

This new recognition of our interdependence is also evident in the 1990s media portrayal of families. While these families provide glimpses of modern togetherness and of postmodern autonomy, the focus is very much on interdependence. Here is the way *Time* magazine described the fall 1993 programs:

> The 28 Fall shows announced by ABC, CBS and NBC over the past two weeks . . . are a conservative, back-to-basics bunch. The theme is old-fashioned, mass-audience entertainment, the kinds of shows the whole family can watch. Sitcoms this fall will favor tight-knit family units rather than funny working places, acerbic yuppies or angst-ridden teens. No quirky small towns, few hard-edged action shows and, surprisingly, only two new series with blacks in leading roles (though several from last year's bumper crop are returning).[11]

A similar trend can be observed in the films of the early 1990s, as described by the *Economist:*

> Qualities long absent from Hollywood pictures are making a dramatic comeback. In line with the new puritanism, the big studios are moving away from the sordid sex, violence and swearing that dominated movies in the 1980's and reverting to foursquare adaptations of literary classics old and new, many of them set in a guileless past.
>
> Symptomatic of the change is that Martin Scorsese—a director whose name with films such as *Mean Streets, Taxi Driver,* and *Good Fellas,* was most closely associated with the tone of brute force and profanity—has harked back in his latest film to the 19th century. It is an adaptation of the most famous novel by Edith Wharton—for which she won a Pulitzer Prize in 1921—and is most appropriately called *The Age of Innocence.*[12]

The value of interdependence not only integrates nuclear-family togetherness with permeable-family autonomy, it also brings together the unilateral and mutual authority relationships of the earlier family forms. In nuclear families, togetherness was a unilateral subordination of self to family. By contrast, in permeable families autonomy was a relation of mutuality—each person looks out for himself and expects other family members to do the same. Once we have attained the value of interdependence, we recognize that these two directions of caring and authority are not mutually exclusive but rather part of a larger whole. Interdependence is founded on a sense of being both one and many, of being both different from everyone else and like them at the same time. This value of interdependence thus supports the vital family members in their appropriate use of both unilateral and mutual authority.

Perceptions of the Vital Family

As the vital sentiments of committed love, authentic parenting, community, and interdependence become more common, they are affecting our perceptions of parents. To be sure, the perception of parents as in need of techniques is still very strong, and the stream of "How-to" books is unabated. Yet there is an enlarging awareness of the importance of knowledge about child development as well as technique. Books that emphasize development such as those by Selma Fraiberg, Penelope Leach, Benjamin Spock, and T. Berry Brazelton have outlived the "How-to" books and, if anything, are growing in popularity.[13]

In addition, school-sponsored programs such as Parents as Teachers, which is in operation in more than fourteen states, are training parents in their homes about child growth and development as well as about effective parenting techniques. Parent-training programs are now present in all states and come in many different forms, from early intervention for parents with children at risk to programs for prospective mothers.

Increasingly, parents are beginning to combine a concern with technique with an understanding of child development. Magazines such as *Parents* and *Parenting* have monthly sections that deal with issues common to children at different age levels. Other parenting magazines are copying this feature, and more and more books are combining a focus on development with suggestions regarding technique. The combination of child development information and technique encourages parents to engage in what might be called *creative parenting.* Parents can combine technique and child development in original ways, in keeping with their unique personalities and their child's personal disposition.

Many postmodern parents, of course, still rely much too heavily on technique and do not improvise as much as they might. Nonetheless, as parents begin to get more information about child development as well as about techniques, there will be many more opportunities for creative parenting. This is particularly true as parents feel more authentic in their role. As parents sense that they can be genuinely themselves, they will also feel more confident and secure about their parenting. This will encourage them to combine, in creative and innovative ways, their knowledge of technique with their knowledge about children in general and with their special understanding of their own unique child.

Creative parenting thus results in new childrearing strategies that are at once unilateral in coming from the parent but mutual in their respect for the child's level of mental ability and his or her particular needs and interests. They are developmentally appropriate strategies.

I see some encouraging signs that we are beginning to change our perception of children as well as parents, though we are far from being there yet. In the recent movie *Sandlot,* boys are depicted as playing baseball without adult supervision; getting into trouble with a neighbor; getting sick from chewing tobacco; and beating a neighborhood team. While the movie is set in the modern era, it nonetheless reflects a new recognition of the importance of preserving childhood as a special period of life. It also highlights the value and importance of child-initiated and child-run activities.

The agreement of some television producers to limit the amount of violence in their programs and to offer objectional shows at a later hour are other small steps in the direction of preserving childhood as a protected time. The growing concern about violence and about the dangers of guns in the hands of children and youth has led to the passage of the Brady Bill and to programs such as Toys for Guns and Premiums for Guns aimed at getting guns off the streets.

We are beginning to look at children as *growing in competence*, but as not fully competent in all domains. In the educational field, this new perception of children has been introduced under the term "developmentally appropriate practice."[14] The concept of developmentally appropriate practice resurrects some of John Dewey's ideas of progressive education and combines them with knowledge about mental development provided by the work of Jean Piaget. It argues that the curriculum must be adapted to the growing needs, abilities, and interests of children.

In British Columbia, the entire school system—from kindergarten to grade thirteen (they have a thirteenth high school grade in Canada)—is going to developmentally appropriate practice. Team teaching, portfolios of the child's work, and product assessment are being encouraged, and grades and testing are being used only sparingly. In Kentucky, the state has mandated "multiage" grouping in the early grades, which encourages flexible curricula and thus reinforces developmentally appropriate practice. Multiage classroom groupings are being introduced in local public schools in cities as large as Cambridge, Massachusetts, and in small towns like Scarborough, Maine. In other communities, developmentally appropriate Montessori programs have been incorporated into several public schools as an option for parents. Small steps, but they are something.

At a more general level, other events will perhaps help to take some of the academic pressures off of our schools and our children. Japan's current economic difficulties and our own economic resurgence may quiet some of those who argued that our educational system was the reason for our failure to compete with Japan. In Japan the educational philosophy is "The nail that sticks up gets hammered down," while in America it is "The squeaky wheel gets the grease." And in fact it is the flexibility and openness of our educational system, its emphasis on helping each child attain the best of his or her talents and abilities, that is at the heart of our adaptability as a nation and the basis for our continued economic and social success.

Indeed, even some of the comparisons in educational achievement between our students and those in Japan and other countries have been shown to be misleading.[15] We can, and must, do better educationally, but not by copying Japan or any other country. We will improve when we focus on what we do best, gearing our educational standards and goals to the developing needs and interests of children and youth. The programs mentioned earlier that have been initiated by Comer, Levin, and Sizer are all of this kind. They encourage flexible programming, child- and teacher-created curricula, and portfolios of students' work in combination with a circumscribed use of testing and grades.

The move toward accepting a perception of children as growing in competence will reinforce parents and teachers in their efforts to employ appropriate authority. That is to say, it will permit us to see that children are, in many cases, in need of adult guidance, direction, rules, and limits (unilateral authority). But it will also enable us to appreciate that there are times and circumstances when children should have choices and make a contribution to familial or classroom decisionmaking (mutual authority). Hence, the vital family perception of children as growing in competence encourages and supports the employment of creative parenting, the practice of developmentally appropriate teaching, and the use of appropriate authority.

Unfortunately, the evidence for a new perception of adolescence is less compelling than the evidence for a new perception of parents and children, but there is some. Interestingly, a number of examples come from college campuses as much as from high schools. More and more universities and colleges are returning to *loco parentis* and are providing organized activities for their students. This is in contrast with a decade ago, when students were left pretty much to their own devices, on the assumption that they were sophisticated and fully capable of organizing their own social lives. After years of having to take students to the hospital every weekend for detoxification, colleges and universities now recognize that even young adults can benefit from some adult-organized activities. Many colleges and universities now take the initiative in organizing rock concerts, field-trips, and other social events.

At the high school level, the needs of low-income, nonmainstream students for adult mentors are beginning to be addressed. Many communities now link at-risk teenagers with adults who offer support, guidance, and tutoring as preparation for employment or college. The national black fraternity Kappa Alpha Psi, with support from the Urban League, matches fraternity brothers with inner-city boys ages eleven to fifteen. The college students serve as Big Brothers, tutoring their charges, coaching them in recreational activities, and engaging them in community service. Such programs clearly recognize that adolescents are *growing in sophistication* but are not fully there yet.

Large urban schools, too, are beginning to appreciate the need of adolescents for more personal recognition than is possible in the comprehensive high schools. In Manhattan, the New Visions project divides large high schools into smaller, more manageable units of 500 students each. These smaller units make it possible for students and teachers to know one another much better, and this enhances the sense of community. At the same time there is also recognition that in some ways today's young people are more sophisticated than those in the past. In Minnesota, eleventh- and twelfth-grade students are allowed to take some, or all, college-level courses.

In keeping with the Minnesota initiative and the new perception of young people, I believe that a reorganization of our high schools is long overdue. Teenagers are different today from what they were when the present high school format was introduced. The current structure presupposes adolescent immaturity and makes little provision for the postmodern sophistication of young people. It is certainly true that the introduction of school health clinics and sex and drug education speak to the new sophistication of adolescents. But something more radical is needed. Young people see themselves as mature in many ways, and in many ways they are. This might be recognized by making the high school, at least grades eleven and twelve, more like a junior college. Giving young people more freedom and responsibility for their own learning is one way of recognizing that postmodern adolescents are indeed sophisticated in some ways.

As with the perception of children as growing in competence, the perception of adolescents as growing in sophistication allows for the integration of the unilateral and mutual authority relationships. Once adolescents are perceived as growing in sophistication, there is room both for the unilateral laying down of rules and limits and for mutual agreement on many matters of taste and interest. Looking at adolescents as growing in sophistication is thus congruent with the perception of creative parenting that combines intuition and technique, unilateral and mutual authority.

In describing the emergence of the vital family, I realize that I have proposed a rather ideal pattern not unlike that of the nuclear family ideal. Yet this model, I hope, leaves room for much greater diversity, particularity, and irregularity than was true for the nuclear family. Moreover, although the vital family incorporates what is beneficial in both the nuclear and the permeable family, it is not superior to them—only different. Human diversity is such that the nuclear family is best suited to some, the permeable family to others, and the vital family to still others. My hope is, however, that the increasing presence of the vital family, and its reflection by the schools, media, legal system, and helping professions, will moderate both nuclear and permeable sentiments. Put differently, my hope is that the prevalence of the vital family will help redress the need imbalance in *all* families.

Reducing the Stress on Children and Youth

As I have argued throughout this book, changes in the family will come about only when there are corresponding changes in the social institutions that impact upon the family. And, as I tried to demonstrate in the preceding section, this is indeed beginning to happen, albeit slowly. In the meantime, the needs of many millions of children and adolescents continue to go unmet, with the resulting stress and the perpetuation of the new morbidity.

Are there some ways that we, as individuals as well as members of social institutions, can contribute to reducing some of the extraordinary demands upon children and youth? I believe that there are, and in this closing section I want to elaborate on what we can do *now*, individually and collectively, to refurbish the conception of child and adolescent development; to expand the range of normality for children and adolescents; and to provide more space for young people to play, work, and socialize.

It is my firm belief that the most important single thing we can do—as parents, teachers, and health professionals—is to *reinvent our adulthood*. Perhaps because of the heady discovery of the stages of adulthood, and the parallel denigration of the stages of childhood and adolescence, the all-important sense of difference between children and adults has diminished. Too often today, I encounter situations where parents appear to be afraid of their children. At an airport recently, I heard a little girl's voice behind me say, "Leave me alone, I told you not to bother me." Thinking she was talking to a younger sibling, or to her doll, I looked around to discover that she was talking to her mother. Her mother looked cowed by her daughter's assertiveness. This mother does neither her child nor herself a good service by not making it very clear to her daughter that a mother is not to be addressed in such a manner.

Children are the young of the species and, like the young of all species, they need adult guidance, direction, and protection. While we cannot reinvent adulthood for everyone, we can do it for ourselves as parents, teachers, and health professionals. At Tufts University, I teach the large undergraduate course in child development. The first day of class students are given a syllabus that tells them the readings, the term paper requirements, the due dates, and the penalties for late papers. I also tell the students that they are free to chat with one another, but not in my class; that they are free to catch up on their sleep, but not in my class; and that they are free to read the newspaper, but not in my class. Throughout the semester if anyone breaks these rules, I stop the classroom proceedings until the rules are again in force. I should not have to teach good manners to college students, but I regard it as my adult responsibility to the majority of students who are obeying the rules. I should say, too, that students never address me by my first name. It is certainly not my place to tell other faculty how to run their classes, but in my own classes I can certainly exercise my unilateral authority.

Asserting one's adultness does not mean being an ogre or a drill sergeant. It does mean that we appreciate that children, adolescents, and even young adults may not yet have a set of internalized rules and standards, nor a good set of controls over their emotions and behavior. The only way they are going to get these internalized rules and standards is from us. Yes, young people may not like us when we set rules and standards, and that is too bad. When we worry about our children liking us, however, we put our needs ahead of our children's needs. When we try to be pals with our children instead of parents, we deprive them of their most important source of internal rules, limits, standards, and controls. Our abrogation of the responsibilities of adulthood is the single most powerful contributor to the new imbalance and to the stress that imbalance puts on children.

A second action we can take is to attend to, and appreciate, each child's uniqueness. This was much easier to do in the modern era, when children were regarded as innocent, than it is today, when children are regarded as competent. The notion of competence suggests the possession of skills and knowledge that can be assessed and compared to some external standard. Too many parents and too many educators today are so concerned about the age at which their children begin reading, or doing math, or using the computer that they sometimes miss the child for the skills. It is in this way that we have narrowed the range of normality for children both at home and at school.

We can do a number of things as parents to rediscover the uniqueness and specialty of each of our children. When my sons were young and I was doing a lot of traveling, they took turns accompanying me on trips. At these times, we had the opportunity to really get to know one another. Even without traveling, parents can find opportunities to know their children as individuals. Shopping and recreational trips can be individualized so that every child gets his or her turn to have time alone with one or both parents. Attending to, and supporting, each child's individual interests and inclinations is another way of appreciating his or her individuality. As parents and teachers we need to emphasize who our children *are* and what they *can* do, rather than who they are *not*, and what they *cannot* do. By focusing on each child as a unique and special person we help expand the range of normality for all young people.

There are things that can be done at school as well. I believe that the now largely abandoned daily or weekly circle meetings of the whole class are valuable and should be reinstituted, particularly at the elementary school level. In the circle meeting each child has an opportunity to talk about a personal project, family activity, or event that is meaningful to him or her. Something comparable is valuable even at the college level. In the Community Field Placement course that I teach on occasion, the entire class period is spent with each student talking in turn about the events of the preceding week at his or her field placement. Such talking is an important mode of learning. Indeed, John Dewey wrote that "learning is the re-presentation of experience." When children or youth talk about their experiences (re-present them), they and the other students learn about, and come to appreciate, the wide range of normal variation among their peers.

A final action we can take to redress the new imbalance is to begin to share our adult spaces with children and youth. This is not easy. Our sense of self and identity has a strong territorial component. Most wars are fought, in whole or part, over the possession of land. The current confrontations in Israel and the former Yugoslavia are good examples of the close link between identity and territory. The same holds true for our individual work, play, and home spaces. As postmodern adults, we keenly appreciate our need for a home study, for an exercise area, and for a place to pursue one or another hobby. It is more difficult for us to understand that children need their special spaces, too. But they do. Whenever possible, we should set aside some place in our homes, other than the child's room, that is exclusively for the child's use and outfitted with his or her own activity material. Even in small homes, a reading or quiet corner with large pillows on the floor, books, and tape player can give children a sense of their own place.

In schools there are ways to give children a sense of their own space as well. Many experienced teachers begin the school year with a relatively empty classroom and proceed to fill it during the year with the children's own work. In this way it becomes the children's room and not just the teacher's. Parents need to join together and fight for the reinstatement of recess and outdoor time. Children are not built to be sitting all day; they need to run about, climb, play, and build. Many schools have well-outfitted and protected areas that are very much underused. But these are safe children's spaces, and children should have access to them not just during the school day but after school and over the weekends as well.

In many European countries, there are child areas in public places. One morning, while having breakfast at a harborside hotel in Helsinki, I heard a rumbling sound that I could not identify. I looked around and there was a child's play area right in the restaurant. All over Scandinavia one finds similar child play areas on ferries, in railway stations, and at airports. We would not have to give up too much adult space to put play areas in our own transportation centers. If we did this, we would be relieved of the intrusion of children running and yelling down the corridors of airports and train stations. Healthy children are active children, and we need to provide places for them to run and play.

With respect to adolescents, is it really impossible to set aside some space in our malls exclusively for teenagers? Is it really too much to ask that our golf courses, our tennis courts, and our health clubs be opened to adolescents at specified times reserved for them? I know the fear is that young people will destroy these facilities. Yet when I attend rock concerts with my sons, I am impressed at how well behaved the young people are. It is their space, and hence they do not defile it. Perhaps if we shared more of our space with young people, if they felt they had some investment in it and the opportunity to use it, we would see less graffiti, and less destruction. The disfranchisement of adolescents from places of their own is at least one reason teenagers vandalize adult enclaves.

All of the adult initiatives that I have described above reflect a common orientation, what Erik Erikson called *a sense of generativity*. When we think beyond ourselves, when we begin to do things for the next generation out of a genuine commitment to their future well-being, we give evidence of this sense of generativity. In the postmodern world, the sentiments, values, and perceptions of the permeable family tend to undermine this sense of generativity. Our postmodern failure to commit time and energy to meeting the needs of the next generation has resulted in the new morbidity.

My hope is that the loss of our sense of generativity was a transient aberration, a short-lived by-product of our rapid transition into the postmodern world. Now that we are coming to accept the special ties of the vital family, these should refurbish our commitment to the upcoming generations. In the end, our surest guarantee of redressing the new imbalance and of reducing the inordinate stress on our children and youth is a revitalized sense of generativity, and a new appreciation of what it means to be an adult.

Notes

Index

Notes

1. Family Imbalance: From Nuclear to Permeable

1. David T. Ellwood, *Poor Support: Poverty in the American Family* (New York: Basic Books, 1988).
2. Friedrich Froebel, *The Education of Man* (New York: D. Appleton & Co., 1887). Maria Montessori, *The Montessori Method* (New York: Schocken Books, 1911/1964).
3. Aristotle, "Rhetorica," in Richard McKeon, ed., *The Basic Works of Aristotle,* translated by W. Roberts (New York: Random House, 1941), p. 1403.
4. Philippe Ariès, *Centuries of Childhood: A Social History of Family Life* (New York: Knopf), p. 329. "Once he had passed the age of five or seven, the child was immediately absorbed into the world of adults: this concept of a brief childhood lasted for a long time in the lower classes . . . Childhood was extended beyond the years when the little man walked on a 'Leading string' or spoke his 'jargon,' when an intermediary stage, hitherto rare and henceforth more and more common, was introduced between the period of the robe with a collar and the period of recognized adult: the stage of the school or of the college."
5. Glenna Matthews, *Just a Housewife: The Rise and Fall of Domesticity in America* (New York: Oxford University Press, 1987), p. 181.
6. Ernst Mayr, *One Long Argument: Charles Darwin and the Genesis of Modern Evolutionary Thought* (Cambridge: Harvard University Press, 1991).

7. Lenore Radloff, "Sex differences in depression: The effects of occupation and marital status," *Sex Roles* 1: 249-265.
8. Philip R. Nader, ed., *School Health: Policy and Practice* (Elk Grove Village, Ill.: American Academy of Pediatrics, 1993), p. 140.
9. D. Middlebrook, "Becoming Anne Sexton," *Denver Quarterly,* June 1984, pp. 23–34, 23f.
10. Stephanie Coontz, *The Way We Never Were: American Families and the Nostalgia Trap* (New York: Basic Books, 1992).
11. Betty Friedan, *The Feminine Mystique* (New York: Norton, 1963).
12. Neil Postman, *The Disappearance of Childhood* (New York: Delacorte Press, 1982). Marie Winn, *Children Without Childhood* (New York: Pantheon, 1983). David Elkind, *The Hurried Child: Growing Up Too Fast Too Soon* (Reading, MA: Addison-Wesley, 1981/1988).
13. National Commission on Excellence in Education, *A Nation at Risk: The Imperative for Educational Reform* (Washington, DC: U.S. Department of Education, 1983), pp. 8–9.
14. Children's Defense Fund, *Children 1990: A Report Card, Briefing Book, and Action Primer* (Washington, DC: National Association for the Education of Young Children, 1990), pp. 5–6.
15. Task Force on Youth Development and Community Programs, *A Matter of Time: Risk and Opportunity in the Non-School Hours* (Washington, DC: Carnegie Council on Adolescent Development, 1992).
16. Gary Putka, "Tense Tots," *Wall Street Journal,* July 6, 1988, p. 1.

2. Family Ties: From Modern to Postmodern

1. David Elkind, *The Hurried Child: Growing Up Too Fast Too Soon* (Reading, MA: Addison-Wesley, 1981/88). David Elkind, *All Grown Up and No Place to Go* (Reading, MA: Addison-Wesley, 1984). David Elkind, *Miseducation: Preschoolers at Risk* (New York: Knopf, 1987).
2. E. Mavis Hetherington and W. Glenn Clingempeel, *Coping with Marital Transitions: A Family Systems Perspective* (Chicago: University of Chicago Press, Monographs of the Society for Research in Child Development, 1992). J. Wallerstein and S. Corbin, "The child and the vicissitudes of divorce," in Melvin Lewis, ed., *Child and Adolescent Psychiatry: A Comprehensive Textbook* (Baltimore: Williams & Wilkins, 1991), pp. 1108–1118.

Ellen Galinsky, James T. Bond, and Dana E. Friedman, *The Changing Workforce: Highlights of the National Study* (New York: Families & Work Institute, 1993). E. Greenberger and W. A. Goldberg, "Work, parenting, and the socialization of children," *Developmental Psychology,* 25 (1989): 22–35. L. W. Hoffman, "Effects of maternal employment on the two parent family," *American Psychologist,* 44 (1989): 283–292. C. M. Buchanan, E. E. Maccoby, and S. M. Dornbusch, "Adolescents and their families after divorce: three residential arrangements compared," *Journal of Research on Adolescence,* 23 (1992): 261–291. Nicholas Zill, *Happy, Healthy, and Insecure* (New York: Cambridge University Press, 1986). Urie Bronfenbrenner, *The Ecology of Human Development: Experiments by Nature and Design* (Cambridge: Harvard University Press, 1979). David T. Ellwood, *Poor Support: Poverty in the American Family* (New York: Basic Books, 1988). Christopher Lasch, *Haven in a Heartless World* (New York: Basic Books, 1977). D. Popanoe, "American family decline, 1960–1990," *Journal of Marriage and the Family,* 55 (August): 527–555. H. A. Liddle, "Family psychology: The journal, the field," *Journal of Family Psychology,* 1:5–22. Judith Stacey, *Brave New Families* (New York: Basic Books, 1990). Arlene Skolnick, *Embattled Paradise: The American Family in an Age of Uncertainty* (New York: Basic Books, 1991).

3. Michel Foucault, *The Order of Things: An Archaeology of the Human Sciences* (New York: Pantheon, 1971).
4. Noam Chomsky, "Human nature: Justice versus power," in Fons Elders, ed., *Reflexive Water: The Basic Concerns of Mankind* (London: Souvenir Press, 1974), p. 172.
5. "It is not by studying human nature that linguists discovered the laws of consonant mutation, or Freud the principles of the analysis of dreams, or cultural anthropologists the structure of myths. In the history of knowledge, the notion of human nature seems to me mainly to have played the role of . . . designating certain types of discourse in relation or in opposition to theology, or biology or history." Michel Foucault, "Human Nature," in Elders, ed., *Reflexive Water,* p. 171.
6. Steven Connor, *Postmodernist Culture: An Introduction to the Theories of the Contemporary* (New York: Basil Blackwell, 1989). Steven Best and Douglas Kellner, *Postmodern Theory* (New York: Guilford Press, 1991). Scott Lash, *Sociology of Postmodernism* (London: Routledge, 1990). Richard Rorty, *Phi-*

losophy and the Mirror of Nature (Princeton: Princeton University Press, 1979). Lawrence E. Cahoone, *The Dilemma of Modernity: Philosophy, Culture, and Anti-Culture* (Albany: State University of New York Press, 1988). Jean François Lyotard, *The Postmodern Condition: A Report on Knowledge* (Minneapolis: University of Minnesota Press, 1984). Jacques Lacan, *The Language of the Self: The Function of Language in Psychoanalysis,* translated with notes and commentary by Anthony Wilden (New York: Delta, 1968). Jacques Derrida, *Dissemination,* translated with an introduction and notes by Barbara Johnston (Chicago: University of Chicago Press, 1981). Fredric Jameson, "Postmodernism, or the cultural logic of late modernism," *New Left Review,* 146 (1984): 53–66. Jean Baudrillard, *L'Echange Symbolique et la Mort* (Paris: Gallimard, 1976). Alex Kozulin, "The concept of activity in Soviet psychology: Vygotsky, his disciples and critics," *American Psychologist,* 41, 3: 264–274. L. S. Vygotsky, *Thought and Language* (Cambridge: MIT Press, 1962). L. S. Vygotsky, *Mind in Society* (Cambridge: Harvard University Press, 1978).

7. Sigmund Freud, *The Future of an Illusion,* translated by W. D. Robson Scott (Garden City, NY: Doubleday, 1927/1957).
8. J. S. Migdal and J. T. S. Keeler, "Bridging the divide," *Items,* Social Science Research Council, 47, 4: 87. "For social scientists like us, weaned on the grand theoretical schemes of the 1950s and 1960s and then trained in the middle level theories that followed in the 1970s and 1980s, the recent challenges to comparative studies have been unsettling. The same forces that have set ethnic group upon ethnic group in the political arena have also chipped away at the conceptual foundation of the cross-cultural comparisons in the academic sphere. That foundation was rooted in the pervasiveness and coherence of an explicitly or explicitly acknowledged modern global system. Within the boundaries of such a system, the thread of modernity allowed for the exploration of similarities and the pondering over differences across a wide variety of cases. But as the system expanded to incorporate people in the far reaches of the world, it also seemed to implode, cracking the foundations of commonality that underlay comparative analysis."
9. Oswald Spengler, *The Decline of the West* (New York: Knopf, 1939). Arnold J. Toynbee, *A Study of History,* 12 vols. (London: Oxford University Press, 1934–1961).
10. Michel Foucault, *Discipline and Punish: The Birth of the Prison* (New York:

Pantheon, 1977). Michel Foucault, "Truth and Power," in Paul Rabinow, ed., *The Foucault Reader* (New York: Pantheon, 1984), pp. 51–75.

11. Jean François Lyotard, *The Postmodern Condition*. Jurgen Habermas, *The Philosophical Discourse of Modernity: Twelve Lectures* (Cambridge: MIT Press, 1987).
12. Friedrich Nietzsche, *Human, All Too Human: A Book for Free Spirits*, translated by R. J. Hollingdale, introduction by Erich Heller (New York: Cambridge University Press, 1986). Ludwig Wittgenstein, *Letters from Ludwig Wittgenstein, with a Memoir*, edited by Paul Engelmann and translated by L. Furtmuller (New York: Oxford University Press, 1967). Sören Kierkegaard, *Stages on Life's Way* (Princeton: Princeton University Press, 1945).
13. Howard Gardner, *Frames of Mind: The Theory of Multiple Intelligence* (New York: Basic Books, 1985).
14. Ithiel de Sola Pool, *Technologies without Boundaries* (Cambridge: Harvard University Press, 1990), p. 15.
15. William Josiah Goode, *World Revolution and Family Patterns* (New York: Free Press, 1963), p. 3.
16. Clifford J. Sager, H. S. Brown, H. Crohn, T. Engel, E. Rodstein, and L. Walker, *Treating the Remarried Family* (New York: Brunner/Mazel, 1983), p. 24.
17. Arlene S. Skolnick and Jerome H. Skolnick, *Family in Transition: Rethinking Marriage, Sexuality, Child Rearing, and Family Organization*, 2nd ed. (Boston: Little, Brown, 1977), p. 237.
18. Sigmund Freud, "Family Romances," in J. Strachey, ed., *Collected Papers*, vol. 5 (London: Hogarth, 1950), pp. 74–78. Karen Horney, *New Ways in Psychoanalysis* (New York: Norton, 1939). Harry Stack Sullivan, *The Interpersonal Theory of Psychiatry*, (New York: Norton, 1953). Erich Fromm, *Escape from Freedom* (New York: Holt, Rinehart, and Winston, 1941).
19. Talcott Parsons, *Societies: Evolutionary and Comparative Perspectives* (Englewood Cliffs, NJ: Prentice-Hall, 1966).
20. David Elkind, *The Hurried Child* (Reading, MA: Addison-Wesley, 1981/1988).
21. Suzanne K. Steinmetz and Murray A. Straus, eds., *Violence in the Family* (New York: Harper & Row, 1974). Skolnick and Skolnick, *Family in Transition*. Lloyd DeMause, ed., *A History of Childhood* (New York: Harper & Row, 1975).
22. J. Dobson, *Parenting Isn't for Cowards* (Waco, Texas: Word Books, 1987).

Sara McLanahan and Gary Sandefur, *Growing Up with a Single Parent: What Hurts, What Helps* (Cambridge: Harvard University Press, 1994).

23. Diana Baumrind, *Current Patterns of Parental Authority* (Washington, DC: American Psychological Association, *Developmental Psychology Monograph*, 4, 1 (1971): 1–103.
24. Jeanne Bodin and Bonnie Mitelman, *Mothers Who Work: Strategies for Coping* (New York: Ballantine, 1983), p. 13.
25. Arlie Russell Hochschild, *The Second Shift: Working Parents and the Revolution at Home* (New York: Viking, 1989), p. 258.
26. Sylvia Ann Hewlett, *When the Bough Breaks: The Cost of Neglecting Our Children* (New York: Basic Books, 1991).
27. Victor Fuchs, *Women's Quest for Economic Equality* (Cambridge: Harvard University Press, 1988).

3. Family Feelings: From Child-Centered to Parent-Centered

1. Edward Shorter, *The Making of the Modern Family* (New York: Basic Books, 1977).
2. Ibid.
3. Glenna Matthews, *Just a Housewife: The Rise and Fall of Domesticity in America* (New York: Oxford University Press, 1987).
4. Vivian Gornick, *Fierce Attachments* (New York: Simon & Schuster), p. 23.
5. Sloan Wilson, *The Man in the Gray Flannel Suit* (New York: Simon and Schuster, 1955), p. 206
6. Shorter, *Making of the Modern Family.*
7. A. Fields, *Life and Letters of Harriet Beecher Stowe* (Boston: Houghton Mifflin, 1897), p. 98.
8. Philip A. Wylie, *A Generation of Vipers* (New York: Rinehart, 1942). Nancy Rubin, *The Mother Mirror: How a Generation of Women Is Changing Motherhood in America* (New York: Putnam, 1984), p. 64.
9. Caroline Zinser, "The best daycare that ever was," *Working Mother,* October 1984, pp. 76–78.
10. John Bowlby, *Child Care and the Growth of Love* (New York: Pelican, 1953), p. 16.
11. Burton White, *The First Three Years of Life* (Englewood Cliffs, NJ: Prentice-Hall, 1975).

12. Martha Wolfenstein, "The image of the child in contemporary films," in Margaret Mead and Martha Wolfenstein, *Childhood in Contemporary Cultures* (Chicago: University of Chicago Press, 1955), p. 291.
13. Shorter, *Making of the Modern Family.*
14. Christopher Lasch, *The Minimal Self: Psychic Survival in Troubled Times* (New York: Norton, 1984), p. xiv.
15. Shorter, *Making of the Modern Family.*
16. Ann Swidler, "Love and adulthood in American culture," in Neil J. Smelser and Erik H. Erikson, eds., *Themes of Work and Love in Adulthood* (Cambridge: Harvard University Press, 1980), p. 136.
17. H. A. Kessing, "The pop message: A trend analysis of the psychological content of two decades of music," in Rolf E. Muuss, ed., *Adolescent Behavior and Society* (New York: Random House, 1974), pp. 543–549.
18. The Boston Women's Health Book Collective, *Ourselves and Our Children: A Book By and For Parents* (New York: Random House, 1978), p. 33.
19. Betty Friedan, *The Second Stage* (New York: Summit Books, 1981).
20. Catherine R. Albiston, Eleanor Maccoby, and Robert H. Mnookin, "Joint legal custody: Does it affect nonresidential fathers' contact, coparenting, and compliance after divorce?" *Stanford Law and Policy Review,* 1 (1990): 167–179.
21. Mary D. Ainsworth, M. Blehar, E. Waters, and S. Wall, *Patterns of Attachment: A Psychological Study of the Strange Situation* (Hillsdale, NJ: Lawrence Erlbaum Associates, 1978).
22. K. A. Clarke-Stewart, "Infant day care: Maligned or malignant," *American Psychologist,* 44 (1989): 266–273.
23. E. Mavis Hetherington and Ross D. Park, *Child Psychology: A Contemporary Viewpoint* (New York: McGraw-Hill, 1993), p. 232.
24. Suzanne K. Steinmetz and Murray A. Straus, eds., *Violence in the Family* (New York: Harper & Row, 1974). *Child Abuse Statistics* (Denver: American Humane Society, 1987). M. E. Wegman, "Annual summary of vital statistics," *Pediatrics,* 80, 6 (1986): 817–826.
25. Christopher Lasch, *Haven in a Heartless World* (New York: Basic Books, 1977).
26. G. Gerbner, L. Gross, M. Morgan, and N. Signorielli, "The mainstreaming of America: Violence profile no. 11," *Journal of Communications,* 30 (1980): 10–29.

27. B. S. Greenberg, S. Fazel, and M. Weber, *Children View Advertising* (New York: Independent Broadcasting Research Report, 1986).
28. C. K. Atkin, R. S. Greenberg, and S. McDermott, "Television and racial socialization," paper presented at the meeting of the Association for Education in Journalism (Seattle, 1978).
29. Lasch, *The Minimal Self,* p. 45.

4. Family Values: From Togetherness to Autonomy

1. Glenna Matthews, *Just a Housewife: The Rise and Fall of Domesticity in America* (New York: Oxford University Press, 1987), p. 181.
2. Peggy Charren, *Changing Channels: Living Sensibly with Television* (Reading, MA: Addison-Wesley, 1983), p. 55.
3. Bruno Bettelheim, *The Uses of Enchantment: The Meaning and Importance of Fairy Tales* (New York: Knopf, 1976).
4. Bruno Bettelheim, *A Good Enough Parent: A Book on Child-rearing* (New York: Knopf, 1987), p. 366.
5. Jean Jacques Rousseau, *The Emile of Jean Jacques Rousseau: Selections,* translated and edited by William Boyd (New York: Teachers College Press, 1956). J. A. Green, *The Educational Ideas of Pestalozzi* (New York: Greenwood, 1914). Charles DeGarmo, *Herbart and the Herbartians* (New York: Charles Scribner's Sons, 1895). Friedrich Froebel, *The Education of Man,* translated by W. N. Hailmann (New York: D. Appleton, 1887). John Dewey, *Democracy in Education: An Introduction to the Philosophy of Education* (New York: Free Press, 1916/1944).
6. Lawrence Arthur Cremin, *The Transformation of the School: Progressivism in American Education: 1876–1957* (New York: Vintage, 1961), p. 349.
7. James M. Sawrey and Charles W. Telford, *Educational Psychology: Psychological Foundations of Education* (Boston: Allyn and Bacon, 1964), p. 146.
8. Diane Ravitch, *The Troubled Crusade: American Education, 1945–1980* (New York: Basic Books, 1983), p. 46.
9. Blackstone, 235 US 237 (1897).
10. *Youth, Transition to Adulthood,* report of the Panel on Youth of the President's Science Advisory Committee (Washington, DC: Superintendent of Documents), p. 30.
11. Ibid., p. 31.

12. Ibid, p. 32.
13. Sigmund Freud, *The Ego and the Id* (London: Hogarth, 1927/1957).
14. Robert Weiss, "Growing up a little faster: The experience of growing up in a single child household," *Journal of Social Issues,* 35, 4 (1979): 98.
15. Paul L. Wachtel, *The Poverty of Affluence: A Psychological Portrait of the American Way of Life* (New York: Free Press, 1983). Tom Wolfe, "The me decade and the third great awakening," in Tom Wolfe, *The Purple Decades: A Reader* (New York: Farrar, Straus & Giroux, 1982), pp. 265–296. Christopher Lasch, *The Culture of Narcissism: American Life in an Age of Diminishing Expectations* (New York: Norton, 1979).
16. Daniel Yankelovich, *New Rules: Searching for Self-Fulfillment in a World Turned Upside Down* (New York: Random House, 1981). Robert N. Bellah, R. Madsen, W. M. Sullivan, A. Swidler, and S. M. Tipton, *Habits of the Heart: Individualism and Commitment in American Life* (New York: Harper & Row, 1986).
17. *The American Family under Siege* (Washington, DC: American Research Council, 1989).
18. Charren, *Changing Channels*, p. 55.
19. Harry F. Waters, "Family feuds," *Newsweek,* April 23, 1990, p. 58.
20. David Elkind, *Children and Adolescents: Interpretive Essays on Jean Piaget* (New York: Oxford University Press, 1981).
21. Sheila A. Egoff, *Thursday's Child: Trends and Patterns in Contemporary Children's Literature* (Chicago: American Library Association, 1981), p. 71.
22. Eugene F. Provenzo Jr., *Video Kids: Making Sense of Nintendo* (Cambridge: Harvard University Press, 1991), p. 118.
23. Ibid., p. 117.
24. B. Neugebauer, ed., *Alike and Different: Exploring Our Humanity with Young Children,* rev. ed. (Washington, DC: NAEYC, 1992).
25. H. M. Marschall, "The development of self concept," *Young Children,* 44, 5 (1989): 48.
26. Philippe Ariès, "The sentimental revolution," *Wilson Quarterly,* 6, 4 (Autumn 1982): 51.
27. *American Jurisprudence,* 2nd ed., vol. 48 (Rochester, NY: Lawyers Cooperative), p. 462. "An act amounting to assault and battery is not punishable if done by a teacher in moderate exercise of his disciplinary authority over a pupil, as for example, where the punishment inflicted by the

teacher consists only with a whipping by a switch, or with a ruler or with something in the nature of a stick."

28. *Belloti v Baird*, 431 US 861 (1977). *Goss v Lopez*, 419 US 565 (1975). *Smith v Organization of Foster Families for Equality and Reform*, 431 US 816 (1977).
29. Bruce C. Hafen, "Exploring test cases in child advocacy," review of Robert Mnookin, "In the interest of children: Advocacy law," *Harvard Law Review*, 100, 2 (December 1986): 447.
30. Ariès, "The sentimental revolution," p. 51.
31. Thomas J. Paolino and Barbara S. McCrady, eds., *Marriage and Marital Therapy: Psychoanalytic, Behavioral, and Systems Theory Perspectives* (New York: Brunner/Mazel, 1978). Salvador Minuchin, *Families and Family Therapy* (Cambridge: Harvard University Press, 1974). Philip J. Guerin, Leo F. Fay, S. L. Burden, and J. G. Kautto, *The Evaluation and Treatment of Marital Conflict* (New York: Basic Books, 1987). George Levinger and Oliver C. Moles, *Divorce and Separation: Context, Causes, and Consequences* (New York: Basic Books, 1979). Clifford J. Sager, H. S. Brown, H. Crohn, T. Engel, E. Rodstein, and L. Walker, *Treating the Remarried Family* (New York: Brunner/Mazel, 1983).
32. Bernard Brown, ed., *Found: Long Term Gains from Early Intervention* (Boulder, Colo.: Westview Press for AAAS, 1978).
33. Ernest L. Boyer, *Ready to Learn: A Mandate for the Nation* (Princeton: Princeton University Press, 1991).
34. Robert J. Sternberg and John Kolligian Jr., eds., *Competence Considered* (New Haven: Yale University Press, 1990). Abraham H. Maslow, *The Farther Reaches of Human Nature* (New York: Viking, 1971). Heinz Kohut, *The Restoration of the Self* (New York: International Universities Press, 1977). James F. Masterson, *The Narcissistic and Borderline Disorders: An Integrated and Developmental Approach* (New York: Brunner/Mazel, 1981).
35. Carl R. Rogers, *Client-Centered Therapy: Its Current Practice, Implications, and Theory* (Boston: Houghton Mifflin, 1951).

5. Parents: From Intuition to Technique

1. John Locke, *An Essay Concerning Human Understanding.*
2. Jean Jacques Rousseau, *Emile* (New York: Appleton, 1911).
3. James Mark Baldwin, *Thought and Things or Genetic Logic,* 2 vols. (New

York: Macmillan, 1906). Wilhelm Preyer, *L'Ame de L'Enfant* (Paris: Felix Alcan, 1887). James Sully, *Studies of Childhood* (New York: Appleton, 1903). Milicent Washburn Shinn, *The Biography of a Baby* (Boston: Houghton Mifflin, 1900). Elizabeth M. Lomax, Jerome Kagan, and Barbara G. Rosenkrantz, *Science and Patterns of Child Care* (San Francisco: W. H. Freeman & Company, 1978), p. 67.

4. Benjamin S. Bloom, *Stability and Change in Human Characteristics* (New York: Wiley, 1964). Joseph McVicker Hunt, *Intelligence and Experience* (New York: Ronald Press Co., 1964). Jerome S. Bruner, *The Process of Education* (Cambridge: Harvard University Press, 1960).
5. Benjamin Spock, *Baby and Child Care,* rev. ed. (New York: Hawthorne Books, 1968).
6. As the pediatrician Arnold Gesell wrote: "Genetic sequence is itself an expression of an elaborate pattern. And the relative stability of both the prenatal and the postnatal ontogenesis [that is, development] under normal and even unusual conditions must be regarded as a significant indication of the fundamental role of maturational factors in the determination of behavior." Arnold Gesell, "Maturation and infant behavior pattern," *Psychological Review,* 36 (1929): 307–319.
7. John Broadus Watson, *The Psychological Care of Infant and Child* (New York: W. W. Norton, 1928), p. 114.
8. Ibid., p. 128.
9. Spock, *Baby and Child Care.* T. Berry Brazelton, *On Becoming a Family* (Reading, MA: Delacorte, 1992). Penelope Leach, *Babyhood: From Birth to Age Two* (New York: Knopf, 1976).
10. Haim Ginott, *Between Parent and Teenager* (New York: Macmillan, 1969), pp. 79, 81.
11. Nancy Salamin and Martha Moraghan Jablow, *Loving Your Child Is Not Enough* (New York: Viking, 1988), p. 112.
12. Jerry J. Bigner, "Parent education in popular literature, 1950–1970," *Family Coordinator* 21 (1972): 313–319. C. Stendlar, "Sixty years of child training practices," *Journal of Pediatrics,* 36 (1950): 122–134.
13. Diana Baumrind, "Parental disciplinary patterns and social competence in children," *Youth and Society,* 9, 3 (1978).
14. Selma H. Fraiberg, *The Magic Years: Understanding and Handling the Problems of Early Childhood* (New York: Scribner, 1959), p. i.

15. Arnold Gesell and Frances Ilg, *The Child from Five to Ten* (New York: Harper, 1946), p. 6.
16. Spock, *Baby and Child Care*, p. 7.
17. M. Kirshenbaum and D. Foster, *Parent/Teen Breakthrough* (New York: Penguin, 1991), p. 129.
18. C. E. Schaefer and Theresa Foy DiGeronimo, *Teach Your Child to Behave* (New York: Plume, 1991), pp. 60–61.
19. Susan Isaacs, *The Nursery Years* (New York: Schocken, 1932/1968), p. 134.
20. Fraiberg, *The Magic Years*, p. 218.
21. Haim Ginott, *Between Parent and Child* (New York: Macmillan, 1965).
22. Adele Faber and Elaine Mazlish, *Liberated Parents/Liberated Children* (New York: Grosset & Dunlop, 1974), pp. 3–4.
23. Adele Faber and Elaine Mazlish, *How to Talk So Kids Will Listen, and Listen So Kids Will Talk* (New York: Avon, 1980), pp. 20, 24.
24. Thomas Gordon, *Teaching Children Self Discipline* (New York: Random House, 1989), pp. 53–54.
25. D. W. Winnicott, *The Child, the Family, and the Outside World* (Reading, MA: Addison-Wesley, 1987), p. 162.
26. Dorothy Cohen, *The Learning Child* (New York: Pantheon, 1972), pp. 304–305.
27. Ginott, *Between Parent and Child*, pp. 3–4.
28. Faber and Mazlish, *How to Talk So Kids Will Listen*.
29. Gordon, *Teaching Children Self Discipline*, pp. 107–108.
30. Isaacs, *The Nursery Years*, pp. 74–75.
31. Fraiberg, *The Magic Years*, p. 127.
32. Bruner, *The Process of Education*, p. 22.
33. S. Lehane, *Help Your Baby Learn: 100 Piaget-based Activities for the First Two Years of Life* (Englewood Cliffs, NJ: Prentice-Hall, 1976). Glenn Doman, *Teach Your Baby to Read* (London: Jonathan Cape, 1965). Sidney Ledson, *Teach Your Child to Read in Sixty Days* (New York: Norton, 1965). Joan Beck, *How to Raise a Brighter Child* (New York: Pocket Books, 1975). Susan Ludington-Hoe, *How to Have a Smarter Baby* (New York: Rawson, 1985). Siegfried Engelmann and T. Englemann, *Give Your Child a Superior Mind* (New York: Cornerstone Library, 1966).
34. Ludington-Hoe, *How to Have a Smarter Baby*, p. 24.
35. Seymour Papert, *Mindstorms: Children, Computers, and Powerful Ideas* (New York: Basic Books, 1980), p. 15.

36. Ibid., p. 16.
37. Robert S. Siegler, *Children's Thinking,* 2nd ed. (Englewood Cliffs, NJ: Prentice-Hall, 1991), p. 53.
38. Ibid., p. 53.
39. S. Bernstein and A. Hollister, "Babies are smarter than you think," *Life* (July 1993): 49–54.

6. Children: From Innocence to Competence

1. Alisdair Roberts, *Out to Play: The Middle Years of Childhood* (Aberdeen: Aberdeen University Press, 1980), p. 26.
2. Sheila A. Egoff, *Thursday's Child: Trends and Patterns in Contemporary Children's Literature* (Chicago: American Library Association, 1981), p. 7.
3. Leonard Carmichael, ed., *Manual of Child Psychology* (New York: Wiley, 1946).
4. Marie Winn, *Children without Childhood* (New York: Pantheon, 1981), pp. 6–7.
5. P. Farhi and L. K. Farhi, "The new children's books, grimmer than Grimm," *Washington Post,* September 3, 1989, p. C5.
6. Ibid.
7. John Dewey, *The Child and the Curriculum: The School and Society* (Chicago: University of Chicago Press, 1915/1956), p. 7.
8. John Dewey and Evelyn Dewey, *Schools of Tomorrow* (New York: Dutton, 1915/1962).
9. D. H. Stewart, "Children's preferences in types of assignments," *Elementary School Journal,* 47, 2 (1946): 93.
10. E. J. Swenson and C. G. Caldwell, "The content of children's letters," *Elementary School Journal,* 49, 2 (1948): 149–159. N. T. Lyons, "Relating reading to individual differences," *Elementary School Journal,* 49, 7 (1949): 389–414.
11. Rudolf Flesch, *Why Johnny Can't Read—And What You Can Do about It* (New York: Harper & Brothers, 1955).
12. Jerome Bruner, *Toward a Theory of Instruction* (Cambridge: The Belknap Press of Harvard University Press, 1966), p. 21.
13. Graham Nuthall and A. Alton-Lee, "Research on teaching and learning: Thirty years of change," *Elementary School Journal,* 5 (1990): 547.
14. S. J. Thornton and R. N. Wenger, "Geography, curriculum, and instruc-

tion in three fourth grade classrooms," *Elementary School Journal,* 90, 5 (1990): 515–532. D. A. Frisbie and K. Andrews, "Kindergarten pupil and teacher behavior during standardized achievement testing," *Elementary School Journal,* 90, 4 (1990): 435–448.

15. Iona Opie and Peter Opie, *The Lore and Language of School Children* (London: Oxford University Press, 1959), p. 121.
16. Ibid., pp. 17–18.
17. Quoted in C. Perlmutter, "Competitive sports," *Children* (1982): 35–38.
18. Ibid., p. 36.
19. Pat McInally, "Little Leaguers beware: curveballs dangerous," *Boston Globe,* Monday, July 6, 1987, p. 39.
20. The National Injury Surveillance System, *Consumer Product Safety Commission.*
21. Sigmund Freud, "The Aetiology of Hysteria," in Sigmund Freud, *Collected Papers,* vol. 1. (London: Hogarth Press, 1924), p. 212.
22. Sigmund Freud, *An Autobiographical Study* (London: Hogarth Press, 1935), pp. 60–61.
23. Jeffrey Masson, *The Assault on Truth: Freud's Suppression of the Seduction Theory* (New York: Farrar, Straus & Giroux, 1984).
24. M. Hickey, "Protecting children against sex offenders," *Ladies' Home Journal,* April 1957, p. 13.
25. Ibid., p. 31.
26. S. X. Radbill, "A history of child abuse and infanticide," in Ray E. Helfer and C. Henry Kempe, eds., *The Battered Child* (Chicago: University of Chicago Press, 1968), p. 19.
27. Alice Miller, *Prisoners of Childhood* (New York: Basic Books, 1981).
28. N. D. Reppucci and J. J. Haugaard, "Prevention of child sexual abuse: Myth or reality," *American Psychologist,* 44, 10 (1989): 1274.
29. Ibid., p. 1274.

7. Adolescents: From Immaturity to Sophistication

1. A. Bandura, "The stormy decade: Fact or fiction," *Psychology in the Schools,* 1 (1964): 224–231.
2. G. Stanley Hall, *Adolescence,* vols. 1 and 2 (New York: Appleton and Co., 1904), p. 14.

3. Erik H. Erikson, *Childhood and Society* (New York: Norton, 1950).
4. Erik H. Erikson, *Identity, Youth, and Crisis* (New York: Norton, 1968), p. 134.
5. L. Kutner, "When young adults head back home," *New York Times*, July 14, 1988, p. C8.
6. Daniel Offer and Judith B. Offer, *From Teenage to Young Manhood* (New York: Basic Books, 1975).
7. Robert J. Lifton, "Proteus revisited," in Sherman C. Feinstein and Peter Giovacchini, eds., *Adolescent Psychiatry*, vol. 4 (New York: Jason Aronson, 1976), pp. 21–35.
8. Heinz Kohut, "Thoughts on narcissism and narcissistic rage," in *Psychoanalytic Study of the Child*, vol. 27 (New York: International Universities Press, 1972), pp. 360–401, 365.
9. A. C. Kinsey, W. Pomeroy, C. E. Martin, and P. H. Gebhard, *Sexual Behavior in the Human Female* (Philadelphia: W. B. Saunders, 1953).
10. C. E. Irwin and M. Shafer, "Adolescent sexuality: negative outcomes of a normative behavior," in D. E. Rogers and E. Ginzberg, *Adolescents at Risk* (Boulder: Westview Press, 1992), p. 37.
11. Arnold Gesell, Frances L. Ilg, and Louise B. Ames, *Youth: The Years from Age Ten to Sixteen* (New York: Harper & Row, 1956), p. 258.
12. Ibid., p. 258.
13. N. Cobb, *Adolescence* (Mountain View, Calif.: Mayfield, 1992), pp. 329–330.
14. Ruth Strang, *The Adolescent Views Himself: A Psychology of Adolescence* (New York: McGraw-Hill, 1957), pp. 432–434.
15. Ellen Greenberger and Laurence Steinberg, *When Teenagers Work* (New York: Basic Books, 1988), p. 66.
16. Ibid., p. 103.
17. J. D. Salinger, *The Catcher in the Rye* (New York: Buccaneer Books).
18. Margaret Mead, *Culture and Commitment* (Garden City, NJ: Natural History Press, 1970).
19. As Shorter puts it: "The cultural categories which shape adolescent orientations to their own social milieu are largely autonomous inasmuch as they are embodied in a system of meanings whose implications are not immediately obvious to adults." Edward Shorter, *The Making of the Modern Family* (New York: Basic Books, 1977), p. 460.

20. G. Shwarz and D. Merten, "The language of adolescents: an anthropological approach to youth culture," *American Journal of Sociology,* 72 (1967): 453–468, 460.
21. Hans Sebald, *Adolescence: A Sociological Analysis* (New York: Appleton-Century-Crofts, 1968).
22. C. James, "The Peter-Pan generation makes room for small fry," *New York Times,* July 23, 1989, p. H11.
23. N. Howe and W. Strauss, "The new generation gap," *Atlantic,* December 1992, pp. 67–89.
24. R. Borne, quoted in Howe and Strauss, ibid., p. 80.

8. Diagnosing Disorder: From Sex to Stress

1. Sigmund Freud, "Three contributions to the theory of sex." In A. A. Brill, ed., *The Basic Writings of Sigmund Freud* (New York: Modern Library, 1938).
2. Thomas Szaz, *The Myth of Mental Illness: Foundations of a Theory of Personal Conduct,* rev. ed. (New York: Harper, 1987).
3. Jerome C. Wakefield, "The concept of mental disorder: On the boundary between biological facts and social values," *American Psychologist,* 47, 3 (1992): 373-388.
4. Hans Selye, *The Stress of Life,* rev. ed. (New York: McGraw-Hill, 1976).
5. Sigmund Freud, "Character and anal eroticism." In J. Riviere, ed., *The Collected Papers of Sigmund Freud,* vol. 11 (London: Hogarth, 1953), pp. 45-50. "General remarks on hysterical attacks," ibid., pp. 100-104.
6. Peter Blos, *On Adolescence* (New York: Free Press, 1962), p. 235.
7. Freud, "General remarks on hysterical attacks," p. 150.
8. Alfred Adler, *The Education of Children* (New York: Greenberg, 1930), p. 7.
9. Melanie Klein, *The Psychoanalysis of Children.* Translated by A. S. Strachey and H. A. Thorner (London: Virago Press, 1932/1989), pp. 9-10.
10. Sigmund Freud, *The Interpretation of Dreams.* In A. A. Brill, ed., *The Basic Writings of Sigmund Freud* (New York: Modern Library, 1938).
11. Sigmund Freud, "Analysis of a phobia in a five-year-old boy." In J. Riviere, ed., *The Collected Papers of Sigmund Freud,* vol. 111 (London: Hogarth, 1953), pp. 149-295.

12. Salvador Minuchin, *Families and Family Therapy* (Cambridge: Harvard University Press, 1974).
13. Harry Stack Sullivan, *The Interpersonal Theory of Psychiatry* (New York: Norton, 1953). Harry Stack Sullivan, *Conceptions of Modern Psychiatry* (New York: Norton, 1940).
14. Karen Horney, *The Neurotic Personality of Our Time* (New York: Norton, 1937). Karen Horney, *New Ways in Psychoanalysis* (New York: Norton, 1939). Karen Horney, *Our Inner Conflicts: A Constructive Theory of Neurosis* (New York: Norton, 1945).
15. Karen Horney, *Self-Analysis* (New York: Norton, 1942).
16. Erik H. Erikson, *Childhood and Society* (New York: Norton, 1950).
17. Heinz Hartman and Rudolf M. Lowenstein, "Comments on the formation of psychic structure," in *The Psychoanalytic Study of the Child, 3/4* (New York: International Universities Press, 1949).
18. Eric Berne, *Games People Play: The Psychology of Human Relationships* (New York: Grove Press, 1964). Martin Shepard, *Fritz: An Intimate Portrait of Fritz Perls and Gestalt Therapy* (New York: Dutton, 1975).
19. Hans Selye, *The Stress of Life.*
20. H. R. Schaffer and P. E. Emerson, "The development of social attachment in infancy," *Monographs for the Society of Research in Child Development,* 29, 3 (1964): serial no. 4. S. B. Crockenberg, "Infant irritability, mother responsiveness, and social support influences on the security of infant-mother attachment," *Child Development,* 52 (1981): 857–865. M. J. Levitt, R. A. Weber, and M. C. Clark, "Social network relationships as sources of maternal support and well being," *Developmental Psychology,* 22 (1986): 310–316.
21. Martin Bax and Ronald Charles MacKeith, "Minimal brain damage: A concept discarded," in MacKeith and Bax, eds., *Minimal Cerebral Dysfunction: Papers from the International Study Group* (London: Heinemann, Little Club Clinics in Developmental Medicine 10, 1963).
22. Marilyn Machlowitz, *Workaholics: Living with Them, Working with Them* (Reading, MA: Addison-Wesley, 1980), p. 22. Melody Beattie, *Codependent No More* (New York: Harper, 1987). Salvador Minuchin, *Family Healing* (New York: Free Press, 1993).
23. Minuchin, *Family Healing,* p. 39.

24. V. Satir, *The New Peoplemaking* (Mountain View, CA: Science and Behavior Books, 1988), p. 4.
25. Ibid., p. 5.
26. J. Szapocznik and W. M. Kurtines, "Family psychology and cultural diversity," *American Psychologist,* 48, 4: 400–407.

9. Stress among Youth: The New Morbidity

1. Robert James Havighurst, *Human Development and Education* (New York: Longmans, 1953).
2. Jean Piaget, *The Psychology of Intelligence* (London: Routledge & Kegan Paul Ltd., 1950).
3. Nancy Bayley, "Individual patterns of development," *Child Development,* 27 (1956): 45–74.
4. David Wechsler, *The Measurement and Appraisal of Adult Intelligence,* 4th ed. (Baltimore: Williams and Wilkins, 1958), p. 135.
5. Betty Friedan, *The Feminine Mystique* (New York: Norton, 1963), p. 21.
6. E. Mavis Hetherington and Ross D. Parke, *Child Psychology: A Contemporary Viewpoint,* 3rd ed. (New York: McGraw-Hill, 1993), p. 317.
7. Robert S. Siegler, *Children's Thinking,* 2nd ed. (Englewood Cliffs, NJ: Prentice-Hall, 1991).
8. Carl R. Rogers, *Client-Centered Therapy: Its Current Practice, Implications, and Theory* (Boston: Houghton Mifflin Company, 1951), p. 487.
9. Abraham Maslow, *Motivation and Personality* (New York: Harper & Row, 1954).
10. Daniel Levinson et al., *The Seasons of a Man's Life* (New York: Knopf, 1978).
11. Gail Sheehy, *Passages: Predictable Crises of Adult Life* (New York: Dutton, 1976).
12. Judith Viorst, *Necessary Losses* (New York: Simon and Schuster, 1986), p. 18.
13. Paul B. Baltes, Hayne M. Reese, and John R. Nesselroade, *Life-span Developmental Psychology: Introduction to Research Methods* (Monterey, CA: Brooks/Cole, 1977).
14. J. Horn, "Organization of data from life-span development of human

abilities," in L. R. Goulet and Paul B. Baltes, eds., *Life Span Developmental Psychology: Research and Theory* (New York: Academic Press, 1970).

15. Baltes, Reese, and Nesselroade, *Life-span Developmental Psychology.*
16. Gesell, *Youth,* p. 26.
17. William T. Grant Foundation Commission on Work, Family and Citizenship, 1988.
18. David Elkind, *The Hurried Child* (Reading, MA: Addison-Wesley, 1981/1988).
19. Ernest Boyer, *Ready to Learn: A Mandate for the Nation* (Princeton: Princeton University Press, 1991), pp. 92–93.
20. Robert J. Haggarty, Kenneth K. Roughman, and Barry I. Bless, eds., *Child Health and the Community* (New York: Wiley, 1975).
21. National Center for Education Statistics, *Youth Indicators, 1993: Trends in the Well Being of Youth* (Washington, DC: U.S. Government Printing Office, 1993).
22. William H. Deitz and Seymour L. Gotmaker, "Do we fatten our children at the TV set? Television viewing and obesity in children and adolescents," *Pediatrics* 75 (1995): 807.
23. *Youth Indicators, 1993.*
24. Ibid.
25. D. P. Gardner and Y. W. Larsen, *A Nation at Risk.* National Commission on Excellence in Education (Washington, DC: U.S. Government Printing Office, 1983).
26. *Code Blue: Uniting for Healthier Youth.* The National Commission on the Role of the School and the Community in Improving Adolescent Health, The National Association of State Boards of Education, and The American Medical Association (1990).
27. Fred M. Hechinger, *Fateful Choices* (New York: Carnegie Corporation of New York, 1992).
28. Peter D. Rodgers and Hoover Adger Jr., "Alcohol and adolescents," in M. Schydlower and P. D. Rodgers, eds., "Adolescent substance abuse and addictions," *Adolescent Medicine: State of the Art Reviews*, 4, 2 (1993): 295–304.
29. Ibid.
30. Carl L. Tishler, "Adolescent suicide: assessment, risk and prevention," in

R. B. Brown and B. A. Cromer, eds., "Psychosocial issues in adolescents," *Adolescent Medicine: State of the Art Reviews,* 3, 1 (1992): 51–59.

31. Hechinger, *Fateful Choices,* pp. 72-73.
32. Stanley K. Henshaw, Asta M. Kenney, Debra Somberg, and Jennifer Van-Vort, *U.S. Teen Pregnancy Statistics* (New York: The Alan Guttmacher Institute, 1992).
33. Willard Cates Jr., "The epidemiology and control of sexually transmitted diseases in adolescents," in Manuel Schydlower and Mary Ann Shafer, eds., "AIDS and Other Sexually Transmitted Diseases," *Adolescent Medicine: State of the Art Reviews,* 1–3 (1990): 409–428.
34. David Elkind, *Children and Adolescents: Interpretive Essays on Jean Piaget,* 3rd ed. (New York: Oxford University Press, 1981).
35. Esther J. Jenkins and Carl C. Bell, "Adolescent violence: Can it be curbed?" in Brown and Cromer, "Psychosocial Issues in Adolescents," pp. 71–86.
36. Sylvia Ann Hewlett, *When the Bough Breaks: The Cost of Neglecting Our Children* (New York: Basic Books, 1991).
37. Gardner and Larsen, *A Nation at Risk.*

10. A New Balance: The Vital Family

1. David Popenoe, "American family decline, 1960–1990," *Journal of Marriage and the Family,* 55 (August 1993): 527–555.
2. Judith Stacey, "Good riddance to 'the family': A response to David Popenoe," *Journal of Marriage and the Family,* 55 (August 1993): 545–547.
3. *The HIV/AIDS Pandemic: 1993. Overview,* document WHO/GPA/CPN/EVA/93.1 (Geneva: Global Program on AIDS, 1993).
4. "AIDS research: The mood is uncertain," *Science,* 260 (28 May 1993): 1254–1293.
5. M. Scott Peck, *The Road Less Traveled* (New York: Touchstone, 1978).
6. Betty Friedan, *The Second Stage* (New York: Dell, 1981).
7. *Beyond Rhetoric.* Final Report of the National Commission on Children (Washington, DC: U.S. Government Printing Office, 1991).
8. For these terms see A. Maslow, *The Further Reaches of Human Nature* (New York: Viking Press, 1971) and Robert J. Rieger, *Looking Out for Number One* (New York: Fawcett, 1991). For criticism of this view see Shan Guisinger

and Sidney Blatt, "Individuality and relatedness: Evolution of a fundamental dialectic," *American Psychologist* 49, no. 2 (1994): 104–111.

9. "The wonders of workflow," *Economist,* December 11, 1993, p. 80.
10. G. Sykes and P. Plastrik, *Standard Setting as Educational Reform* (Washington, DC: ERIC, 1993).
11. W. Tynan, "The networks come home," *Time,* May 31, 1993, p. 62.
12. "Hollywood's heartthrobs," *Economist,* December 11, 1993, p. 97.
13. T. Berry Brazelton, *Touchpoints* (Reading, MA: Addison-Wesley, 1992); Penelope Leach, *Your Growing Child: From Babyhood through Adolescence* (New York: Knopf, 1986); Benjamin Spock, *Baby and Child Care* (New York: Pocket Books, 1981).
14. S. Bredenkamp, *Developmentally Appropriate Practice* (Washington, DC: NAEYC, 1990).
15. *Youth Indicators, 1993.*

Index